We share in these pages information on
~ How The Mind Works
~ What Spirit is & How To Communicate With It
~ Why The Soul Is Here & Where It's Been
~ The Future & Enlightenment In It

We gathered this information through the altered state
knowledge of many minds, spirits, and souls.
The tales in this book are true.
Master of Light & Master of Spirit are real.
We are real, too.

We gave manuscripts of this book to six people.
One person is very mystical. One is metaphysical.
One is more open than closed.
One was more closed than open.
One is a seeker. One just likes to read.
Some of their wrtitten comments follow:

"I LOVED the part about your car tires -
nothing happens just by accident ~ *Wonderful!*
Chemo bath of Clorox - *Valuable!*
Cesarean births - *Wow!*
Ultra sounds produce cell damage - *Wow!*
The answer to 'how can I forgive them?' - *Outstanding!*
Ectoplasm - *Totally interesting!*
This entire book is OUTSTANDING and INTERESTING!
I can't wait to own it. I will cherish it
and <u>STUDY</u> it for the rest of my life!."
~ * ~
"You lived with Bette Midler in Greenwich Village in the 60's?!
WOW! You seem so normal."
~ * ~

"I am finally getting that my Higher Self knows all.
I can't wait to own this book and read this part over!"

~ * ~

"Very understandable reading and the personal stories were positive,
useful and very moving. A very positive and loving book."

~ * ~

"Your book has unique insights on the journey of life.
It's a good book for people who are interested
in life's deeper meaning."

~ * ~

"I would recommend this to people who are on a path
and searching. It makes you want to look at
the blocks in your own life, knowing you can change them."

~ * ~

"The stories on both of you were of great interest
and totally fascinating."

~ * ~

"Most of the people I work with don't know anything
about the material in your book. I like
to discuss it with them and share my views."

~ * ~

"I would recommend this to people who had symptoms of
illnesses they want healed and to others who are
interested in getting touch with the Higher Self."

~ * ~

"This book contains straightforward, easy-to-understand information
that can be easily applied to ones life."

~ * ~

"I would say this is 'THE KEY' - showing the major
role the mind has towards the ability to deny or have self love."

~ * ~

""It appeals to me that the book uses real cases from various people to
teach its concepts. I'm also interested in anything that explains hypnosis."

"This book has the keys to lifting the veil."
~ * ~

"I liked that it's about getting knowledge and guidance from the best possible source - our own true self."
~ * ~

"It's intriguing and exciting."
~ * ~

"Very understandable reading for somewhat complex subjects. Positive-useful-moving case histories."
~ * ~

"Unique insights on the journey of life."
~ * ~

"I think your personal sagas are of critical importance for the masses. People are scared to death of their own divinity. Reading a story of how two seemingly ordinary individuals discovered and embraced their own divinity was extraordinarily empowering."
~ * ~

"I thought the personal information did a great job of demonstrating the guidance that's available to all of us."
~ * ~

"Really enjoyed the bio on you two.
Enjoyed you sharing your own vulnerabilities."
~ * ~

"I am finally getting that my higher self knows all. I can't wait to get this book and read this part over and over. It is awesome. If only everyone could read and fully understand this."
~ * ~

"I loved the book. Master of Light's Chapter is even more wonderful. So simple and profound. When is Light's book, Book Two, coming out?"
~ * ~

We Asked Our Readers To Describe This Book:

"Gives the delineation of levels of mind and spirit"

"Explains when body, mind, and spirit come together."

"How the soul is like time - no doors, or barriers, or limits -
always available and open to investigate."

"Written by the authors with their own personal younger life stories
and how they, too, realized the effects negative and positive conditions
laid upon them. How they saw as adults it was necessary to take
responsibility to seek and learn understanding for correcting and
finding their release from their inner duality."

"It is a straightforward, matter-of-fact information supported by
people's actual experiences. "

"It's new age; it talks about abuse and your higher self, it explains alot
of unanswered questions about life."

We Asked What Kind Of People They Would Recommend This Book To:

"Metaphysically inclined."

"To my good friends, especially the ones
who show an interest in the things that interest me."

"To people I know who are on a path and
searching and to people who have been abused."

"People who seem interested in life's deeper meaning."

"To people with symptoms of illness and anyone interested in getting
in touch with the Higher Self."

"Anyone but my mother, father, brother, or sister.
Their opinions no longer interest me."

Odyssey
Of The
Soul

A Trilogy

Book One
Apocatastasis

by

Pamela Chilton, C.Ht.   Hugh Harmon, Ph.D.
&
MASTER OF LIGHT

Quick Book
Publishing

First Printing: December 1997

Library of Congress Catalog Card Number: 97-92477

ISBN: 0-9659891-0-0

Published and distributed in the United States by
Quick Book
Publishing
(800) 403-4325
10 Venus Drive
Rancho Mirage, CA 92270

Printed by McNaughton & Gunn, Inc.
Printed on recycled paper

Typesetting by Christy J. Keller

Cover Design and Illustrations: Dorothy Okada Nakatsui

Table of Contents

INFORMATION PAGES

APPENDIX

Book List

(The following pages are on
tear-out sheets for your convenience.)

Proclamation

Master of Light's Plan of Light

Rachael's Story

Dedicated To Spirit

For
Those Who Seek
The Answers To
The Past
The Present
The Future

Chapter 1

The Master Within

There is a part of you that knows everything there is to know about you. It can tell you why you are in this world and where you were before you came here. It can state both the Universal Truths and the Personal Truths you need to know to get to where you want to go. It can talk about your future, your present, and your past. It can tell you about the people in your life ~ why you are involved with them, what you might want to learn from them, and what you have to teach them. It can help you become closer in your relationships or help you cut the ties that bind you to them. This part knows a great deal more about you than any psychic ever could. Further, it can heal you instantly, although it may take you longer to allow, or even hold onto, the healing.

This part of you is the you that always was and ever will be. It is your Higher Self, though others may know it by other names. God Self, Over Soul, High Self, Atman, Spiritual Self, Whole Self, True Self, Guardian Angel - by whatever name you choose to call it, it is very real. And it is you. It is the you that has never lost its divine connection to or awareness of that which is greater than Man and Woman and the Sum of their Parts and their Works. That which is the Source, The Prime Creator. Your Higher Self is that which was created, in the beginning, by The Prime Creator. It is of the same likeness as The Prime Creator. It is a Master of The Universe seeking ever greater Mastery. It is Spirit.

Spirit is the unseen essence of all that is. Your Spirit is of such magnificence and power the whole of it could never be contained in the physical dimensions of your body. That is why only a part of your spirit is physically embodied. This embodied spirit is your soul. Your soul and your Higher Self are both spirit - they are simply different aspects of the same Spirit.

Think of a tornado. The top of a tornado is vast and it remains in the heavens generating powerful energies which spiral down into a more narrow, yet still powerful, focus on the earth. This focus - the aspect of the tornado that touches the earth - does the physical "work" of the tornado.

So it is with your spirit. Your Higher Self is vast and it remains "in the heavens" (spiritual realms) generating energies that spiral in decreasing vibratory rates into the more narrow, but powerful, focus of the soul. The soul does the physical work of the spirit. The Higher Self and the Soul remain connected through the Mind.

Mind, Soul, and Spirit consist of subtle energies; energies that vibrate faster than the physical eyes can see. However, like the subtle energy waves of radio, television, and radar, they can be detected, researched, and utilized. Though Western Science is increasing its efforts in such research, much of what is found is not revealed to the general public. Moreover, as long as Western Science remains largely dependent upon government funding and resources, this is unlikely to change.

The reason is power. Governments and those they govern are in a continual power struggle. Governments must institute control of the masses in order to govern efficiently. The masses are wary of this control, and rightly so, for it easily leads to abuses of power. Therefore, citizens of a government _must institute and maintain control_ of systems of checks and balances of power within their governments. Such systems fail when citizens abdicate this responsibility.

When those who govern become accustomed to unchecked power they begin to fear its loss. Corrupted by fear, they consolidate power by manipulating the masses with that which the masses fear most - loss of security. Convince the masses they are dependent upon those in power and those in power gain what they continually seek and crave - more power, more control, more tenure.

Those who love power have much invested in denying the empowerment of others. They have much to gain by keeping others "in the dark". People who are without light fear everything, including their own power. Those who fear are easy to control and manipulate.

Knowledge of the mind and the spirit illuminates the ability of <u>every person</u> to move beyond fear. Such empowerment allows the masses to access their own innate abilities to govern themselves through truth and right action. Such knowledge is unlikely to reach the hands of the masses if it must first pass through the hands of those who love power and control.

Nevertheless, scientific research on the mind and its energies continues. Information does filter to the public. Though largely unheralded in the popular media, books on such research do exist. For instance:

Dr. Harold Saxon Burr researched what he called "electrodynamic mind fields" at Yale and published his results <u>in The Fields of Life</u> (1972).

A colleague of Dr. Burr's, Edward R. Russell, in his book <u>Design for Destiny</u>, (1976), wrote at length about his research in these mind fields and included extensive research done by L.L. Vasiliev, a professor of Physiology at the University of Leningrad. Russell cites compelling evidence that thought is independent of the physical brain and exists in a field which he named the "T Field".

Rupert Sheldrake, a biologist at the University of London called these same fields "morphogenic fields" , which he described as "fields of reality into which everything that is done and thought is fed and which, in turn, influences everything that is done and thought".

Richard Gerber, M.D. in his book <u>Vibrational Medicine</u> (1988) compiles extensive information and knowledge from the physical sciences about the subtle energy fields of mind, body, and spirit.

Fortunately, humans enjoy a long history of not waiting for science or research studies to offer proof and documentation of the existance of energies which are often felt, and sometimes seen, by many. Shamans, Kahunas, Yogis, Spiritualists, Medicine Men, Medicine Women, Sacred Healers, Witch Doctors, - all tribes, cultures, and ages have had those who have knowledgeably used (as well as misused) the subtle energies of the mind, body, and spirit. Written and/or spoken histories of their information and practices exist. If you are interested in exploring some or all of these, buy and peruse <u>The Donning International Encyclopedic Psychic Dictionary</u> (1986) compiled by June G. Bletzer, Ph.D. It is a major compilation of metaphysical exploration.

Metaphysics is a name coined by Aristotle - long considered, with Plato and Socrates, the most influential philosopher in the history of Western thought. Also considered the father of modern biology and physics, Aristotle wrote a treatise on the natural sciences that he divided into two parts. The first part - the study of the natural, visible world - he named "Physika". The second part - the study of immaterial substance and form - was named "Metaphysika", or, literally, the works after the physical works.

Metaphysicians seek knowledge of immaterial substance and form; that is, the subtle energies of mind, body, and spirit. They use this knowledge to understand and work with the inherent abilities of human beings to create and change physical reality. While many metaphysicians are scientists and many scientists are metaphysicians, the study of metaphysics has not, fortunately, waited for scientific proof before exploring and working within the subtle energies. Had the master metaphysician Jesus waited for such "proof", he would have had to wait centuries to perform his miracles.

"Miracles" are what metaphysicians seek to illuminate, define, duplicate, and make common in the experience of human kind. Master metaphysicians Moses, Jesus, Buddha, Mohammad, Krisna, and others whose names are less universally known have demonstrated miracles. Each have taught: "These things I do, you can do also."

A notable Master Metaphysician alive today is a man of India named Sri Sathya Sai Baba. He frequently demonstrates "miracles". Many of these, including the ability to materialize matter "out of thin air", have been well documented by highly respected western researchers. When asked to explain his abilities, he offered these words: "In the case of Science, proof precedes belief. In the case of Spirituality, belief precedes experience."

Opening to the "invisible" world of the subtle energies develops the beliefs that will lead to YOUR miracles. As you open, you will, at your own pace, receive guiding dreams, visions, thoughts, inner voices, and inner teachers. You will be led to "outer" guides, teachers, and books as well. Your powers may open quickly or they may open more slowly. They will open - if you do not force them open - under the guidance of your Higher Self at a pace and in ways that are most comfortable, safe, and balanced for YOU.

Of course, dreams, visions, thoughts, voices, books, guides and teachers - whether "inner" or "outer" - can be deceptive. Mind, soul, and spirit are masters of illusion. Mind, soul, and spirit can harbor doubts, fears, false beliefs, insecurities, denials, emotions, imbalances, ego, lower instincts, and lies.

This book is meant to remind you of your - and others' - power to create. The power to create is the guiding principle of miracles as well as conceit and deceit. Knowledge lights the way through the maze of deceit and conceit. Understanding allows the creation of miracles without chaining the soul, destroying the body, unbalancing the mind, or darkening the spirit.

We wish to share our knowledge and understanding with you. We are Dr. Hugh Harmon, Pamela, and Master of Light. As much of the credibility for this book rests on Dr. Harmon's academic and professional credentials - including 60 years of metaphysical research, and 40 years of clinical practice in "holistic healing" therapies - we share some of his personal journey in Chapter Two. You will learn more of Pamela in Chapter Three. Throughout these pages, you will be guided by Master of Light, and in the last chapter you will learn more of Master of Light. All of the chapters are important, for they lay the foundation for your understanding of the knowledge we share.

We share in these pages what thousands of bodies, minds, souls, and spirits have taught us. We work daily with levels of consciousness many don't even believe exist. We know they exist. We have seen, heard, recorded, observed, and experienced too many miracles, phenomena, healings, transformations, and demonstrations to not believe. We believe.

We don't ask you to believe. We offer you information. All of the stories in these pages are true, (with the *possible* exception of the Three Princes of Serendip, which *may* be true). However, so many people have had such similar experiences, many of the stories (and nearly all of the information) may seem to fit more than one of our clients, students, or research subjects. We assure you all: the names we have used are fictitious and we have been careful to eliminate identifying data.

Some of the stories are painful. It is our hope you will recognize from these stories - as we have - that human suffering has a purpose. Its purpose is, perhaps, best summed up in a word: Apocatastasis.

In ancient times, it is written, alchemists knew the secret of turning base metals into gold. They named this process Apocatastasis. The ancient alchemists were also metaphysicians and they understood that the material and the immaterial worlds mirror one another. Apocatastasis, they realized, was also the transmutation of base experiences into gold - the gold of spiritual illumination. Such illumination was, to the ancient alchemists, the most valuable treasure of all.

The following is a story illuminating the process of Apocatastasis in the material and the immaterial worlds. It is a story, one of many, in the ancient Persian Folktale, <u>The Three Princes of Serendip</u>.

One day, the three Princes of Serendip leave their father, the King, to search for glory and treasures that will honor their father and gain his favor. They do not travel as Princes and, thus, they find much hardship and human suffering along the way. Also, too, they discover, quite unexpectedly, great good in the most unlikely of situations, places, and people. To commemorate finding valuable and agreeable things not specifically sought, the three Princes of Serendip coin a word called "serendipity".

There is another word, an ancient word, used by the Princes to describe the power to transform the tragedies of life by focusing on the good hidden within them. It is told that one day the Princes came upon a great river with rushing, roaring waters. Beside the river a man in fine robes sat weeping and cursing the gods.

"O worthy one," spoke the eldest of the brothers, "what think ye the gods have brought upon thy worthy head?"

"Calamity and catastrophe," wailed the man loudly, cursing the evil that has befallen him.

"Tell us your story," begged the second brother as they gather around the sobbing man.

"Indeed, for perhaps we may be of service to you," announced the youngest of the three.

"None can help me," the man moaned in reply, staring sadly at the rushing river. "For there lies my fortune and my future. I am a merchant and I have gathered many fine things from all the known kingdoms of the world. There I built my palace, beside the banks of the river. Never has the river, in even ancient memory, run over the bank where I built my palace and stored my treasures. But now, behold. It has stolen all my most precious things." Again the merchant began to wail loudly.

The Princes gazed at one another and in unison they joyfully raised their voices to cry: "Apocatastasis!"

Bewildered, the merchant demanded the meaning of such a reaction to his sad tale.

"It is a magical and mystical word," the oldest brother told him, smiling broadly at the merchant.

"It means," added the second brother, whose smile was even wider, "that if you search for the good in this seeming misfortune you will find greater fortune."

"We leave you then with joy in our hearts," the youngest brother announced, his smile the widest of all, "for with this tragedy we know you have been blessed."

With that, the brothers rode away, leaving the merchant to ponder on their words.

Many years later, the Princes returned, stopping at the very spot along the river where last they had left the merchant. A servant ran breathlessly towards them and shouted in greeting: "O good brothers, my Master saw you riding from afar and he invites you to rest and partake of his hospitality."

Following the servant, the Princes came to a great palace built on a high cliff above the river. There, the merchant greeted them, smiling so broadly his teeth sparkle brightly in the sun. "Welcome my friends!" he hailed them, "and thanks be to the gods for your return. I have much to tell you and much for which to thank you. First, please, rest and prepare for the evening meal, at which you shall be my most honored guests."

Later that evening, after all at the palace had gathered to share the finest of wines and most delectable of foods, the merchant stood and bowed to the Princes. "My friends," he began, "when last we met, you gifted me with a word; a strange word, with a strange meaning. A magical, mystical word, you said, and as I pondered upon this, I watched the angry, swollen river. Suddenly, I recalled my boyhood spent along the banks of this river. How I had loved the river! And it had returned my love with friendship. It had shared my play and my dreams. It had even spoken to me, many times. I had forgotten that as a man, but I remembered now, and I became quiet in my heart, listening intently to the rushing waters They were speaking, it seemed to me, of my palace. 'This is not the place,' the river whispered urgently. 'Lift your sights and you will see.'

"I looked above the river. There was a promontory high above it I had not considered this spot before as it was somewhat difficult to reach, but as I gazed upon it I allowed my heart to lift. I realized the river was telling me a more magnificent view of its span would bring me greater joy than sitting along its banks. 'Apocatastasis!' I shouted aloud, and joy filled my heart, even though I had lost all of my treasures and most of my wealth.

"I sent my servants up the mountain to mark out the foundations for the palace I would someday build. My servants, in working the earth, discovered a field of priceless jewels. 'Apocatastasis!' I cried out once again when they brought this news to me.

"With the wealth brought to me by the river, I built a grander palace than any I could have imagined. I invited all that I knew from all the Kingdoms I had traveled to come and partake of the generous hospitality I could now afford.

"My friends have come and they bring treasures that fill my many room; though the company they bring is more precious than these gifts. I feel blessed beyond measure, and the youthful zest of my youth has been returned to me. My friends, my family, my good health - these are my greatest treasures. From my misfortune has, indeed, flowed the greatest good."

Together, the merchant and the Princes raised their wine and in unison toasted as one: "APOCATASTASIS!"

~ NOTES TO YOURSELF ~

Chapter 2

From Bad Billy to Doctor Hugh

I was named Hugh William Harmon, but everyone began calling me Billy early on. I was not initially wanted by my father, but I was loved and revered by him after my birth. I never felt a real closeness or bonding with my mother, perhaps a result of the near fatal diarrhea I suffered the first few months of my life. I could not tolerate milk or soy milk substitutes and was slowly starving and dehydrating to death. Dr. Paul Popono, a renowned naturalist and writer, happened to visit the family. After taking one look at my dehydrated, starving body, he gathered dates from the palms in our front yard, stewed them in water, and put the resulting inverted sugar water in my bottle. After that I thrived, and though I grew up during the depression, I seldom lacked for anything. My grandparents were doting, my older brother and I were close, I had lots of friends, and, perhaps best of all, I raised my very own horse. From the outside, it was an ideal childhood. Yet, I never really felt a sense of completeness within my family, maybe because from the inside it was less than ideal.

My father and mother suffered through so much dissension between them that by the time I was in high school they hardly spoke to one another and although they continued to live in the same house they were rarely in the same room together. I became determined never to marry, terrified I would end up like my father - locked in a dead relationship with a controlling and domineering woman.

My mother was strong, but controlling, domineering, and manipulative. She could and would force us to do anything she needed or wanted done. For me, the worst was when she made me "take care of" the animals. We had a large property in a very small town and people would often dump unwanted pets and strays on our land, knowing the Harmons would take care of them. We did. When the animals got to be too numerous, which never took too long, mother would tell me the animals were slowly starving. She insisted because I loved animals it was my responsibility to take them to the desert and shoot them. I was eight years old when it began. I loved animals deeply. But it was my job to destroy them. Mother convinced me that it was my job and there was certainly no bucking mother in anything. It nearly destroyed me, and I began searching for a way to save the animals.

The only way, really, was to keep them from multiplying. I already knew I could communicate with animals mentally. By using my mind and thinking what I wanted them to do, I could usually get them to do it. So, in my mind, I "told" the females to stop going into heat. It seemed to me there was a change - shorter, less frequent heats, and smaller litters, but they still over-multiplied. However, I was convinced I was communicating better and better with their minds. Such was the beginning of my lifelong interest in the mind and the powers of the mind.

The second major influence on my life's work was my sexual development. My first sexual experience was when I was four years old. I was in my bedroom playing with my toys when an eight year old relative came into the room and began playing a different sort of game with me. One that led to mutual masturbation and oral copulation. I was intrigued by our play and participated willingly. What we were doing felt good. Then he fiercely warned me NOT TO TELL! I wasn't sure what I wasn't supposed to tell or why and I was at an age when secrets were very difficult to keep. I began to feel very burdened by the need for secrecy and wanted to stop.

He would not let me stop, and that confused, scared, and upset me. Now everything felt bad ~ my tummy hurt, my genitals were sore, and my head was aching. I wanted to cry. He began to moan, then he ejaculated. I was terrified. I thought I'd hurt him terribly. Laughing at me, he said he had "done it right", but I hadn't. He continued to tease me, and I began to worry there was something wrong with me. I didn't know who to ask though, because I couldn't "tell". When he left, I was feeling a lot of heavy feelings for a little boy.

Now, it is not unusual, abnormal, or wrong for children to experiment with each other physically. Sexuality is meant to be a process that unfolds gradually and naturally within ones peer group at a pace and level that is comfortable and unforced. It is when one is manipulated, seduced, betrayed, or forced into any activity for which one is not prepared - whether emotionally, mentally, or physically - that it becomes abusive.

My next sexual encounter was when I was six. A playmate, an eight year old girl, pulled me aside, whispering she knew a "good game". The game was vaginal penetration and was of only mild interest to me. There were a lot more fun and interesting things to do and after our brief "play" we ran off to do them. Unlike the experience when I was four, I carry no negative thoughts or feelings from that experience. I hadn't been forced into it. I was able to stop when I wanted. And while I knew it was a "secret" I shouldn't tell any adults, there wasn't much I did by age six that I would tell an adult anyway, so I wasn't burdened with guilt or shame. It had been just another silly and naughty thing we kids would do behind the adults' backs.

When I was eight and a half years old, I was manipulated into sexual activity by an army Master Sergeant living on the Army Air Corp Post near us. I liked being on the Air Corp Post. I also liked the gifts and privileges I was given by the Sergeant and didn't mind too much the favors I had to do in return. Those favors were sexual. He often had me watch while he masturbated himself and sometimes he would masturbate me manually or orally, though he was a very gentle man and made a game of it. I'd been taught to respect adults and the Master Sergeant told me what we were doing wasn't bad. Still, I felt inwardly that something was not right. Perhaps because we always hid in the mesquite bushes and he was always very nervous upon our return to his offices.

This arrangement continued until an Army Provost Marshal, who knew of the man's reputation, began to notice our friendship. The Provost Marshall was a friend of my family and, after restricting me from visiting the base, he told my parents of the Sergeant's reputation and his suspicions of what might have been happening to me. My parents only comment to me after hearing this was, "The Sergeant doesn't sound like a very nice man, perhaps you'd best not see him again."

When I was eleven, I met another man who, like the Sergeant, began to shower me with attention. He was quite a famous actor, with a large, lavish ranch, and he flew his own airplane. I loved it at his ranch. Things were always happening there to excite an 11 year old boy, including lots of parties with famous, and infamous, Hollywood actors and actresses. Best of all, he started taking me up in his PT 19 Army Trainer and teaching me to fly. Unfortunately he, too, began to require sexual favors. I disliked this activity, but I was reluctant to give up the flying lessons and the fun I had at the ranch. As the favors began to escalate, however, I decided the fun and the flying weren't worth it. I just wanted to end the association.

My mother, however, made that almost impossible to do. She was thrilled such a famous person was taking an interest in me and she was hopeful he would make me famous. I could already sing and dance and I could mimic anyone or anything. One of my early childhood playmates had been Shirley Temple and my mother had dreams of my becoming a star like her. I felt quite betrayed by mother. She must have known the man she was pushing me toward was a homosexual. He lived openly with a well-known author and playwright, a man whom everyone knew to be homosexual. I did try to tell her about the things he was making me do, but she would refuse to discuss my relationship with him beyond insisting I promote it as much as possible. She must have known what was going on, especially considering my previous experiences with the Master Sergeant. My sense of betrayal by my mother would continue to haunt me for many years.

When my mother would not listen or help, I turned to another woman. She was a sophisticated woman, a friend of my family and a friend of the actor in question. Though well aware of his sexual orientation, she refused my request for help. Laughing, she told me to *act like a big boy* and handle it myself. Her ridicule shamed me and her refusal to help hurt me. With no one else to turn to, I did "act like a big boy". I told the actor that while I liked him and enjoyed our adventures together - and while I DEARLY loved learning to fly - I wanted to end the sexual stuff. That ended that. I lost my beloved lessons in flying, as well as a great deal of trust in the adults around me.

Years later I would interview a police detective assigned to cover "chicken hawks", the name given to those adult males who sexually prey on young boys. He said he'd spent his life trying to educate parents to the astounding number of "chicken hawks" in their children's lives. "Camp counselors, YMCA instructors, boy scout and cub scout leaders, sports coaches, teachers, priests, even policemen - no field is free of them. Naturally, the hawks will go where the chickens are," he said.

Parents - and other trusted family members ~ **must** establish and encourage, from a very early age, open communication with their children. It is SO VERY easy to manipulate and coerce children, as most children have been taught to respect and obey adults, no matter what. It is very easy to convince a child that what is happening (especially if it feels good at some level) is the child's "fault" or that the child "asked for it" or that the child will "get in trouble" if the child "tells". It is important to teach children to respect adults, but to know that NO adult has the right to do anything that the child must "keep secret". It is my strong belief, and the belief of many in my field of work, that the "secrets" people keep - from themselves and others - bring illness, disease, addictions, and destructive behaviors.

Sexual abuse and molest are powerful secrets that people often feel must be kept. That idea is slowly dying. Sexual abuse and molest are not more frequent today. People today are more willing to talk about it. Being more willing to talk about it encourages more and more of us who have suffered from it to tell our secrets.

Perhaps because of my childhood sexual experiences, I became quite sexually precocious in my early teens. Although I experimented a great deal sexually, I never took advantage of anyone. Sensitized early to abusive, coercive behavior, I was always careful the situation, the girl, and the sex were safe. By age 16, I was quite mature for my age and began dating women in their middle to late 20's. I escorted these women to several of the Palm Springs night clubs frequented by Hollywood celebrities and Palm Springs socialites. Soon, I became a regular, invited to private parties held at the clubs after hours. These parties were frequently little more than orgies, and while I became friends with a lot of the homosexual and bi-sexual entertainers who attended them, I knew I was most definitely heterosexual.

My early sexual experiences with males were negative experiences for me. Not because they had been homosexual experiences, for children often explore within their own genders, but because I had been manipulated, used, and my protests ignored. Such experiences constitute sexual abuse. The shame, anger, guilt, and sense of betrayal, I harbored from those experiences stayed with me for many years and affected me in many ways. Some of those ways were quite convoluted.

A curious and adventurous boy, I was nicknamed "Bad Billy" by a family member. One day, I took a rattlesnake (live, but contained in a one galleon glass jar) on the school bus for my biology teacher, Mr. Batley, who'd asked for "interesting specimens" for class. I proudly showed it to Mr. Batley, who was also the school bus driver, by shoving the jar close to his face. Screaming, he slammed on the brakes, which threw me off balance and caused me to drop the jar, which shattered as it hit the floor. Instantly, girls were standing on the seats and screaming. Boys were shouting and whooping down the aisles. I was chasing after one scared rattlesnake slithering under the seats. After I finally caught it (you grab a rattler *quickly* behind the head to catch it), Mr. Batley threw me off the bus and left me standing there, holding my rattler. I had to walk to school. I left the rattler behind. He was happy to stay.

After that, everyone began calling me "Bad Billy". The funny thing was, I secretly believed the moniker was given me because I'd been sexually molested. Even though I hadn't told anyone, I felt everyone somehow knew anyway and the name was their way of letting me know they knew. Not an uncommon feeling in sexual abuse survivors. "Bad Billy" began to feel, deep inside, he really was bad.

Years later, rather late in my professional career, I realized the name Bill ~ which I'd been called all my life ~ reminded me at a deep level of "Bad Billy". That name, after all those years, still bothered me deeply. So I changed my name, insisting I be called by my given name, Hugh. Interestingly, those who knew me by Bill and couldn't seem to adjust to my "new" name, drifted out of my life. I was glad. I was happy to put "Bad Billy" behind me.

There have been positive benefits from my early abuse. My experiences sensitized me to the feelings of others, which has been valuable in my clinical practice. I have worked a great deal with survivors of abuse of all kinds and have worked extensively with sexual abuse survivors. I am able to tune in readily to people who have experienced abuse - even if they themselves are not consciously aware of it. I can often guess what the abuse consisted of and at what age - and will most often be right. However, I take great care, because of this, to clear my mind of any preconceptions when dealing with clients so as not to influence their minds or feelings.

Nevertheless, as a clinician and keen observer of human nature and behavior, I cannot help but note the common bonds linking survivors of abuse. Whether that abuse is physical, mental, emotional, spiritual, verbal, or sexual, and whether it is short-term or long-term, the scars run deep and link people of all ages and gender. Very often the shame, anger, and guilt are so deeply rooted there is an inward need for punishment. That need destroys many lives.

It has been my life's work to save lives. As a boy, made responsible for the death of my beloved animals, I'd determined I would become a healer. Because of my interest and skill in communicating with animals' minds, I figured I would become a veterinarian with a psychological bent. However, as I grew, I became more interested in people, so I entered medical school instead.

It didn't take me long to become disenchanted with the medical profession's bias for cutting, burning, and poisoning the body. Discouraged, I wondered when we would be taught "real" healing. Then I took an elective class in medical hypnosis taught by a man named Dave Elman. I was so impressed with the seeming ability of a person to heal quickly with only the power of the mind, I left medical school and obtained a Doctorate in Behavioral Science from the University of Southern California. Later, I added a Doctorate in Religion. Later still, as I became more and more fascinated with Metaphysics, I obtained a Doctorate of Metaphysics from the University of Metaphysics in Los Angeles.

I chose not to practice psychology. The licensing methods of the governing board were restrictive and controlling. They wanted to tell me how I could and could not work with people and wanted me to fill out endless paper work for the privilege of controlling me. (In my opinion, the medical field ought to have taken a look at THAT situation and stopped it right there. We'd be a lot better off today, both patients and doctors.) Besides, I'd already discovered that clinical hypnosis was the most powerful tool available for guiding clients into healing states. So I opened a practice as a clinical hypnotherapist. As word spread of the powerful change and healing being demonstrated through my work, I began being asked to teach other professionals, including medical doctors and psychologists, my "technique".

My so called technique was then - and remains today - teaching others to take responsibility for themselves and their own lives. After working for the past 40 years with literally thousands of people, I KNOW that those who hope and wait for others to save or to heal them are lost. No-one can save or heal another. I have asked many of the medical doctors with whom I've studied, worked, and associated if they have ever really healed anyone. After some reflection, they have (with only one exception) answered: "No, I just keep people alive. They do the rest themselves." Healing, I believe and observe, is an inside job.

It is the same with mental and emotional healing. Most people go to a therapist to be "fixed." The problem with this is twofold: 1) It promotes the mind set that the self is broken. 2) It turns responsibility for the self over to another. While many therapists - whether licensed or unlicensed - are skilled and sincere, others are not. I often remark to the therapists I train that the word "therapist", when separated, is "the rapist". Therapy, when done badly, can feel like a rape, and do just as much damage.

I have come to think of myself not as a therapist or a healer, but as a teacher. I teach what I have learned about the body, the mind, the soul, and the spirit so that others can use my knowledge to heal and improve themselves. I know a great deal and have a great deal to share and to teach. Perhaps the most important message I have to teach is this: Thought creates all that there is. Negative thoughts, whether conscious or hidden, block the unlimited potential for good and promote imbalance of the mind, the body, and the spirit.

No-one likes to admit to negativity. Certainly, I don't. But the fact is, we all harbor negative thoughts and emotions that continue to keep us "stuck" in many areas. While my clinical practice continued to grow and flourish, my personal life did not. When my second marriage became stuck in negativity, I knew it was time to investigate the lack of satisfaction I experienced in my intimate relationships. While there are always many contributing factors leading to the demise of relationships, I was determined to uncover the limiting negative thoughts and emotions I was contributing to my marriages.

That proved difficult to do. While it is true that self-healing is an inside job, it is also true that the mind is capable of setting up powerful resistance to changing "old" patterns of thinking and behavior, even if they are counter-productive. Thus the need for a skilled and knowledgeable therapist to help move one past ones own outer and inner resistance. I needed a therapist who worked with the tools I knew worked. I needed a clinical hypnotherapist. However, while I had trained hundreds of clinical hypnotherapists, none of them possessed my level of skill and knowledge. Of course, none of them had my years of experience either. I tried working with a few "conventional" therapists near me, but became impatient with their more limited techniques. I did know of colleagues who used similar methods and techniques to mine, but they lived at such distances it was impossible to work with them. Even clinical hypnotherapy requires repeated visits for deep rooted healing and change. So I began to work with my personal physician, Warren Jacobs, M.D.

Dr. Jacobs is a true healer. While it is true that no-one can heal another, there are people who can do much to facilitate the healing process. Dr. Jacobs is such a person, and we began to work with a technique we'd learned in a class together called Touch For Health. This technique, pioneered by Dr. John Thie, utilizes the meridian energy flows to help people get in touch with their emotions.

The meridian flows are the pathways of life energy that flow to all organs of the body. They are the same meridian flows worked with in acupuncture and acupressure. I have worked with these same energy flows to perfect a means of correcting allergies without needles or medications. While the Chinese have used an elaborate method of using the meridian flows to correct allergies for centuries, a fellow researcher and I began to investigate Western knowledge of the immune system to find a more simplified method. Later, I continued this research on my own to develop a very simple, quick, and completely painless and non-invasive method of testing and correcting allergic reactions. A friend named it The Allergone Method and Pamela and I use it extensively with our clients.

In literally hundreds of cases of allergies to foods, pollens, mold, dust, hair, medications, animals, chemicals, make-up, colognes, tobacco, alcohol, insects, bites, stings, pollutants, etc. complete relief has been experienced. I've even found people allergic to cold and have successfully balanced them to it. Some people have had allergic reactions to a particular color of flower and not to another color of the same type of flower. Two women were allergic to their husbands. One of the women was allergic to her husband's hair and this situation was easily corrected. The other woman's allergy turned out to be emotional, which we addressed with therapy.

The relief clients have experienced with this method includes completely cleared sinuses and complete elimination of headaches, aches, pains, fatigue, upset stomachs, itchy ears and eyes, skin rashes, hives, chronic sneezing and coughing, food addictions, scratchy eyes and throats, red and swollen eyes and throats, even hyperactivity and the inability to concentrate. Our research shows allergies frequently can be a cause of hyperactivity and attention deficit disorders in children. We find a combination of eliminating the allergies, which is very easy to do with my method, and then some hypnotic suggestions to counteract the negative programming they have received in regards to their "condition" turns these children around completely.

Balancing to all allergens has been of tremendous help to our clients with arthritis, asthma, and diseases involving imbalanced immune systems. A client of Pamela's was successful in healing Lyme's Disease due to tick bites with a combination of this method and two sessions of hypnosis work to bring the immune system back into balance.

How long allergy relief lasts with this method is not yet clear as I have only been using it with myself and my clients for thirteen years. Most clients have, in these thirteen years, remained allergy symptom free to those allergens to which they have been balanced. Other clients have had to be re-balanced to specific allergens when their immune systems have become compromised by stress, illness, or an overwhelming exposure to that allergen. For instance, clients of ours living along golf courses sometimes need to be re-balanced to grass when the golf course is scarified. The same is true for some clients who have been balanced to dust and then been caught out in the open in a dust storm. I, myself, have to be re-balanced to mesquite pollen when it comes in bloom once a year as we sit beneath that tree every morning. Pamela, on the other hand, was also allergic to mesquite pollen, but she has not had to be re-balanced to it in the six years since I balanced her. Re-balancing takes less than a minute.

Balancing to allergens is like any other healing in that encouraging the immune system to right itself may be all that was needed. However, when an emotional need for allergies is present or a subconscious belief in the inevitability of allergies remains, the allergy symptoms may return. For subconscious belief in allergies, EMDR or hypnosis or a combination of these will usually be sufficient. For an emotional need for allergies, regression therapy is effective.

Although it would naturally be upsetting to the allergy drug companies and to those labs who specialize in expensive testing for allergies, I would like to share - not sell - my method. As it is a non-medical process it can be used by many in the healing arts and sciences, but I intend to teach this method only to professional therapists and doctors. While it is a simple method and can do no harm, it is also a method that requires careful intake and investigation if all the allergies are to be discovered and balanced and all emotional factors eliminated. Partial relief may come with the balancing of only some allergies, but all allergies must be balanced for complete relief. It's also important to discern between toxins and allergens. Reactions to toxins cannot be corrected by this method. Fortunately, the body can itself indicate through this method whether a substance is toxic to it or merely an allergen. For instance, we find white sugar is toxic to many and should be avoided by those people. For other people, it is an allergen to which the immune system can be balanced. The same is true with sugar substitutes.

I have already taught this method to a few doctors (one of those an allergy specialist) who came to me for relief of their allergies. However, they have been afraid to use it with their own patients as they don't understand how it works and could not, therefore, explain it to their medical boards. I can explain it. Even if the medical boards don't accept that information, as much of it is based on meridian flows, they can easily see its benefit when they experience it for themselves. As it's non-toxic, non-invasive, and very inexpensive, it would be of enormous benefit to millions of people who suffer needlessly. I would love to see every medical practitioner in the land using it.

In ancient China medical practitioners had great incentive for keeping their patients in good health as they were paid a steady income as long as those they served were well. When a person became ill, that person's family ceased to pay the doctor until he or she became well again. This situation propelled those who practiced medicine to investigate and develop ways of keeping the body healthy and balanced. Keeping the meridian flows of their patients flowing and in balance was one of the most important of those ways for the meridian flows are important not only to the immune system but to all the systems of the body and brain.

Meridian flows are strongly affected by thoughts and emotions. Negative thoughts and emotions can block or diminish these flows, thus depriving the organ associated with that meridian of necessary life energy and leading to weakness or disease in that area of the body. With Dr. Thie's technique it is possible to quickly and comfortably discover which meridian flows are weak and the thoughts and emotions weakening them.

Dr. Jacobs and I refined Dr. Thie's techniques to uncover the experiences creating the thoughts and emotions weakening the meridians. Working with our refined techniques, Dr Jacobs and I discovered I was unable to allow myself an ongoing, satisfying, and fulfilling relationship past a certain length of time with a woman due to feelings of guilt, shame, and anger that I'd carried forward from my negative childhood sexual experiences. These experiences had locked me into the subconscious belief I did not deserve happiness in my intimate relationships. I would subconsciously choose women that would bring me the unhappiness I inwardly thought I deserved. To complicate matters, we discovered I also subconsciously believed all women to be betrayers. My subconscious pattern of behavior was one of "setting up" the women in my relationships to betray me so the relationship would end. If a woman was loving and caring, I would subconsciously begin to act in ways that would eventually cause her to be unloving and uncaring. Towards the end of the relationship I would, sometimes deliberately, cause them to become so angry at me they would either break up with me or wouldn't feel too badly when I left them.

After discovering what is undesirable in ones self, the next step is to change it. Although Dr. Jaycobs possessed superior therapeutic skills, he worked with the body, not the mind. I needed a hypnotherapist. More, I needed a hypnotherapist with my understanding and knowledge of sexual abuse and my level of therapy skills in working with it. I began to program attracting such a person.

I have trained, through my state approved school of hypnosis and hypnotherapy, hundreds of students. These have included medical doctors, chiropractors, therapists, teachers, journalists, business people, sales people, sports professionals, retirees, "alternative" healers, and metaphysical seekers. Some of my many students established their own practices in hypnosis and hypnotherapy. Others put their new knowledge and skills to good use in their professional and personal lives. People have come from all over the country to train with me, but Pamela was the first to come from Hawaii. All of the people I have trained have been special in some way, but Pamela was extraordinary. She was one of those students that seem to "soak" up everything. I had the sense I wasn't teaching her, just reminding her of things she already knew, but had temporarily forgotten.

When Pamela began working with volunteers brought into the advanced classes for supervised sessions, I was startled to observe in her a natural and gifted therapeutic manner that closely matched my own. Further, she seemed to possess an innate knowledge and understanding of the mind that took her beyond what she had learned in class. I was excited by her abilities and began to talk with her about her plans after graduation from the school.

She was, she informed me, a writer with a life long interest in metaphysics and the mind. While she'd planned to use hypnosis in some way, she'd not really considered full time work in the field. Somewhat startled to find herself so gifted, however, and buoyed by my supportive enthusiasm for her abilities, she was considering opening a hypnotherapy practice when she returned to Honolulu. I was thrilled. As a teacher nothing is more exciting than to see gifted students embrace their gifts and training to use them for the benefit of others. I was trying to think how I could teach her even more of what I knew in the short time remaining when it occurred to me that Pamela might well be the one to write the book I had long planned to write.

I am an able writer, but hardly enthused by the process of writing. I lack the temperament, the patience, and the time for re-writes, a necessary process in writing a book. I suggested to Pamela that, in addition to establishing a practice, she might be interested in writing a book of my work - specifically a book on sexual abuse. In that way, she would have access to my written notes, tapes of sessions with clients who had agreed to share their stories, and could even observe sessions. It would be a way of sharing as much of my knowledge with her as possible and getting that knowledge out to all who would benefit from it. Pamela enthusiastically agreed. After graduating from the school she began a short internship with me. Then, taking with her the notes, tapes, and books she would need, she returned to Hawaii.

Over the next two years, we would collaborate often, both on the book and on her growing clinical practice. As I listened to her telephoned reports and read the pages of the book sent back to me, I noted with pride her growth as a therapist and her increasing knowledge of the mind. I noted, also, her increasing contributions to the book and was bemused when she announced, rather defensively, that it was now "our" book. I chuckled inwardly and wondered that it had taken her so long to realize it.

In the meanwhile, I continued with my own work which seemed to be moving in a new direction. Many of my clients had always been referred by doctors and other therapists, but the practitioners were now bringing in these people themselves in order to observe my work with them. I had further refined the techniques Dr. Jacobs and I had refined from Dr. Thie's techniques, naming my refined process Neuro-Muscular Response, or NMR. Using NMR, it became possible to access information from all levels of the mind - cell consciousness, conscious level, subconscious level, emotional levels, 'inner child', past life memory banks - and from the Higher Self. Clients could differentiate between "truths", "programmed beliefs", and "false information." We could discover in one morning or afternoon session all that was out of balance in their bodies and their lives and what needed to be done to regain the balance. Frequently, the one being tested would comment: "Wow! I've just found out more about myself in a couple of hours than I've discovered in years of treatment!" Sometimes the NMR would indicate that working with my techniques was the best method of recovery. Sometimes, it would indicate other techniques and methods. On rare occasions, just discovering what was wrong was all that was needed for the healing or change to occur!

I believe in, and teach, the wisdom of using all of the treatments the body and the mind require or desire. I do not like the terms "mainstream" or "alternative" healing. I prefer the term "compatible" or "holistic" healing. Holistic Health is the awareness that the body and the mind are one and must be treated as one. No process has all of the answers. We must encourage our sharing with one another the knowledge we each gather and link that knowledge for the good of all.

As my professional practice began to change direction, so did my personal life. My second wife, Merrien, and I, recognizing we had grown apart, agreed to divorce. After a period of turmoil and anger, we parted as friends. She had been a large part of the success of my practice and my school. An amazing woman, she had lifted herself out of the despair of her childhood and beyond the damage of her abusive first marriage. She had endured, in that marriage, twenty years of violent abuse at the hands of her husband. When she finally was able to leave him, he broke into her home, intent on murdering her and their children with a gun he had brought. Trying to stop him, her oldest son accidentally killed his father. After that, she slowly and painstakingly rebuilt her life. She let nothing stop her, not even a devastating stroke a few years later.

When told by her doctors she would never walk again and that her sight, hearing, and speech would remain badly damaged, we began working with all the healing techniques I knew. She healed completely and became a powerful force in our community. Even working full-time to promote and support my work, she was active on several community boards and spoke (despite a previously paralyzing fear of public speaking) to numerous clubs and organizations about abuse. Invited to speak, with her children, on the Oprah Winfrey show, she received a generous donation from Oprah for the building of a shelter in Coachella Valley for abused women and their children. She, and I, served on the Board that got the shelter built - thanks to the support, help, donations, and work of many members of the community. That shelter - Shelter From The Storm - is now actively serving many women and children in our Valley.

Oprah was also instrumental in encouraging Merrien to write a book on the story of her abusive first marriage. Merrien did write her story and that book, Twenty Years To Life, is certain to help many understand more clearly and intimately how abusive marriages work and why they can't work as long as the abuse is going on. I am certain her story will inspire others to leave abusive marriages while they still survive the abuse. I am very proud of Merrien Helton Harmon and it was with a mixture of sadness and joy that I watched her go. Sadness because the sharing of our lives was over, and joy that each of us was facing new and exciting change.

My change involved Pamela. During the two years of collaboration by phone and letter, we'd grown to appreciate each other's energies more and more. Now that I was divorced, it seemed a good time to discover if our mutual appreciation was destined to be more than the professional collaboration of good friends. So Pamela moved to the desert and joined me. Thus did a new chapter in my life begin.

Chapter 3

The Path of Spirit

<u>Pamela</u>

I sometimes wonder if Hugh and I joined forces at the best or the worst times of our lives. On the plus side, we were both ready for spiritual growth and personal change - which was good, because we were each about to get plenty of both. On the negative side, he had just gone through a divorce that been drawn out for three long years. While his ex-wife had initiated the divorce, and he had resisted it, the tables had turned somewhere in the middle. Now here I was, arriving less than a month after the divorce had become final. I knew what that looked like, and I knew how difficult it made it for his ex-wife. It's hard enough to let go. It's even harder when the one you're letting go of seems to have found someone new. I'd been on both sides of the "other woman" drama and I had no intention of ever repeating either role.

I'd been the "other woman" at 19 years old when I had an affair with an actor I met on the set of the movie Hawaii. I'd been cast as a missionary's wife in my hometown, Kailua, Hawaii, but was "shipped" with the other missionary wives (one of whom was an unknown Bette Midler) to Hollywood. Both stars of the movie - Julie Andrews and Max Von Sydow - seemed to take a particular interest in befriending and watching out for me in "wicked" Hollywood. Mr. Von Sydow even went so far as to have me "whisked" away by his studio chauffeur when it was brought to his attention that a 'hung over' Richard Harris (who'd just been in a fist fight because of another man's wife) was focusing his attentions on me. I never saw Mr. Harris again.

I also was "locked" out of the set next door, where Elvis Presley was making a move. I'd wandered over there one day still dressed in my demure missionary wife's outfit; bonnet included. Elvis noticed me right away and walked right up to me. He smiled into my eyes, took my hands, and kissed my forehead. "Don't go away," he whispered in a soft, southern voice. I was thrilled. But I had to leave. I'd only had a ten minute break while the next scene was being set up on my movie. I hurried back and bragged to someone what had happened. "Oh, he probably just wants you to party with one of his entourage," I was told. "He does that, you know."

Well, I was 19, and an Elvis Party, no matter what the circumstances, sounded exciting so I hurried back over to the Presley set at my next break. The guard at the door, who had let me pass before, stopped me. "Your name Pamela?" he asked, looking down at his clip board.

I was impressed my name had been discovered so quickly. "Yes, it is," I answered eagerly.

"You can't come in here," he barked, and shut the door. I never did find out which one of my "protectors" managed that one.

Despite their efforts, however, I wasn't "saved". Unbeknownst to me, an actor on our set was watching me closely. It must have been quite clear I was ready for something to happen to me in Hollywood, and he happened. He was very discreet. He had to be. He was married, and I had people watching out for me. Ms. Andrews and Mr. Von Sydow either never found out or they gave up trying to help someone obviously intent on experiencing more than just movie making. Even after I discovered the actor in question was married the affair continued. I, young and dumb, thought his wife didn't understand him, and he didn't love her. She did, and he did. Their marriage lasted another twenty years, during which time he became a big star.

My affair with him ended when I went to New York with Bette Midler. We'd become acquainted on the set and friends the day she tried to teach me to smoke in Grauman's Chinese Theater. I managed to smoke two cigarettes, half of a third, and never smoked again. Bette had bigger plans for us anyway. The first phase of the plan was to take the money we'd made in the movie (slightly over $3,000 each) and conquer New York. She could conquer New York; she had no doubts about that. And she'd take me right along with her. Why go to New York; why not stay in Hollywood? Bette declared herself, "Too Jewish, too short, and too homely for

Hollywood."   (Bette's line, not mine, and NOT my opinion.) "But," she added with astute foresight, "when I'm too famous, they'll HAVE to put me in the movies."   Being in the movies in Hollywood had always been Bette's main plan.

It took Bette only five years to conquer New York. We began those years together, in a once grand, by then seedy, hotel in skid row on Bowery Street. We shared a small room with a sink and a bed and not much else. Bathrooms were down the hall, and going to them at any time of day or night meant stepping over drunks or druggies passed out in the hallways. Bette loved it. It was cheap and adventurous. I hated it. It was too cheap and too adventurous. Besides, we shared the one single bed that dipped to the inside. Whoever slept on the outside of the bed - usually Bette - would roll onto the one sleeping on the inside - usually me. After a week of suffocating in Bette's breasts, I found us a studio apartment, with two beds.

We were so excited to be in New York, living our dreams at last, that we found it hard to sleep, or even read, when we went to bed. We had no TV. We would lie in our beds and talk into the night. Often Bette would sing. (She'd sing in the shower, too, which obviously was beneath ducts that went through the whole building as she would frequently get "requests" in our mailbox the next day for particular songs.) One night we were fantasizing about how we would each accept our Academy Awards for "Best Actress". We discussed whom, beside each other, we would absolutely not want to compete against. We agreed it would be someone "really nice and really sweet". We decided, mutually, on Sally Fields, whom we'd both adored as Gidget and The Flying Nun.

Some time later, we went to see Janis Joplin perform on stage at the Fillmore East. As I watched her, I saw Bette Midler. "It's eerie," I told Bette afterwards. "She could be you." "I know," Bette agreed. "I saw that too." Wouldn't it be weird," I mused, "if you played her in a movie someday?" Fifteen years later, watching the Academy Awards on TV, I watched Bette lose the Best Actress Oscar for her part as Janis Joplin in THE ROSE to Sally Fields.

We lived in that studio apartment a couple of months, just long enough to experience the power outage that knocked out all the electricity in the whole North Eastern Seaboard. Caught uptown, I walked the fifty blocks home. I found Bette in bed reading with a flashlight. "I'm sorry," she apologized, looking up from her book. "I didn't pay the electric bill, and they've turned off our lights." I took her by the hand, pulled her outside, and pointed to the buildings on the street, all dark. "Damn," she quipped, "they're tough. I'll pay it tomorrow."

We moved when I found us a bigger apartment, with a bedroom for each of us, in Greenwich Village. Living in the Village, in the 60's. with Bette Midler! Wild times, right? Actually, the only wild times we shared were the go-go dancing gig at a bar in New Jersey and the night we killed the two "maiden aunts" and their parrot.

The go-go dancing lasted a month or so. We'd dance on a platform "stage" placed on the end of the bar. During our breaks, a country western group would play. It didn't take Bette long to join them. I could hear her yodeling happily on "stage" while I hid in the bathroom and read a book. Somewhere, unless it has been destroyed, there is life size cardboard cut-out of Bette and me, in our identical go-go outfits of black and white mini-skirts, white sweaters, and white boots.

The "maiden aunts", as we took to calling them, lived beneath our sixth floor walkup apartment on the corner of Bedford and Christopher. (The parrot, we were to later surmise, lived directly below Bette's bedroom.) We met the "aunts" as we walked by their door one day on the way up to our apartment. The door opened, and a crisp voice called out, "Young ladies!" Bette and I turned. Two elderly ladies stood there, one tall and lean and the other shorter and considerably less lean. "Our parrot has a bad heart," the taller, leaner "aunt" announced. "Loud noises and sex could kill it." They both stepped back and closed the door.

It is the ONLY time I've seen Bette tongue tied. After a stunned moment, we broke up laughing. "Well," Bette gasped out finally, "Hurrah for the parrot."

After that, the "aunts" took to pounding - with brooms we supposed - on Bette's bedroom floor whenever they deemed the activity above offensive. As just walking across the floor or dropping a book on it could elicit mad "brooming", they were kept quite busy protecting their parrot's sensibilities. Bette and I would often chuckle at the thought of them sitting, broom sticks in hand, with their eyes, ears, and imagination glued to the ceiling.

One night, impulsively thinking to add additional excitement to their lives, we began making "suspicious sounds", including dragging ourselves across Bette's bedroom floor. Suddenly, merciless in our mirth, we leaped together onto Bette's big double bed. The bed broke with a loud crash. We waited breathlessly. No pounding. We looked at each other. "The parrot!" we whispered in tandem. We tiptoed down the stairs and put our ears to the door: dead silence. We had obviously killed the parrot.

It seems we killed the maiden aunts too. We never heard from or saw them again. Every time we passed their door, we'd put our ears on it and listen: nothing. For all we know, they lie there still, two fossilized old ladies, brooms in hand, and a stiff parrot.

The next year, Bette moved out and my boyfriend moved in. Bette's and my relationship had been wounded in a grave misunderstanding. It recovered, but only after our mutually hurt feelings had subsided, which took some time. Even before our friendship resumed, Bette remained generous in her concern for my welfare. She called me to tell me she had talked a casting director into casting me, sight unseen, for a play she'd been cast in upstate. I declined. I didn't want to leave my boyfriend. Bette was horrified. "You'll never get anywhere in this business," she lectured, "if you don't take it seriously."

That was the problem exactly. I didn't take it seriously. I thought I did. But I was really waiting and hoping; waiting for someone to notice me and put me on the stage, for which I had little training, and hoping someone would notice me and put me in the movies, for which I definitely was not in the right place. Still, Bette tried hard to pull me along her path, the path we were both convinced I wanted too. "Your attitude is all wrong," she warned me, with wise and shrewd counsel I would neither understand nor heed. "You present yourself as 'I'm young, I'm pretty, and I think I'm talented. Please give me a chance.' On the other hand," she continued, "I let anyone and everyone know: 'Hey, I'm going to be a star. If you want to hitch yourself to me, this is your chance.' Sure," she conceded, "they all laugh at me, but someday, somebody won't."

Someday came, and everybody laughed ~ and applauded. In the Green Room of the Tonight Show, after Bette's first appearance on Johnny Carson, we looked at each other. Johnny hadn't asked her to sit with him, this first time, but we both knew she'd be back. Her star was definitely beginning its orbit. Neither of us, however, had any inkling she would someday bid

Johnny "Aloha" as his last guest on his last show.

That I was not ready for "show biz", despite Bette's best efforts, became even more clear when she called me to tell me she was leaving Fiddler On The Roof, the Broadway play in which she played one of the daughters. "I've set up a private audition for you with the producer and the casting director," she said, "Be there."

"I can't sing!" I protested, panicking.

"Anyone who can carry a tune can sing," Bette argued. "I TOLD you to take singing lessons when we first got here." She paused, clearly exasperated. "Well, you can act and you can dance. These people can help you, Pamela. Do something, anything. Let them know who you are. It's an opportunity few people get. USE IT!"

I'm ashamed to say I declined yet again. I am so thankful for Bette. She provided me a chance (several chances) to attain what I thought was my dream. Today, I have very few regrets that I did not attain that particular dream for I understand clearly, because of Bette, the sacrifices, focus, discipline, and belief in oneself that being a "star" requires. I did, however, put what Bette taught me to good use. I know how important sacrifice, focus, discipline, and belief in oneself are for making any dream come true. I have also learned, through experience, that the only dreams worth the effort and the hard work are the dreams in which one finds JOY.

I left New York when my joy was seriously disrupted by a broken heart. I loved my musician boyfriend, but he loved his guitar more, so I left him and returned home for a summer of mending. As is too common in the mending of a broken heart, I turned quickly to another man. Ten months later, we had a daughter; a magical being I named Bambi. Yes, there was rhyme (Bambi Birnbaum) and reason (she looked like a little dear, with large, beautiful, soft eyes) to the name. Nevertheless, I can't count the number of people who asked if we were going to name her brother - born three years later - Thumper. We named him Tyson, this soul whose spirit has walked with mine in many lives.

When Bambi was two, I visited Bette in New York. She asked if she could be Bambi's Godmother. I laughed. I thought she was kidding. The "Divine Miss M", a Godmother? Bette, looking crestfallen, replied, "I could help her financially, you know." I was confused. Surely she was joking. Godparents were a "Catholic Thing," weren't they? Too late, I discovered

Godparents were not just for Catholics and Bette had been serious. I had, once again, deeply hurt her feelings. I don't think she's forgiven me completely for that one. I don't think Bambi has either.

My relationship with my children's father lasted five years. Though we cared deeply for one another, we were clearly incompatible. Gifted athletically, he wanted to play sports more than he wanted to play house. While I wasn't certain I wanted to play house, I did know kids were a major responsibility, so I devoted myself to them. Of course, the trouble with devoting yourself to your children is someday they grow up and move away.

I'd held many jobs raising and supporting my children, including "ghost" writing. I wrote a script for a Hollywood producer for a play, The Orbitor, which UNICEF was to stage at the United Nations for "The Year of The Child." The director had a heart attack and as I had not received script credit, I never followed up on whether the play was ever staged. However, the script did bring me an offer of a studio job in Hollywood in the script writing department. This time, I turned down Hollywood. A place where you couldn't breathe the air didn't seem a place to raise children.

I cleaned houses and apartments in Honolulu for seven years instead. In most of those years I cleaned, by myself, ten to twelve residences a week. It was hard work. However, it provided the opportunity to write my own novels instead of the articles and stories I'd been writing for others. I'd mentally work on a book while I scrubbed, dusted, and vacuumed, then I'd write into the night at home.

My kids were patient. They believed me when I said my novel would make our dreams come true. Unfortunately, it didn't happen that way. The first novel I wrote was lousy. The second book was better, but not good enough. The third book was, I thought, good enough. I paid a literary agency to critique it. The verdict: "A dark and extraordinary work.. We took a long time arguing about it. In the end, we decided it is too badly flawed, with the parts considerably greater than the whole. You can imagine our regret in this case." The critique went on for several pages. I couldn't decipher whether they thought my writing was brilliant or awful.

I was devastated. My plan had been to fly to New York, sign the book contract, pick up the kids in Oklahoma, where they were spending the summer with my sister, and all of our dreams would come true. I'd been so certain of our "destiny", I'd given up the house we'd rented for ten years and given away all the furniture. Now what? I sat on the floor and cried all night. The next morning, I knew there was nothing to do but start over again. The kids would have to learn about not giving up when dreams don't come true.

That morning is when Bette called me for the first time in ten years. "Hello, is Pamela Chilton there?" The voice on the phone inquired.

"Yes" I responded and asked who was calling.

"Bette" the voice answered.

"Bette who?" I asked, not recognizing her voice.

"Bette Midler," she said, not recognizing my voice either.

We agreed to meet on a corner in Waikiki, near her hotel. Impishly, I asked, "How will I recognize you?"

Never one to be "up-quipped", Bette answered, "I look just the same, only fatter."

A new momma, Bette looked great. We strolled leisurely through Waikiki, with no one bothering us since people smiled at the adorable Sophie in the stroller, barely glancing at "mom". We ended up near the studio apartment where I was staying, so Bette came up to chat. We laughed, and cried, about old times. Those that know Bette know she is, arguably, an even greater listener than she is an entertainer. That, in itself, is a rare talent.

After Bette and Sophie left, I found several one hundred dollar bills on the rug where we'd been sitting. I called Bette's hotel. "Oh," she said, when I got her on the phone and explained what I'd found, "Sophie is always playing with my hand bag. She must have pulled them out. Why don't you just keep them?" I was puzzled. Why would I keep Bette's money? Then I looked around the apartment. It was tiny and bare. I was only borrowing it, for free, from a friend while the kids were away, so I hadn't bothered to fix it up at all. Bette must have thought I'd fallen on hard times, which I had; just not as hard or in quite the way she envisioned. Embarrassed, I left her money at the hotel for her.

When my children returned, I rented a two bedroom furnished apartment in Waikiki and began cleaning and writing again. I decided no more "dark, extraordinary novels". I began writing about a plain looking, brilliant, girl named Beth, who grows up feeling homely, unwanted, and unlovable. Beth dreams of becoming an actress and moves to New York when she is 19 to pursue her dreams. I sent Bette the first chapter to read. She was aghast.

She felt Beth was a thinly disguised portrayal of her. Worse, she felt I'd betrayed her even more by naming the character Beth. I'd, unfortunately, forgotten about Bette's dearest childhood friend, Beth, who had been killed in an automobile accident. I'd had very good reasons for naming my character Beth, none of which had to do with Bette or her Beth. Nor was the book about Bette. After all, I was smart. I'd grown up feeling homely, unwanted, and unlovable. I'd dreamt of becoming an actress. I had gone to New York at 19 to pursue my dreams. Still, Bette didn't believe me and it added yet another page to the saga of misunderstandings between us.

I gave the first chapter to my best friend, Paula, from High School to read. She, too, thought herself to be Beth, which astonished me. Bette had once been plain, so I could see how she thought herself to be Beth. I had a pretty face, but never pretty enough, and I always had a fat ass and thick thighs, so I definitely thought myself to be Beth. But how did long and lean Paula, with her gorgeous legs and beautiful face think she could be Beth? Perhaps, I thought, Paula, like Bette and I, compared her looks far too harshly with the Asian, Polynesian, and other Island Beauties that surrounded us in Hawaii. I sent the first chapter to an editorial assistant I knew in the Mainland. She thought SHE was Beth! Thus encouraged - clearly women related to Beth - I sent the novel to a New York literary agent.

The phone rang some months later. It was the literary agent. "I've been agonizing what to do about your book," she said. "First, let me say, I'm Beth. I gave it to my assistant to read and she thinks she's Beth. Obviously, we liked the book. But I just don't know what to do with it." I was confused. What else would a New York literary agent do with a book women clearly related to but sell it to a publisher. "This book," she continued, "is what we call a mid-list book. Without a well known author, it is unlikely to make any money for the publisher. Publishing is about profits. I'm sorry."

I was sorry too, but I wasn't ready to give up. Bambi was spending her sophomore year in Germany. Her father had a friend, I'll call Gunther, visiting him from Berlin who worked for an airlines. Gunther said I could fly with him, free, to Germany to visit Bambi for Christmas and fly back with him, free, if I could get to Berlin by New Year's. I decided I would take him up on his offer, but get off the plane in New York. I would rent a room, get a waitress job, and knock on publishers' and agents' doors for two months while Tyson stayed with his dad. I believed in Beth's Book. I was determined I would get someone else to believe in it enough to get it published. Then we'd see just how many women related to Beth.

It didn't work out that way. Bambi, despite the fact she was doing very well in school and adored living in Hamburg with her uncle and aunt, insisted she had to return with me. She wasn't sure why, she said, she just knew she "had to". It meant the end of my New York plans, but I had learned long ago to trust Bambi's instincts. So we traveled through East Germany together as soldiers scrutinized passports and large dogs sniffed under the train at every stop. We didn't leave Berlin on New Years, as planned. We didn't leave the next day either, or the day after that. Gunther, whose flat we were sharing with his girlfriend, had become very nonchalant about returning to Hawaii. We rarely saw him and when we did, he said he was so busy he didn't know when he'd be able to get back to Hawaii. As we couldn't fly back without him (unless we paid, which would be extremely expensive), we just had to wait until he was ready.

Finally, desperate after a month in Berlin surviving mostly on canned soup and filling our time with very long walks every day, I concocted a story. Gunther was a big Bette Midler fan and he knew she was a friend of mine. I told him Bambi and I had decided to stay in L.A. with Bette for a few days on our way home. I told him Bette would pick us up at the airport, and he could meet her. "The only catch is," I told him, "we have to be there this Friday. Otherwise, she'll have to send her driver and you won't get to meet her."

On Friday, we were on the airplane, winging into L.A. I made certain Bambi's and my seating passes for Hawaii in two days were in my pocket. As soon as we landed, I went to the phones to 'call Bette'. After a few moments of pretending to talk into the phone, I hung up, and walked back to our host with a sad face. "Bette is so sorry," I lied, "but she can't be here to meet you after all. She got hung up at the studio." Gunther turned on his heels and left us without a word.

Bambi and I spent the next two days with Yee Sun, my "adopted" daughter and Bambi's "adopted" sister. Yee Sun had lived with us from when she'd left Malaysia at barely 17 years old to go to The University of Hawaii. She stayed with us until her graduation - and wedding - four years later. She became, in that time, a part of our family, hearts, and lives forever.

We did see Bette while we were in town. We met her for lunch near the Roosevelt Hotel, where Bette and I had stayed while making the movie Hawaii. (Bambi and I searched out Bette's star along Hollywood Blvd. and I was delighted to discover it was just across the street from the Roosevelt.) It was the first time Bette had seen Bambi since she was a baby. Bambi told Bette a Jay Leno joke that caused Bette to laugh so hard, she threw back her head and bumped it - hard - on the wooden back of the booth we were sitting in. (The joke: "Have you ever read the expiration date on a loaf of Wonder Bread? It reads, "You should live so long.")

Later that night, I met Bette in a Hollywood Coffee shop. We each ordered a cup of tea. The "you should live so long" faced waitress pointed to a sign: $1.50 minimum per person. "Can you manage that?" she snapped.

Bette - Disney's #1 star - and I looked at each other. "I think I can," she said to me solemnly, "I'll treat."

Afterwards, Bette drove me to Yee Sun's in her suburban station wagon. The only "star" accessory was an elaborate car phone provided by Disney studios. "They like to be able to get in touch with me any time", she apologized. We stopped at the nearest station for gas. Bette pumped it. Then we got lost, driving aimlessly in the midnight hour around the empty streets of Glendale. Finally, we located the house. "You'll always have a friend," she promised as I got out of the car.

"I know," I promised back. "So will you." I knew she'd just told me she'd forgiven the hurts between us. Bette's theme song "Friends" is well penned. Bette has friends because Bette IS a friend.

Almost as soon as we got off the plane in Hawaii, Bambi's appendix burst. Only the doctors didn't realize it until they cut her open. They'd been reluctant to do surgery, thinking it wasn't her appendix, but Bambi, and I, had insisted they do it. Had she remained in Germany, they would have delayed the operation long enough to get written parental permission. She would have died before they'd received it. Bambi's premonition had saved her life.

The next several months became extremely challenging. I'd gambled once again - and lost once again - on a dream. I'd expected to stay in New York and return with a book contract. Now I'd returned with a sick daughter and no money. We didn't even have a house to live in. It took great discipline, and the help of family and friends, to get me out of that mess.

Bette helped me directly and indirectly. Her song, Wind Beneath My Wings, became popular. I'd seen Beaches in L.A. with Bambi, and I couldn't help but note the similarities in the movie to our friendship. No doubt the similarities were, as with Beth in my book, more circumstantial than intentional, but I chose to believe Bette's movie and song were - not coincidentally - in my life at that time to inspire me, and inspire me they did. Working feverishly at two full time jobs, I made my way out of debt. When I had enough to buy an old car and begin cleaning again, I quit both jobs.

Bette called about then, saying she'd had a brainstorm in the shower: she'd figured out a way to help her brother, Danny, and me. Danny, who couldn't cook, loved home cooked meals. Whenever she was in Hawaii, she would fill his refrigerator with home cooked meals. "But I can't get there often enough," she said, "so I thought, why don't I pay you to cook for him." She offered me a scandalous amount of money, especially since I was barely a cook. I took half that amount, bought some cookbooks, and began supplying home cooked meals to Danny.

One day I arrived with Danny's food and found, not him, but his and Bette's sister, Susan. I'd never met Susie before, though I'd heard a lot about her. Unlike the private Bette, she prefers talking to listening, and like the public Bette, she is very entertaining. At one point, she got up and walked into the kitchen. "Oh wow!" I exclaimed, "you've got Bette's walk!!"

She paused, turned with hands on hips, and said, "My dear, I'm the older sister. She's got MY walk."

Cooking for Danny for a year, plus cleaning six days a week allowed me to save enough to pay for Bambi's first Semester in Community College and for me to take a three week intensive course in hypnosis in Glendale. I'd discovered the school while I was in L.A. Hypnosis as a career seemed to me a better way than cleaning to support my writing. I would leave my kids under the watchful eye of my sister, who lived with us, and would leave three weeks worth of meals for Danny. I sent in my deposit money for the school.

Next, I went to the library reference room, to look up in the Glendale Yellow Pages places I could stay while I was at the school. I was writing down names of motels when a voice whispered in my ear, "Palm Springs". I turned around. No-one was there. I began looking at the Glendale Yellow

Pages again. Again a voice whispered, "Palm Springs." I looked up. Again, no one was there. I wondered about it, but psychic experiences are not that unusual for me, so I decided to ignore the voice in my ear. Besides, I had no reason to go to Palm Springs. I looked down at the Glendale phone book. This time the voice shouted in my ear: "PALM SPRINGS!"

I got up and looked for the Yellow Pages for Palm Springs. When I found it, I returned to the table, sat down, and opened it to Hypnosis Schools. There was a hypnosis school, The Academy For Instruction In Mind Motivation, in Palm Desert, right next to Palm Springs. (I'd have never known where Palm Desert was, which was why - I figured out later - the voice kept saying Palm Springs.)

When I got home, I called for the brochure, which arrived three days later. The courses - Master Hypnotist, Hypnotherapist, Age Regressionist, Past Life Therapist, Sexual Abuse and Multiple Personality Disorder - all interested me very much. However, taking all of the courses would take three months. How would I ever get away for three months? My sister could keep an eye on Tyson, but what about rent, utilities, and food while I was gone? What about rent, utilities, and food in Palm Desert? Besides, I would need $1,800 more than I had saved for the courses in Glendale. Going to Palm Desert was impossible, I decided. But the "voice" bothered me. Why had it insisted on leading me to Palm Desert?

I decided to walk and swim along the beach in Waikiki, something I frequently did when I had things to figure out. (In the very early mornings, double rainbows usually arch over the emerald green and turquoise blue sea off Waikiki. Frequently, there are triple rainbows.) As I strolled along Kalakaua Avenue on my way to the beach, I passed a man going in the opposite direction. As he passed me, the thought 'he's psychic, follow him' popped into my head, so I turned around and followed him. One block later, I was feeling pretty foolish, but when he turned into the International Market Place, I turned too. He stopped at the giant banyon tree, then turned and stepped into it, disappearing behind branches and roots. Cautiously, I walked up to where he'd disappeared. Inside the tree were a small table and two high backed rattan chairs. Above them, a sign on an overhanging branch read, "The Psychic Tree". The man I was following, sat down on one of the chairs. He placed a sign 'Psychic In' on the table and under that a sign with his name, "Tony". Then he looked up at me and smiled.

"Would you like a tarot reading?" he asked.

I sat down, pulled brochures for both schools out of my beach bag, laid them on the table, and said, "I just want to know which one I should go to."

He looked down at the brochures and closed his eyes. After a moment, he opened them and reached for the Palm Desert brochure. "This one", he said, and placed it in my hand.

"Are you sure?" I asked, looking down at it worriedly. He'd picked the school I couldn't afford.

He closed his eyes again. "A voice I haven't heard before," he said, "is saying, 'don't question, go'." He opened his eyes and studied my face. "How about a tarot reading anyway?" he suggested. I agreed.

He spread the cards out, after I'd cut them three times. Studying them, he asked me, "Do you know Bette Midler?"

I was startled. "Why?" I asked.

He shrugged. "Her name popped in my head. I'm a BIG fan of hers," he added, studying the cards. "Are you a writer?"

"Are you getting that from the cards?" I asked.

"Partly. You also seem to have someone with you who is talking to me in my head. I think that's who said Bette's name." He pointed at a card. "Your mate is there, too."

"Where?" I asked, staring stupidly at the cards..

"Palm Desert. I can't tell if he's married or not, but he's definitely your mate."

"I'm not interested in that," I said (and meant it), "what does it say about my writing?"

"You're a prophet," he said, tapping a card. "Your books will be very important." He looked up at me. "What have you written?"

I thought about the books I'd written. Hardly prophecy. I decided he wasn't so hot at tarot cards, although the "voice" in his head intrigued me. How had it known about Bette?

"Do you get anything else about the school?" I asked impatiently.

"Don't question, go," he said and scooped up the cards.

I went home and called the school in Palm Desert. "I'll be there," I said. Next, I called Bette's offices. Bette was on a trip and couldn't be reached. So I left a message with her offices that Danny would have a month's worth of meals when I left, but Bette had only two weeks to get back to me and let me know if she needed me to find someone else for him. I followed that up with a letter as I could never be certain Bette got my messages. Actually, I could never be certain she got my mail either. She'd made remarks in the past that made me wonder if she'd ever read any of my letters.

Next, I worked out a plan with Bambi and three of her friends. I had decided when I returned from California, I would get a smaller place for Tyson and me, so Bambi, now 18, and three of her friends, who were all looking for a place to live together, could take over my lease. In the meanwhile, if they all wanted to share Bambi's room and pay the rent on the room, I could afford to hold onto the house for three months They eagerly accepted. Including my sister, there would now be five adult women in the house while I was gone. Tyson, age 15, might feel outnumbered, but he and the house would be taken care of, I hoped.

I'd already received a week's subscription to the Palm Desert Newspaper that I had ordered. Rooms in private homes were readily available and I had just enough for one month's rent, deposit, and food. I would have to get work to pay for the last two month's rent and food. The only problem remaining was the additional $1800 I needed to pay for the courses. I decided I would just have to trust the money would come in somehow.

"What do you mean, it will come in somehow!" my best friend, Faye, exclaimed incredulously. "You have a week . What do you think, you'll just walk to your mailbox one morning and there will be a check for $1800?"

"Why not?" I retorted flippantly. "All I know is I'm supposed to be in those classes. I have no doubt that I have done all I can to make that happen. The Universe will have to do the rest." The very next morning, I went to my mailbox. There was a postcard in it:

Edward C. Noonan
Mi$$ing People Locator
Carmichael, California

Our service has located an ASSET belonging to the ADDRESSEE of this postcard. If you know the location of the addressee, please contact this office immediately. If the addressee is unknown, please return this card to your postal carrier. 10% FEE

On the other side of the post card was a phone number. When I called, Mr. Noonan answered. He was, he said, a special investigator and he had located money for me in the California General Fund. He would do the necessary paper work, mail me the papers for a notarized signature, then, after I'd mailed those back to him, he would send me a check, minus his 10%.

"That seems fair," I said cautiously, "what money?"

"Twenty-five years ago, you were in the movie 'Hawaii'," Mr. Noonan replied.

"Yes," I agreed. "I was."

"Well, you've been collecting residuals from it ever since. The Screen Actor's Guild couldn't locate you so the money has been going to the California General Fund."

"How much is it?" I asked.

"Minus my fee, $1800," Mr. Noonan answered.

I gave him his 10%, plus twenty bucks for dinner. I'd have given him more if I could. He was, after all, an angel.

I was to meet another angel on my first night in Palm Springs. I arrived in Palm Springs in the afternoon, in August. Desert heat is not like island heat. It is dry; and very, very HOT. I discovered Palm Desert was some distance away, so I checked into the Spa Hotel for the night while I figured out how to get to Palm Desert. After a soak in the hot springs (I was disappointed it was in a concrete tub), I was feeling nauseous and lightheaded, so I skipped dinner and went to bed.

Sometime in the night, I had a dream. The dream was of four women - myself, Bette, a friend of mine, and a friend of Bette's. In the dream Bette was lamenting about good and evil and the pain people suffer. I put my arm around her to console her. An invisible voice spoke loudly, reprimanding me. It said, "We're trying to teach her something here."

I replied, "Oh, yes," and removed my arm. My friend patted Bette's hand, which I resented. My thought was, if I can't console her, why should she? She's not even a friend of Bette's. Then I recognized she was as much a part of Bette as Bette's friend and I were, or anyone else was for that matter. I looked at the three of them and announced, "Knowledge leads to understanding. Understanding leads to self-mastery. And self-mastery leads to God."

At that moment, I woke. I realized my bed was rocking and the room was filled with Light. In the middle of the room was a very tall Angelic Being. It didn't have wings, but it was surrounded with Light. "You are about to begin a journey," the Being said, smiling at me. As strange as it seems, I nodded, closed my eyes, and went back to sleep.

The next morning, as I awoke, I immediately thought of what had happened in the night; I knew it had been real. My mind drifted back to an experience two years before, while I was meditating.

While still In New York, I'd read There Is A River, by Thomas Sugrue. It was the biography of Edgar Cayce, often called America's greatest seer. After that, I read all of the Edgar Cayce books I could find. The books renewed my spiritual faith and taught me to meditate. For me, meditation is a time of inner silence when my mind is absent of all thought, visions, dreams, and voices. (Those happen in between meditations.) I have long noted that when I am meditating, life's challenges are still present, but they are so much easier to meet. When I am not meditating, I struggle. So for twenty-five years, I have meditated more days than I have not.

On that morning, my mind had been on an Edgar Cayce book I'd been re-reading the night before. Something in it had triggered deep within me an absolute acceptance of the reality of God. I'd shut the book in great excitement, my heart joyfully leaping as I thought, "There IS a God!" As I sat to meditate, I could feel that feeling again. I closed my eyes with the thought, "God Is" filling my mind and joy filling my heart. Then a voice spoke. It seemed to be my voice, but it spoke without my volition, and it was different somehow: like a still, quiet voice. It said, "I will lift thee up and use thee." My eyes flew open. I was certain I'd just heard from God.

In an interesting survey I read in The Reader's Digest, I think, a large majority of the people surveyed believed they had heard at some time in their lives the voice of God. Now I was one of them.

I became more convinced it had been God when I heard that same voice again, a couple of months later, as I was floating on my back in the blue-green sea off Waikiki, lazily kicking my feet. I had been pondering for several days an argument with a beloved friend, who had stated one could only be "saved" by believing in the divinity of Jesus Christ. Her belief had astounded and saddened me, leaving out as it did billions of people and implying anyone God had created needed to be "saved'. As I stared up at the clouds, however, I wondered if I was the one being closed minded. Suddenly, I heard "that voice" again. It said:

"The Lord Thy God Is One. Whether Man Calls Me By God, Jesus, Buddha, Mohammed, Yea, Even Krishna, It Is I. For I Am With Man Always. As Long As A Man Believes And Acknowledges That Which Is Greater Than The Sum Of His Parts And His Works, That Which Is His Creator, He Worships Me. For My Name Man Has Never Known, And Could Not Utter. I Am That I Am. And I Am With Thee Always."

I swam back to shore, climbed out, and having nothing to write on or with, I walked the few blocks to my apartment, hoping I could remember the words. I needn't have worried, the words were etched in my mind.

I'd been waiting ever since for God to lift me up and use me. I'd expected something spectacular to happen right away. It hadn't. I wondered if it was happening now. I took a city bus into Palm Desert; eager to discover my destiny.

The very first day of class I discovered the answer to life's greatest (for me) puzzles: Why some prayers are answered and many, seemingly, are not. Why bad things happen to good people. Why some people heal and others do not. Why miracles happen, and why they don't. Why some people are psychic a lot and others are never psychic at all. Why mystical voices, visions, and angelic beings are not commonplace. The answer, I discovered, was the subconscious mind.

Now all I had to do was learn everything I could about the subconscious mind.

Dr. Harmon is a wonderful teacher. Incredibly knowledgeable, he teaches as all Masters teach: simply, with gentle guidance, and wise counsel. He also teaches with great humor, and I became more and more enchanted with his stories of "Bad Billy", the adventurous lad he had been. I knew he was teaching us, as he shared his personal journey, how the soul grows.

As I continued my exploration of my own soul, I began to do "automatic" writing. I designated one hand for my "emotional mind" and the other my "spiritual mind". I placed the pen on a piece of paper and asked if any emotions would like to express themselves. I got page after page of 'o's, just like we used to do in grade school when we first learned penmanship. Then I got LOTS of pages of letters of the alphabet. I quickly learned that my hand didn't like to lift off the paper between words or lines, so I turned the paper sideways to give myself more room. Eventually the letters began to make words, though the words didn't add up to anything meaningful. Bored, I quit practicing.

The next day I tried again. Only this time, I put the pen in my spiritual mind hand and placed it on the paper. Immediately, my "hand" wrote my name. I stared at the paper. I hadn't thought of writing my name, or had I? And if I had, why had I? I put the pen to paper again. My hand moved fluidly across the paper. The writing was very messy and large, and the words ran into one another, but the message they spelled were clear. It said: "We are here." I lifted the pen and stared at the words. "Who is here?" I asked aloud and put pen to paper again.

This time my hand wrote: "Spirit."

I asked aloud, "Who and what kind of Spirit?"

"Your guides," they wrote.

I asked for names. I was given two, Rama (pronounced Rah MA´) and Ramet (pronounced Rah MAY´). I was told these spirit guides were aspects of my Higher Self and the Higher Self of my mate.

"What mate?" I asked. "Where is he?"

"Bebe is near," they wrote.

They also advised me to quit job hunting and concentrate on my studies. "Have faith," they wrote. "Your needs will be provided." Three days later, an opportunity to house and cat sit for two months presented itself. I took it happily and continued to do automatic writing (though for me, the thought comes and then I write it, my hand doesn't write it "automatically") with my spirit guides. (Unfortunately for my emotional mind, I did not return to it. Too bad for me, for had I done so, I've little doubt my therapy would have begun sooner and progressed much faster.)

The next two months were heavenly. I went to class, read the class books, swam daily in the pool, had many mystical experiences, and discovered hummingbirds. (We don't have hummingbirds in Hawaii. I think they are as delightful as I imagine fairies would be. Actually, I think they ARE fairies embodied in earth forms.) Though I was as content as I think it is earthly possible to be, I wondered, as the weeks rolled by, what had happened to BeBe. I didn't really care if he didn't show up - intimate relationships had proved more curse than blessing in my life - but I hated to think my guides had been wrong.

Too soon, the courses were coming to a close. We had less than two week left when a fellow classmate, Shirley Smith, and I went dancing to celebrate our coming graduation. Dr. Harmon and his wife, Merrien, joined us. An excellent dancer, Dr. Harmon danced with each of us. When it was my turn, he put his arm around my waist. I leaned into him and my knees buckled. Not only did he have to hold me up, he had to practically drag me across the dance floor. As I'd been bragging earlier about my dancing prowess, I was quite embarrassed. I think he wondered whether I was a liar, drunk, or both.

When I got home that night, I was very confused. I knew what had buckled my knees: sexual energy. Where had that come from? I had not felt any kind of energy like that from or towards Dr. Harmon all through the classes. Besides, Dr. Harmon was married, though it was no secret the marriage was dissolving. Merrien Harmon had informed several of her friends of her desire for a divorce, and that news had, as such gossip usually does, spread rapidly. I decided I was simply experiencing a classic crush on the teacher; albeit, a bit late. My crush, however, seemed to get worse with each passing day.

Just before graduation, Dr. Harmon called me into his office. He asked me about my plans when I returned to Hawaii. I told him I was thinking of opening, thanks to his encouragement, a practice as a hypnotherapist. He told me that was exactly what he'd hoped, and that I could call him on the phone as often as I needed or wanted his support and guidance. I was thrilled. Then he asked me to help him with his book. I was more than thrilled. He also told me we would always be friends, good friends. I was certain he was telling me he was aware of my crush and was gently discouraging me. Hurt and embarrassed, I mumbled a "thank you" and left.

I returned home and whipped out my pen and paper. "Who IS this BeBe," I demanded, still feeling angry and hurt. "Why hasn't he appeared?"

"You call him Bad Billy," the guides wrote. I sat in shock, staring at the words. I went back over my automatic writing - which I kept in a large spiral notebook - and found 'BeBe'. Staring at it, I could see that what I thought were two small 'e's' could easily be two large, messy periods. Still, the Guides had been wrong: Dr. Harmon clearly was not my mate. At that moment, the phone rang. It was Dr. Harmon.

"I don't know why I'm doing this," he said quietly. I held my tongue. There was a moment's silence, then he said, "Do you have something to tell me?"

"Yes," I said, and took a deep breath. "I have a crush on you. Will you help me get over it?"

"No," he said softly. There was another moment of silence, then he spoke again, "It will take some time. Will you stay here in the Desert while Merrien and I work out our divorce?"

"No," I said, wishing I could. "You go through your stuff without me. I'll wait in Hawaii. I'll return when you're divorced."

It took two years.

Merrien changed her mind about the divorce. She and Hugh had been friends a long time, much longer than they had been mates. He'd helped her completely recover from a devastating stroke when the doctors had considered such recovery impossible. She realized how much she had come to depend on him and she decided she wanted a separation, not a divorce. Hugh reminded her she had asked for the divorce, telling him they had grown apart and she was eager to be on her own. She was right, he said, they had grown apart and he, too, was eager to be on his own. He didn't mention me.

I spoke with Hugh by phone daily as we collaborated on the book. I could hear in his voice his sincerity when he said he wanted to be with me, but felt he had to stay with Merrien until she was emotionally ready to accept the divorce. He asked me for patience. Had it not been for my guides, I'm not certain I would have had the patience. "Trust" they wrote. "Believe" they wrote. "He is your mate," they wrote. "Have faith. Be BeBe's Bride."

I continued to write on the book and see clients. Not wanting to invest in an "official" office because I would be leaving soon - I thought - I'd made a hypnotherapy room out of the Master bedroom after Bambi and her friends had left. They had been very upset when I'd returned and broken my promise to let them take over the lease. I didn't blame them. But I'd returned home penniless and had no-where else to go. It was them or me, and I had Tyson to consider.

I had also managed to antagonize Bette. She had not gotten either my phone message or my letter and she felt I'd let her down with Danny. She also felt I'd been overcharging her for Danny's food and cooking. I didn't even bother to remind her how expensive food is in Hawaii, and gas, nor that she had offered me twice the amount, which I had turned down. Besides, I suspected she was more upset about Hugh than she was about Danny. She'd called me a couple of times in Palm Desert and I'd been highly enthusiastic about Dr. Harmon.

"Is he coming on to you?" she'd demanded, incensed by the idea of a teacher - a married teacher - compromising a student.

"Of course not," I replied, indignantly. "There isn't a hint of sexuality between us."

It was hard explaining from that remark - which had been absolutely true at the time - how we had gotten to the point of him getting a divorce and me waiting in the wings. So hard, I didn't even try.

After a year and a half of waiting for the divorce, I rebelled. I began to believe I could trust neither my guides nor Hugh. I started dating a man who was earnestly pursuing me. It was my father who checked my rebellion. "A marriage," he told me gently, "is difficult to end, even when it is time to end it. It is even more difficult when a business partnership is involved. If you love him, trust him." I sat down, after my talk with my father, and told my guides I had to have a sign that would help me to believe.

While in Palm Desert, I had been swimming in the pool and thinking of the mate my guides had 'promised". 'How will I know this man?' I'd asked aloud. At that moment, I'd looked up and right in front of me, at the end of the pool, was a rose bush, covered with roses. 'He will be a man of roses,' I heard myself think. When the class went to Hugh's home for our graduation dinner, there in his back yard was a huge rose garden. "Fifty-four rose bushes," he told us proudly. "I'm a man of roses." Later, I received a package from him in Honolulu. Opening it, I found a perfect live French Lace rose. I hadn't even told him my rose story.

"You have until noon to provide a sign," I announced imperially to the guides. Impatient with them and myself, I went to look for a present for a friend's birthday. In the store, I was riding up the escalator, eyes straight ahead. Slowly, the largest bouquet of roses I'd ever seen came into view right at the top of the escalator. I stepped off and stared at them. Then I smelled them. Smiling - I recognized a sign when I saw one - I went to buy my present, noting the store clock as I passed it. It read 11:59 A.M. When I came back, the roses were gone! Were they real? I wondered and asked a sales lady passing by if there had been roses at the top of the escalator a few minutes ago. "Oh yes," she said brightly. "They were ordered for a state dinner. You're lucky you saw them, they were only here for a minute or two."

Three months later, Hugh and Merrien were divorced. I turned the lease on the house over to my son (now out of High School) and his friends, then flew back to Palm Desert to join Hugh. It was too soon. Hugh was stressed - mentally and emotionally - as well as exhausted - physically and financially - from the divorce. Though it had begun amicably enough, it had ended with rancor on both sides. Despite this, they were still working together. Merrien had helped him build his practice and school. She was reluctant to leave. He was reluctant to have her leave. They had worked out a testy truce at the office.

I was shocked. I'd left my Hawaii practice, which had been doing very well indeed, to start a practice as Hugh's partner. Merrien, well aware of my arrival in town and my relationship with Hugh, was not willing to have me even walk in the front door. I was not willing to walk in the front door either, until she left. As far as I was concerned, this was the woman who had "cost" me two years with Hugh. I was not in the mood to consider her feelings or reflect on how valuable and important those two years apart had been for me. I had built up my own Practice and become secure in my own therapist abilities. I'd also had more time with my children, though I'd spent too much of it moping around, waiting impatiently for my "real life" to begin. (If I could impart only one piece of advice for all girls and women, it would be: Your "real life" is NOW, with or without a boy or a man in it. Enjoy every moment.)

Hurt and feeling betrayed by Hugh, I "holed" myself up in my townhouse. I pretended I was working on the book, but really, I was worrying about my relationship and my savings. Hugh had been generous in the divorce settlement, leaving himself barely enough money to maintain the offices and rent a small apartment for himself. Not that I expected him to meet my expenses. My father raised me to be self-sufficient, and self-sufficient I am. Nevertheless, my savings were shrinking.

Hugh would arrive at the end of the day with food he would cook in my tiny, ill-equipped kitchen. He pretended he didn't miss his spacious home, his beloved rose gardens, or his gourmet kitchen. It was clear, however, as I watched him trying to please me, that he was as miserable as I. Though I was sympathetic, and tried to be understanding, inwardly I was fuming. I, too, had suffered loss: I'd left behind clients I cared about, an island I loved, and most difficult of all, my beloved family. Now I was being cheated of a courtship as well.

<u>Hugh</u>

Stuck in the middle of the anger and pain of both an ex-wife and a future wife, I was under a great deal of stress. Financial concerns added to my stress, which hammered at me daily, especially in my neck. The pain was becoming intolerable, even with my healing techniques. I couldn't understand why the neck was getting the best of me; I'd met and conquered every challenge to my body in the past.

As a young man, I'd had a strong and healthy body; only I'd damaged it repeatedly with strenuous - even dare-devil - exploits. My back had been fractured three times: Falling off the roof as a kid. Playing football in High School. While serving in the army. Consequently, by the time I was forty, an x-ray revealed three ruptured discs, with one of them completely destroyed. Of course, the medical doctors wanted to do an operation to fuse my spine, but I told them I would heal it myself. They shook their heads and warned me the discs would continue to deteriorate. Since the subconscious mind controls the body, I began telling my subconscious to heal the discs in my back. I continued this message daily by imaging the discs whole and healthy. The pain went away. Seven years later another x-ray revealed three perfectly shaped, normal discs.

In my 50's, I began to have difficulty breathing. No-one seemed able to determine the cause, though it was getting so bad I was having difficulty walking across a room without having to stop to catch my breath. Finally I found a doctor specializing in thoracic medicine; which is how I met Dr. Warren Jacobs. He took X-rays and discovered interstitial fibrosis, an almost invisible fibrous growth that slowly fills the lungs, thus limiting - and eventually eliminating - the ability of the lungs to absorb oxygen. I was told medical science could stop the growth with the use of steroids, but nothing could reverse the damage already done. I thanked Dr. Jacobs. Now that I knew what was wrong, I could fix it. I also knew my subconscious mind could do more than stop the growth, it could reverse the damage already done.

The second step in any healing (after discovering what is broken, ill, or out of balance), is to find the emotion or emotions that caused and/or are contributing to the injury, illness, or imbalance. I sat in a hot tub, closed my eyes, and began to name emotions. As I named anger, my chest constricted; when I named resentment, it constricted again. Still in a light self-hypnotic state, I asked to know the source of the anger and resentment. Immediately, my mind returned to a visit I'd made to a very close friend, some six months prior. I'd clearly seen serious errors he was making in an important business matter and had tried to share my observations with him. This, despite the fact that as a therapist, I knew better than to offer unasked for help. I tried to help him over the next several weeks. Not only did he refuse my help, he would - each time I tried to bring the matter up - consistently hold newspapers or magazines in front of his face to shut me out! Remembering, I could feel the anger and resentment all over again. That I could feel the emotions now was a sure indication I'd not released them.

Emotion is energy, powerful energy. It is the energy that combines with thought to manifest physical reality. Negative emotions, like my anger and resentment, manifest negative conditions. Suppressing my anger and resentment had caused my lungs to fill with a fibrous growth that could kill me. What I had to do now, in order to reverse that, was to release those emotions.

I thought of my friend. I reminded myself he, like everyone, possessed a direct line to better guidance than I, or anyone else, could offer. I could not know whether he had accessed that guidance directly, indirectly, or not at all. I could not know if his Higher Self had guided him to make the very errors he had made in order to grow or even to offer an opportunity for others to grow. I reminded myself that it had been my error to offer unasked for advice and my error to have let his childish reaction to that offer affect me. Certainly it had been my error, and loss, to let that incident affect my love for him. Shutting down love had caused my body to begin shutting down the very breath (lungs) of life. I thought of my friend and our bond since childhood. I thought of all I loved and admired about him and as I let my buried love re-surface, I felt the anger and resentment melt away in its warmth.

The inward healing of my emotions accomplished, I now needed to attend to the damage already done. As I thought of the fibrous growth in my lungs, the thought of a large oak tree flashed in my mind. Realizing the oak tree was the interstitial fibrosis as imaged by my subconscious, I asked my subconscious how to get rid of the oak tree in my lungs.

I suddenly thought of a workshop I'd taken with Dr. John Ott who had done great research with light and time frame photography. His work had been used to create the fantastic images of rapidly blooming plants in the movie Fantasia. The thought occurred to me of using that technique to reverse the growth of the oak tree; i.e., the interstitial fibrosis. Like a movie reel in my mind, I reversed the growth of the oak tree, shrinking it down into the acorn from which it had grown. I asked myself what to do with the acorn. Knowing that composting is a returning of organic matter back into the vital prime energy of nature, I composted - in my mind - that acorn back into my vital prime energy; then I thanked my subconscious mind for making it happen.

I got out of the tub and dried myself off, accepting completely that what had been set in motion would indeed manifest, as that is the law of physics. Every day after that, I simply thanked the creative energy of the Universe in order to remind myself - and my subconscious - that completion of the healing was imminent. In seven weeks, my lungs were completely healed. The fibrous growth was gone and the damage to my lungs completely reversed.

For forty years I'd been demonstrating the power of the subconscious mind to heal anything, including financial limitations. Now, for the first time, I seemed incapable of harnessing that power. Angry, stressed, and in a great deal of pain, I thought of Pamela. She had, in an amazingly short time, become the therapist I'd long been seeking. However, I believe all men fear women to some extent and sometimes fear to a greater extent the women they love. I'd run away - in one form or another - from all the women in my life. This one, I did not want to lose. It made for an interesting dilemma: In order not to lose Pamela, I would need therapy, but the only therapist whose skills I could trust was Pamela.

It can be argued that a personal relationship interferes with therapy, and to complicate matters, we discovered as we moved into the intimacy of our relationship that Pamela would, herself, need therapy. Using NMR, we quickly uncovered Pamela's early childhood sexual abuse. As we did so, Pamela began to remember. Healing from sexual abuse is challenging; it requires very special skills and techniques on the part of the therapist. I would trust no one else with Pamela's therapy, even as I would trust no-one else but Pamela with mine. We both knew that once sexual abuse is uncovered, sexual intimacy can trigger even more memories and trauma. This proved true of Pamela, so we agreed to delay our sexual relationship until she was healed. Clearly, Pamela and I were being heavily challenged in all directions.

It is a tribute to our skills as therapists, but just as importantly, it is a tribute to the type of therapy we do, that our relationship survives those challenges. Hypnotherapy is client centered, not therapist centered, which diminishes a great deal of the transference clients are apt to place on a therapist. Thus a personal relationship is far less likely to be compromised by the therapy, and the therapy far less likely to be compromised by a personal relationship.

<u>Pamela</u>

Three months after I arrived, Merrien left the offices, and I happily began to set up my practice. There were still many challenges to be met, however, so in addition to our own therapy work, Hugh and I began channeling our Higher Selves for guidance.

Channeling, like religion, suffers from the company it sometimes keep. However, to trance channel does require preparation and precaution. A spirit can name itself anyone or anything. Spirits do lie. How does one know whether a spirit is telling the truth? How does one know a Spirit's information is to the higher good? Intuitive knowing is one way, reason another. Yet ego is quick to stifle both intuition and reason when it wants desperately to believe. Anyone who would channel spirit would do well to anchor first with The Higher Self and to rely on its guidance, wisdom, protection, and discernment.

One day, as Hugh's Higher Self was speaking through him, it did something quite unexpected. "One moment," it said, and paused. Then, after a moment or two had passed, another energy began to speak. (Since the voice box of the channel is being used, the voice of anyone using that channel will sound, of course, like the channel's voice. However, syntax and grammar may vary greatly, as will the manner of speaking.)

"He is to close the doors to this place and leave," the voice said. "It is time to begin teaching."

"Who speaks?" I asked.

"Spirit."

"What spirit?"

"Higher Spirit."

"Teach what?" I inquired.

"Teach what the Spirit brings through you, Pamela. Teach the messages of God. Teach how to heal and to feel and to be a part of that message. Teach the Word. And the Word IS the Word. And ALL the Words are the Word. And the Word will come like a breath through Pamela."

I wasn't certain what to make of that, but I proceeded on doggedly with the "important" matter at hand. "Move where?" I asked.

"I am aware," the 'voice' continued, 'there is a one story, yes pink, rather large building that needs to be occupied by such as yourselves."

"Do you know how we would find this place?" I asked.

"I see it," Spirit answered.

"Hmmm, big help" I thought and pressed on with, "Is it here in this valley?"

"Yes."

"Is there something near it Hugh might know?"

"Yes."

"What is it near?"

"I don't know the terms."

"Is there a landmark nearby?"

"Trees."

"Trees," I repeated, thinking how unhelpful this Spirit was being.

"Openness. Acres of land."

"Is it near the mountains?"

"Not near the mountains."

Are there other buildings around it?"

"Some distance away."

"Is there a road name?"

"I see none."

"Do you know directions?" I pressed, feeling frustration creeping in.

"I see northwest."

"Northwest of the valley?"

"North northwest IN the valley."

"Thank you. And Spirit, shall we continue our therapy practices?"

Spirit replied: "Some people are open to therapy and they will benefit. Others are not open, and so would not benefit. Teaching ALL how they can and may benefit is wise for you to do. Many people are not willing or ready for change."

Hugh stretched and opened his eyes. I explained to him what had happened, as he does not stay in his body when he channels and is not aware of what has occurred. I read to him what Higher Spirit had said then remarked, "Not very precise directions were they?"

Hugh was looking at me as though I had sprouted horns. "Just who or what, exactly, do you suppose this Higher Spirit is, my dear?" He asked me, his voice calm, but distinctly cool.

I looked at him, shocked. "You mean you don't know?" (I thought he knew everything.)

"I don't trust spirits," he said slowly, "that tell people what to do, nor do I intend to ever allow anyone, especially spirit, to mind my business. I've worked hard and long to build up this center. I'm NOT going to close the doors. And if I were, which I'm not, it wouldn't be to go wandering around the countryside spouting about God."

"Oh," I said. "Would you be open to some NMR?"

NMR of Hugh's Higher Self said the Spirit we had heard from was from a level higher than the Higher Selves and that it had spoken truthfully and accurately. "Hmmmph," was Hugh's only comment.

The next day Hugh suggested I speak to his Higher Self while he was in trance and ask directly about the spirit that had spoken and its information. I agreed and guided him into trance. When I had accessed his Higher Self, I asked if the spirit that had spoken to us the day before could be trusted.

"Indeed," replied the Higher Self, "it is Higher Spirit and it will speak now."

Again, the spirit from the day before began speaking. It said: "If you do not move, Jeremiah will have his way."

I knew who Jeremiah was. Hugh had explained him as a friendly spirit that hung around the offices. He played with the lights a great deal, particularly in sessions with clients who knew of his presence. I'd seen far too much evidence of Jeremiah, and his abilities, to doubt his existence.

"How will Jeremiah have his way?" I asked.

"He will burn down the building you are now in," said Higher Spirit,

"How soon?" I asked.

"Two weeks, in your time," was the answer.

Afterwards, when I read what had been said, Hugh was furious. "I refuse to be told what to do AND threatened with consequences if I don't do it!" He protested vehemently. "This spirit does not sound very spiritual to me. I don't trust it."

On the other hand, he trusted NMR and his Higher Self. Again, NMR testing - done VERY precisely under Hugh's careful scrutiny - said the information given by the Spirit that had just spoken was accurate.

I found Hugh an hour later, staring at the client files, research records, equipment, supplies, and books that filled his suite of offices. The thought of even the possibility of losing all of it to fire was intolerable. Nor was there any denying Jerimiah's ability to manipulate electricity. There had often been electrical shorts - causing lights in various rooms of the offices to dim or blink - that no electrician could isolate or explain. Even as we stood there, the lights above us began to blink in an irregular pattern! Swallowing hard, Hugh looked at me and I looked at him. "Rancho Mirage and Palm Springs are north-west of here," he said slowly. "They are urban and expensive areas. Do you realize how much a place with acres of open land would cost? It's impossible right now. We need to get more information about this Spirit and why it is directing us to move there. And if it is, we need to have better directions on finding it." So, I guided Hugh into trance once more and asked for the Spirit that was guiding us to move.

"I am here," it said.

"I shall call you Master of Spirit," I began, "as you are of Higher Spirit and are clearly a Master."

"Very well," Master of Spirit responded.

"I would like to know more about you. Who are you exactly and why are you addressing us?"

"I am the knowledge with no name. You are the ancient catalyst. Maybe now he can take the knowledge out of my place to those who are ready to receive or to benefit. He has fear. The fear can only be reversed through the opposite. The opposite is love. He needs to address love. As was given, you are that love. You are the catalyst. Help him find reason to address the blocks. He must learn trust. Otherwise, fear will block all off."

"Can you give us more precise directives for finding the pink building of which you spoke?" I asked.

"Fear holds you back. If you believe, it will appear. If you scour and scrub, with nose to the floor, you will not see the place that I describe."

After Hugh came out of hypnosis, I read back to him what Master of Spirit had said. "Well, let's find it then," he said with a sigh and opened the newspaper to rentals.

"I'll call," I said, "you start making the moving arrangements." I called every ad in the paper for rental or leased houses. I'd already figured out Master of Spirit was talking about a house because we certainly couldn't afford offices in Rancho Mirage or Palm Springs in addition to my townhouse and Hugh's apartment. We would just have to live together (about time, I thought) and have our offices in our home. I asked each person who answered if the house advertised was pink. While a surprising number offered to paint their houses pink, not one of the houses was already pink.

I called the very last ad in the paper. The Realtor said, "No, that house isn't pink." As I was about to hang up, she said, "Oh wait a minute. Everyone around here refers to it as the pink house, but I don't know why. It's locked, but if you'd like to go look at the outside, you could call me back if you're interested. It's on Venus Drive in Rancho Mirage." I took the address, chuckling at the thought of two hypnotherapists on Venus Drive in Rancho Mirage. At the end of the day, Hugh and I drove out to look at it.

It was at the end of a dead-end street, and there were two restaurants some distance away. There were trees in front, but the house definitely wasn't pink. It was beige-white with a terra-cotta tile roof. We walked around to the back of the house. There was a swimming pool, a large yard with several trees, and a brick wall surrounding all of it. Beyond the brick wall were acres of open land. Hugh laughed. "Well," he said, still chuckling, "no-one said it would be OUR land."

Wanting to see the inside of the house and knowing sometimes Realtors forget to lock up houses after they show them, Hugh tried the back French door. It was locked tight. We walked around the house, trying the side doors; they were locked, too. When we walked to the back again, Hugh said we'd have to wait and see the house the next day. We started to walk away, when I stopped. "Wait," I said. "I know this is the house. If I'm right, Master of Spirit will open the door."

I walked to the French door, put my hand on the knob, turned it down, and the door opened. Hugh jumped at least a foot. "I just tried that!" He protested, ashen faced, "And it was locked tight."

"I know," I said, quietly. "Let's go in."

We carefully slipped through the vertical blinds that draped the French doors and stepped into the living room. The wall to wall carpeting in the living room was pink. The tiled floors around the living room were pink. The white walls, in the glow of the setting sun reflected all that pink. It was like walking straight into a pink cloud. "No wonder they call it the pink house," we said in unison. (Later, when Hugh replaced some light fixtures, he discovered the walls had once been pink as well.)

The next day we did another session with Master of Spirit. The first thing I asked was: "Is the house we found yesterday the house you have led us to?"

Master of Spirit: "Yes."

"Was that you that opened the door?" I asked.

"Shocked you both."

"It isn't pink outside." I protested.

"Didn't say outside," Master of Spirit replied and added that we were to offer the owners $200 a month less than they were asking as they would take that amount.

After the session, Hugh was again dubious. "The amount they are asking is already below market value," he argued. "Why would they go even lower?" Nevertheless, we called the Realtor and offered $200 a month less.

"Impossible," she retorted. She called back two hours later and asked when we could sign the lease. The owners had agreed to the lower amount if we would do our own gardening. Hugh, the man of roses, beamed.

We were all moved in by the deadline Master of Spirit had set. We'd given away three offices worth of furniture, as we'd have no room for them.

We kept two offices of furniture to turn the spare bedroom into my office and the small, formal dining room into Hugh's office. Still, Hugh was very unhappy having his practice in his home. He didn't consider it professional. I was comfortable with the idea. I'd practiced out of my home in Hawaii without any problems, and this was a far nicer home. Besides, hadn't Master of Spirit told us we would be doing more teaching of the masses than individual therapy work? I pointed this out to Hugh and that's where he put his foot down. "We do teach, we have a school," he said firmly, surveying the living room to see how many students we could comfortably seat.

"I don't think the school is what Master of Spirit had in mind," I chided.

"Spirit does not run our lives," he responded. "We do."

I shook my head and raised my eyebrows, but said nothing. While I believed Master of Spirit, I trusted Hugh. I would, I decided, wait to see what else Master of Spirit had to say. As it turned out, it had a great deal to say.

Master of Spirit

"You are here, as are others, for a very important mission. You are here to help save humans. Nature has had enough of humans. They do not honor or respect Nature, which supports them, but seek, instead, through corruption and greed, to destroy their beautiful earth. This cannot last. Humans face destruction on a massive scale. Destruction they have brought upon themselves. Many think they can escape this destruction by preparing for it. This is not true. All humans will be destroyed if the destruction comes. And Man will return to the pre-historic age to begin the struggle through evolution once again. A struggle on a planet that must slowly rebuild itself, for Man's destruction will destroy great land masses. This future can still be averted. Some people have lost faith it can be done, and have given up hope. Others teach and preach denial; saying this future has already been averted, or that humans are not in peril on such a massive scale. These people, and the spirits that guide them, are well meaning, thinking they are helping to avert disaster. This, too, is folly. Humans have chosen, by their actions, this future. Humans must exert their will, NOW, to change that which they have created. Spirit will help, but it cannot over-rule the human will, for the path of choice is the path of earth souls. Choice is your birth right. You must choose. You must choose knowingly, each of you. No-one can hide your choices from you, or lead you blindly to them. Choose. Choose now. Choose wisely. You must teach the people what Spirit teaches you"

"When," I asked Master of Spirit, "will this destruction come?"

"Soon, it has already begun," was the answer. "Move now."

How? That's what Hugh and I wanted to know. We were two people, obscure people at that. How were we to convince people we weren't crazy. How were we to convince people Master of Spirit was real and its information accurate? How would we support ourselves sharing with people information that would, we had no doubt, make us very unpopular? Most importantly, how were we to tell them they could change the future in the short time remaining when we didn't know how ourselves? We took our concerns to Master of Spirit:

Master of Spirit

"You, Pamela, know how. You are one of the Masters to bring the information to save the populace, if it is willing to be saved. If not, you will have done your work and return. The education is the work, the learning processes and information made available. Each must teach themselves, or move out of the way for the earth will not tolerate this any longer. There is a cloaked figure, that seems to be of another dimension, from ancient times of earthly records, that is with you, and will guide you in teaching how [humans] may effectively change the path the human race is taking now. She may be recognized as a Master or may serve her time as a Master incognito. She will indeed serve as she has now, and has been serving for many years. This is not an easy task for any Master, for they resist greatly the Master's teaching. She will be very famous for her work, whether it is recognized or not by the human, but by the Masters, who respect each other greatly. She has a Master's highest role. The word, in ancient times, of human record, is Ra. Ra, meaning the God like energy, which like a mantle of authority to the Master, rides her yoke gently, but steadfastly. As to how you will change the future in the short time left, the one that shall do this, with the aid of enough human minds, joins you now. Heed this one well."

As Master of Spirit stopped speaking, a subtle, but definite, radiance spread across Hugh's face, and a blue light that I had often noted around Hugh when he taught or channeled began to spread throughout the room.

"Look around, what do you see?" Hugh's voice, sounding different from Master of Spirit or his Higher Self, asked.

"I see blue," I answered.

The voice laughed. "Then call me Blue, although I am all colors, for I am Light."

"How can we help you?" I asked.

The voice began to laugh heartily. "I am here to help you," it said, when it stopped laughing. "For I am Light."

"How can you help us then?" I asked. (It would be years before I realized Light has consciousness and that "Blue", as we affectionately called Light for several months, IS that consciousness.)

"I will be with you. We have much to do. Ask for me when I can be of service."

We have asked many times for Master of Light, as we eventually called him. (Master of Light spoke for the first five years through Hugh, so we refer to Master of Light as male, though "he" is, of course, genderless.) One of the first things we asked for, from Master of Light, was financial support for our "mission". We thought it a reasonable request.

Master of Light reminded us of what we already knew: spirit can only work through and with human consciousness to affect the earth planes and material matter within it. The financial funds for our work would come, we were told, but only after we cleared our own subconscious minds of mental and emotional blocks to receiving it and had totally focused our conscious efforts on the work we were to do for Spirit. [And humankind.]

Meanwhile, other spirits appeared, asking to help in any way they could. Knowing we would need to have someone with promotional skills to help us, I asked the spirit world to "bring us the world's greatest promoter". We got Mike Todd. (Actually, I'd meant someone IN body. With spirit, as with the mind, it is necessary to be specific.) Mike Todd is as forceful a spirit out of a body as I imagine he was while in the body. I asked him for advice.

Mike Todd: "You're too scattered. You're not focused. If you're going to do this work, you have to focus. Keep your focus! This is big work. This is big things. This is NOT to be played with. I'm not going to put this thing together. I'm only here to help. Spirit and love and belief are powerful. People in the United States are the most giving in the whole western world. There's nobody like a sucker in the USA to give money to a good cause. They're really willing to help. But you've got to give THEM something. You need to say this is what we're doing, this is what we're heading towards, we need your help. SPIRIT NEEDS YOU. Each one has a special place, special abilities and skills. It'll work. It'll work. What better goal could you have then saving the world as you know it, as I know it. But you need to get money and influence. You have to have some big names involved. Sorry, but nobody knows you guys very well. I'll see if I can get Elizabeth. See if we can prime her. You may meet her."

"Good," I said, "You can help me learn how to speak to her."

"Easy."

"With her involved, maybe Michael Jackson will help?" I suggested.

"Liz always was for the underdog, but she always admired the winner. She has duel, no, more than that, she has lots of interests. But she always did like the ones who came from the bottom to be the winner."

"I can see why she likes Michael so much," I said, "what do you think of her husband Larry?"

"I don't know what HE'S got. Maybe she's slowing down a little." Mike Todd laughed.

"Will you be there when she crosses over, Mr. Todd?" I asked him.

"Wouldn't miss it. We'll all be here. And it's Mike Todd. Not Mr., not Mike: Mike Todd."

"Oh, okay, now, about promoting this," I remarked, "I know Bette Midler. She's a friend of mine. I'm certain this is her mission, too."

"I like Bette."

"And I think Opra Winfrey is important, very important, to this project," I added.

"Biggest listening audience. She's rational, sympathetic, empathetic, rational. People relate to her. Rational. Relate. Got it?"

I said "yes" but I didn't really get it. What I wanted to know was how we could get in touch with Elizabeth Taylor. Mike Todd promised to get back to us on that.

"Well?" I asked at our next meeting.

"Well, what's holding you up?" He demanded. "You've got to get on the fast track with this thing. That's what I'm good at if you'll give me something to work with."

"What about Elizabeth, can she help?"

"I tried to get her attention, but she's not paying attention. Why don't you call her? You need her."

True, but what would we say? "Hello Ms. Taylor. We've been talking to your husband, Mike Todd, and he suggested we call you to help us save the world." I pointed out the difficulty of this to Mike Todd.

"Well, I'll try talking to her again," he said. "But she doesn't listen to me very well. How about Bette Midler. You said you know her."

True, as well, but after some reflection, I'd realized Bette probably wouldn't believe us any more than Elizabeth Taylor would. In fact, she'd probably worry about my sanity. After another meeting or two, Mike Todd, impatient with our stodgy ways, left us.

We thought of reaching people through television. But it would take time, we realized, to build up an audience, and time was running short. Self-help and motivational seminars, even hypnosis shows, were out. They, too, would take more time then we had, and more self-promoting then we wanted to do. We realized the best way to get the message out was a book.

We'd almost finished the book on sexual abuse. We needed, however, a different kind of book. We needed a book about spirit and the mind. We needed a book that explains who we are and the work we do, so people realize the information we bring is real, not fantasy. We needed a book that describes how physical reality, and thus the future, are created and can be changed. We needed a book to present Master of Light's plan to save humans. This is that book.

Before you read Master of Light's plan in Chapter Eight, you will want to read the chapters preceding it, for they bring you knowledge, Knowledge that leads to understanding. Understanding that leads to self-mastery. Self-mastery that leads to Light. And with Light, YOU will alter the future.

Chapter 4

Spoonbending

"Spoon bending?" The young woman in Dr. Harmon's office frowned at him. "What does bending spoons have to do with it?"

"Let me put it this way, Clarissa," Dr. Harmon answered, smiling, "Albert Einstein once stated it was his observation that even the brightest of individuals use no more than ten percent of their minds' abilities. Well, it has become obvious as we learn more and more of what the mind can do that Dr. Einstein was either wrong, or he deliberately overstated that percentage for reasons of his own. My own opinion is that humans use, as a matter of course, no more than maybe one one-thousandth percent of the mind's total ability. For instance, what enables people to walk barefoot on burning coals heated to a temperature that melts lead and aluminum?"

"I read some place it's because the body releases little jets of water through the bottoms of the feet and that cools them down," Clarissa suggested, still frowning.

Doctor Harmon laughed. "I've heard that too. Makes you wonder if the ones promoting that theory realize what steam is all about, doesn't it?"

Now Clarissa smiled again. "Oh, yes. I see what you mean."

"Good. Then you also see, even when we DO manage to demonstrate for ourselves the remarkable powers of our minds, we immediately try to reason the demonstration away. Even if we have to bend our reasoning minds to do it."

"Which brings us right back to spoon bending!" Clarissa noted, laughing.

"Very good, my dear," Dr. Harmon acknowledged, joining her laughter. "Which affords me the opportunity to explain the unexplainable by telling you about my classes in spoon bending, as they are popularly called. It is really a course in psychokinesis which is the ability to mentally affect physical objects. It is exciting to watch as even the most ardent skeptics observe their own minds altering physical matter."

"Does everyone's spoon bend?" Clarissa asked.

"Most everyone's, and that percentage increases when I use the suggestion given me by my friend Dr. Freda Morris, a former professor of Psychology at UCLA. Which was, to put young children in with the group as a wonderful catalyst to making it all happen. You see, young children's spoons always bend quickly and easily."

"They do?" Clarissa asked with interest. "How?"

"We suspect it is because they believe, without any doubt, that it will happen. We tell them if they look at the spoon and imagine it bending, their spoons will grow very soft, very fast, and bend easily with just the slightest touch. Almost as soon as we are done telling them, they start, and - just like that - it happens. That, in turn, makes believers out of some of the adults and THEIR spoons begin to bend. Pretty soon, the whole class has spoons made out of putty and they are laughing and joking as they bend the metal every which way, some even tying them in knots."

"You're kidding!"

"I assure you, I am not. Of particular interest are the staunch left-brained adults." Doctor Harmon cleared his throat and looked under his bushy brows at Clarissa, who laughed again. "They desperately try to rationalize how they are accomplishing the 'inexplicable'. Sometimes to the point of denying what they are doing even as they are doing it! One of my favorite stories is the engineer who observed with a real note of desperation in his voice, 'Well, yes, it SEEMS to be this spoon gets much softer when I keep saying bend, bend, bend.'

"Meanwhile, another student, - a lovely, elderly lady from Arkansas - kept exclaiming, 'Why land a goshin', this ole spoon just feels like taffy!'

"The engineer became quite upset, insisting, 'This is not happening. Metal does NOT soften like this just by holding it and thinking it will bend.'

"Afterwards, the engineer brought me his bent spoon and insisted I come to his plant later that week - which I did. When I arrived, he handed me a piece of tempered steel that he said was known to be absolutely impossible to bend by human hands. Maybe that was true, but by focusing my MIND on bending it, I was able - with my hands - to bend it easily."

"Really?" Clarissa, leaned forward. "What do you think happened? I mean, seriously, how did you do it?"

"The same as with the spoons, Clarissa. I focused my mind on the metal softening in my hands. Then, when it softened, I bent it easily. What happens exactly is not really known. Not yet anyway."

"Well, what do you think is happening?"

"I thought you weren't interested in spoonbending," Dr. Harmon teased.

"I am now," Clarissa answered firmly. "If the mind can protect the body from burning on 1500 to 1700 degree coals and bend steel - like you say it can - then what else can the mind do that we don't know about or understand?"

Dr. Harmon beamed at her. "Exactly. Very good, Clairissa. I do know this, the engineer and I examined the steel I'd bent using the power of my mind. There was no stretching on one side and pressuring, or compacting, on the other side, as would be expected when a piece of metal is bent with physical or mechanical power. Also, when metal bent with the mind is examined under a micron microscope, we see that the random locking of the molecular structure has become more linear. Meaning, the molecules are now in little rows that allows the metal to bend without the breaking or pressuring seen in metal bent by muscular or mechanical strength. So one possible explanation is that our minds realign the molecular structure of the metal."

"Wow. So," Clarissa summed up. "The purpose of classes like fire-walking and spoon bending is to demonstrate the power of one's mind."

"Yes. Then we teach how to avail oneself of that power in order to effect changes."

"You mean like healing," Clarissa commented, as she mused over what he had just said.

"Healing, as well as other changes; like the improvement you are seeking in your marital relationship."

Clarissa's face flushed as she remarked, "I love my husband, I just don't like sex."

"I understand that," Dr. Harmon assured her and gently added, "I also understand you wouldn't be here today if you didn't want to change that."

"Well," Clarissa flushed even more deeply, "he deserves a wife who enjoys his attentions. He likes sex. A lot," she added with an anger in her voice that did not escape Dr. Harmon's notice.

"How would you evaluate your husband's sexual skills?" Dr. Harmon asked. The matter-of-fact and comforting tone of his voice visibly relaxed Clarissa, and the blush had left her cheeks.

"Excellent. He is not my first lover, so I know."

""And you? Have you been checked medically to see if you have a hooded clitoris or some other condition that might be negatively affecting your sexual pleasure?" Dr. Harmon asked.

The question, though intimate, was presented in such a clinical and detached manner, that Clarissa answered easily. "Yes, I've had a thorough check-up. My doctor is the one who recommended you," she added.

"Good. I noted that you put that on your intake form. How would you assess your relationship with your husband, Clarissa? Forgetting about the sexual relations."

"If only we could, forget the sexual relations," Clarissa mumbled glumly, "then it would be great."

"Yet, you deserve a pleasurable sex life, Clarissa," Dr. Harmon gently reminded her. "So maybe we need to find out what's blocking you from doing that, and change it, hmmmm?"

"I'd like to." Clarissa's eyes were misty. "But how?"

"I don't how. You'll have to tell me."

"If I knew THAT, I wouldn't be here." Clarissa's eyes had shifted quickly from misty to steely.

"You may not know consciously, Clarissa, but some part of your mind does know."

"You mean my subconscious mind?" Clarissa asked.

"I see you know something about the mind. What do you know about the subconscious?" Dr. Harmon questioned her.

"I know the subconscious mind is the emotional mind. I've read it holds the memories, controls the body, and directs the processes of the body and the brain."

"My, Clarissa. You are much better informed than most of my first-time clients. I'm impressed."

"Well, I've been working on this, uh, sexual problem, for some time. And, I think I know what's wrong." Now Clarissa was staring at Dr.

Harmon with a fixed gaze. He waited, without speaking, for her to continue. A few moments passed. "I think I was sexually abused!" Clarissa blurted out finally.

"Do you have conscious memories of such abuse Clarissa?" Dr. Harmon asked.

"No."

"What leads you to suspect it then?"

"Well, the fact I hate sex for one thing. And just a feeling I have."

"Tell me about that feeling," Dr. Harmon settled back in his chair. His face and manner displayed an open and non-judging attitude. Clarissa felt relieved. He seemed as interested in finding out the truth as she was. She didn't want to believe she'd been sexually abused, and he didn't seem to have leaped to the conclusion she was, despite her suspicions.

"Well," Clarissa began, "it was my grandfather, my mother's father. I always felt really funny around him. My mother is the one who told me about sex, only she didn't tell me very much. She was too embarrassed. Then, while she was talking, I kept seeing my grandfather, which really confused and upset me. So I couldn't look her in the eye, which I think embarrassed her even more. So I guess I didn't get a very good introduction to sex." Clarissa clasped her hands tightly in her lap and continued. "I love my church, but its attitude towards sex certainly isn't helpful. Sex is the original sin and all of that. I figured out for myself that if sex is sinful or only to be used for procreation, then God wouldn't have designed us for pleasure. At least, the possibility of pleasure." Clarissa smiled wryly, took a deep breath, and continued. "My first time was pretty awful. It was, oh, I don't know, furtive and clumsy and over so quickly. I hardly felt anything beyond a short stabbing pain. After that, I avoided the guy almost as much as he avoided me. My reputation at school was shot, though, and I had to ignore a lot of smirks and smutty comments." Clarissa shuddered. "It was just so icky. We moved away not long afterwards, thank goodness. My next time was with a boyfriend. I'd gone with him for some time and he was hassling me to start. I didn't want to; I was afraid after the first time."

"Was that experience better?" Dr. Harmon prompted Clarissa after she'd remained silent for several moments.

"What? Oh, yes, well, it was better, but not great. I really couldn't understand why everyone made such a fuss about sex. He seemed to enjoy it though. We went together for two years and the sex was okay. I mean, I couldn't really feel anything, but it wasn't upsetting either."

"Upsetting? You mean it didn't hurt you?" Dr. Harmon asked.

"I mean I didn't really care I wasn't feeling much. With my husband though, it's different. He wants me to enjoy it. He's always asking me what would please me more than he's doing. I can't imagine what more he could do! I feel so angry at myself that he has to work so hard. My marriage is important to me. I just keep," Clarissa's voice trailed off.

"You keep what, Clarissa?" Dr. Harmon prompted again.

"I know it sounds really stupid," Clarissa mumbled in a small voice, looking down at her hands in her lap, "but I just keep thinking about my grandfather." She looked up at Dr. Harmon. "Do you think he abused me sexually, Doctor? Is that why I can't relax enough to enjoy myself?"

"Clarissa, you are a very smart woman. You are right, a large part of the problem is that your prior experiences with sex have convinced you that it is not something you are going to enjoy. So your belief - reinforced each time you don't enjoy yourself - is proven correct every time, because you expect it to be."

"Like the spoon bending," Clarissa observed.

"Exactly. What the mind expects tends to be realized. And while certain kinds of tensions in specific areas of the body are helpful to sexual pleasure, a nervous body, stressed mind, and uptight feelings are definitely working against you. So the inability to relax is another stumbling block."

"Can you fix that?" Clarissa asked hopefully. "Can you teach me to relax and enjoy myself?"

Dr. Harmon smiled. "I can certainly train you in relaxation techniques that will prove helpful if you allow yourself to use them."

"Why wouldn't I?" Clarissa demanded. "If you teach me to relax, I can overcome my feelings. I've been meditating and praying about this. I'm also doing affirmations and visualizations."

"Good, that is all very helpful in creating positive expectations and behaviors," Dr. Harmon agreed.

"Well, none of it has helped so far, but I'm hoping hypnosis will add to their effectiveness," Clarissa responded.

"It's certainly true most, if not all, methods for creating positive change either involve hypnosis or are more effective with it," Dr. Harmon agreed again. "However, in this case, Clarissa, it is likely you will have to eliminate your negative beliefs and patterns about sexual relations first, before you can successfully establish the positive changes."

"Why is that?" Clarissa asked.

"Simply put, when new programming contradicts old programming, the subconscious resists the new programming. Hypnosis can change this unless the emotional levels of your mind have a strong attachment to the old programming, then the subconscious will block anything - including will power, hypnosis, or anything else - that tries to change it."

"So what can I do?" Clarissa protested. "Give up?"

"No, far from it," Dr. Harmon reassured her. "What will work is to convince the part of the mind that is attached to the old programming to let go of its emotional attachment to it."

"How do we do that?" Clarissa asked. "It sounds difficult."

"It's sometimes complex, but not difficult. At least, no more difficult than struggling with the things in your life that no longer serve you. The rewards far outweigh the temporary discomfort of giving up old habits and beliefs. Many of our clients continue to come in to see us long after the need for therapy has ended because they enjoy the transformations they keep creating for themselves. Pamela calls what we do 'soul work'. It does seem to be a means of accelerating soul growth, as well as personal satisfaction and fulfillment."

"So what I'm doing might have worked if I didn't have any subconscious resistance to them working, right?" Clarissa pressed.

"Yes, if you've been doing them correctly," Dr. Harmon cautioned her. "For example, people often program the subconscious to bring to them exactly the opposite of what they want because they fail to realize the importance of images to the subconscious mind. For instance, when you say or think the word 'sugar', an image of sugar is projected on the screen of the mind. The subconscious links this image to stored data in its memory banks about sugar. If some of that data is connected to desire or will then desire and will are triggered. The subconscious acts upon images to which desire or will are attached."

"So that means," Clarissa spoke slowly and thoughtfully, "that affirming 'no sugar' projects an image of sugar to the subconscious, thus triggering a desire for the sugar."

"Exactly. The data stored in the subconscious indicates a desire and will for the sugar, not the contrary."

"But wouldn't an image of sugar - like in a bag, a cup, or a spoon - with a large line drawn through it work?" Clarissa asked. "And why wouldn't the words 'no sugar' project such an image?"

Dr. Harmon shrugged. "Maybe it does, we don't really know. However, we do know when people say 'no sugar' or draw a line through a mental image of a substance they crave, the cravings for that substance increases, not decreases. It's much more effective to begin building a new data bank of the desired change and attach will and desire to that image."

"In other words," Clarissa interjected, "if I wanted to weigh less, which I do, I should suggest the weight I want to weigh, not keep saying 'fat go away' which I've been saying, That just keeps bringing up the image of a fat me."

"You got it," Dr. Harmon said, nodding in agreement. "Now close your eyes a moment and think of the words sexual intimacy."

Clarissa did so, then a moment later sighed dejectedly. When she opened her eyes, Dr. Harmon said gently, "You just demonstrated perfectly how the mind works. As you thought of the words, your conscious mind projected the thought forms, or images, on the screen of the mind. Your subconscious mind is visual, even though you are not, Clarissa, and it responded instantly to that projected image. It linked that image to your stored data, or beliefs, about sexual intimacy. Then, as it is the seat of the emotions and in control of the body, it responded emotionally and physically to those beliefs. You sighed."

"I had a feeling of hopelessness," Clarissa added.

"Noted," Dr. Harmon responded. "Your subconscious beliefs are that you do not enjoy sexual intimacy. Emotionally, you hold little hope of doing so soon."

"I'm not trying to escape the subject," Clarissa said, neatly escaping the subject, "but how do you know I'm not visual?"

"I watch the movement of your eyes," Dr. Harmon told her. "Whether you are speaking or listening, they look straight ahead or side to side. They seldom shift upwards - which would indicate a visual person - or downwards - which would indicate a kinesthetic person. You have to see a person speak to hear them."

"That's true!" Clarissa exclaimed. "It drives me crazy when my husband tries to talk to me from across the room, or worse yet, from another room. He thinks I'm being controlling when I ask him to look at me when he speaks to me."

"You aren't," Dr. Harmon assured her. "You are watching his lips mouth the words. That's very important for auditory people. Tell me, does your husband speak rapidly, leave sentences unfinished, and jump quickly from idea to idea?"

"Yes, that drives me even crazier!" Clarissa exclaimed again. "What does that mean?"

"He's visual. Watch his eyes next time and you'll see what I mean. His eyes will shift upwards as he speaks. He's seeing pictures, so he doesn't need all the words. Your need to hear all of what he sees probably drives him a little crazy, too," Dr. Harmon said laughing. "Just understanding how the other communicates will help your relationship a great deal."

"It will help me at work, too," Clarissa said, fascinated. "I'm a teacher. I'm going to see to it the auditory kids sit in the front of the class where they can see and hear me clearly."

"Wonderful! Also suggest they read their studies aloud when they do homework. Even recording as they read and listening to it again helps auditory students a great deal. The kinesthetic kids need to learn by doing. A logical sequence of steps or ideas is always important to them and auditory people. Kinesthetic people like to be touched and get close to people, unless an emotional aversion has been created to this for some reason."

"Well, that explains another person at work. He always stands too close to me and touches my arm alot, but he never says or does anything suggestive. I've had a hard time figuring him out."

"Probably kinesthetic," Dr. Harmon agreed. "Watch his eyes and his hands. If he glances down frequently and touches his own body frequently, he's kinesthetic."

"My husband uses his hands alot," Clarissa added, "he kind of paints pictures of what he's saying."

"Yes, visual people do that. Kinesthetic people speak with their hands, as well, though the hands tend to stay at waist level and below. Most people have some of all three kinds of communication, but do tend to be predominately of one type," Dr. Harmon added. "Some will switch, depending on whether they are listening or speaking. It's helpful to be aware of that, too. All relationships, personal and professional, improve when the other person's mode of communication is understood and used."

"Is that why visualization is so frustrating for me?" Clarissa asked. "I never see anything."

"That's right, and you may not see anything in hypnosis either, especially if frustration gets in the way. Simply imagine - in hypnosis and with visualization, which is often used in hypnosis - of what you would see if you could see what the words are saying. Or just think of the words. Your subconscious will see them as they are projected on the screen of the mind. You don't have to worry about that. Just be certain, when you use visualization or self-hypnosis, that you are thinking of what you do want, as we discussed, and not what you don't want. That's true of prayer, as well," Dr. Harmon added. "Pray for what you want."

"But doesn't God know what you mean when you pray?" Clarissa protested.

"I don't know what God knows, but I do know how the mind works. When you pray, you are projecting words or thoughts as images on the screen of your mind. Prayer brings in spiritual energy for the use of the subconscious in manifesting the images you are projecting, unless, of course, there is an inner block or resistance to getting it."

"So that's why prayers aren't always answered," Clarissa said. "We block them ourselves."

"That's right, prayer is not magic. It works, or doesn't work, according to the principles of the mind. After all, the mind is what the Creator gave us for creating our own destinies. We just have to learn to use the mind wisely and knowingly."

"So, to get back to imaging. What would a person who is trying to heal their body of a disease imagine? The body fighting off the disease?" Clarissa asked.

"That just puts the focus on the disease," Dr. Harmon answered. "It's much more powerful to focus, by word, thought, and deed, on a healthy body."

"What if a person is so sick they just can't imagine being well?" Clarissa asked. "Or like with me, I've never been slender so I have a hard time thinking of myself as slender, or believing in it."

"The first step in healing or change of any kind is to acknowledge what one wants to change," agreed Dr. Harmon. "The second step is to discover what created the condition in the first place and what continues to contribute to its existence. Once those things have been found, understood, and corrected, then one can begin to take the steps that will create the transformation."

"I understand," Clarissa said, nodding. "You're saying the emotional causes for illness and or weight have to be addressed first and then the changes can occur. I imagine it's the same with addictions and phobias and that kind of thing, isn't it?"

"Yes," Dr. Harmon agreed, "it's the way the mind works. Addictive behavior can be controlled with drugs, medication, and coping mechanisms, but to end the desire for them, the emotional factors that created and continues to trigger them must be addressed. Fears and phobias are emotionally driven, too. There always seems to be, in my experience, a beginning point for these things. An experience that first created the thoughts and beliefs to which the emotions became attached. Thought is the creator of our reality. Physicists and metaphysicians tend to agree on that."

"How early in life do experiences begin to affect us, Dr. Harmon?" Clarissa asked.

"We make up our minds about an astonishing number of important matters very early in life, Clarissa. Often without even realizing it. Take reading minds, for instance."

"Reading minds? You mean being psychic, knowing other people's thoughts, that sort of thing?"

"Yes. Everyone is psychic at the subconscious levels of mind. The subconscious mind 'reads" not only the images on your screen of the mind, but on everyone else's minds as well. Most babies and very young children read minds quite readily and easily. They are taught, however, to suppress this ability."

"Why?" Clarissa asked curiously, "and how?"

"Humans like to keep secrets. We are taught from very young, by our families, culture, and society, that secrets are important. It happens as easily as a child asking mommy why she's mad at daddy, or asking daddy why he's feeling sad. Now, the child can see, mad and sad thoughts in their minds, so when the response is 'I'm not mad' or 'I'm not sad', the child perceives the message is 'Stay out of my mind'. After repeated messages of that kind, children learn reading what someone else is thinking is not acceptable. So they learn to suppress the ability. The subconscious mind continues to 'read' minds, but it has been given the instruction not to bring this information to the conscious awareness."

"But do children and babies really understand what they are seeing?" Clarissa asked dubiously.

"I have, in forty years of clinical research and practice, done over 50,000 regressions. Many have been to early childhood, birth, the womb, even to conception. I didn't believe memory could go back so far when I first began my clinical practice. But it kept happening spontaneously, to myself and other therapists, when we would suggest in hypnosis that a person go to the root of a problem, or find the cause of a symptom."

"People have memories of the womb?" Clarissa asked incredulously.

"One client, a middle aged man," Dr. Harmon recounted, "was speaking, in a regression, of floating in and out of his body while in his mother's womb. He described, in vivid detail, a violent argument his parents were having. He even described the dress his mother was wearing - a brightly colored dress with large stripes. Afterwards, he expressed his doubts about the regression, feeling he 'must have made it up.'

"The next week he returned and reported that he'd called his mother and asked her about the argument. Shocked, his mother replied, 'But you couldn't know about that! Your father and I never spoke of that matter again.' When he described her dress, there had been a long pause. Shakily, she'd told him, 'I threw that dress away as soon as you were born. I looked like an elephant in a circus tent in that dress. I even tore up the one picture of me in it when I threw it out. How could you know these things?'

"Another client, a woman," he continued, "spoke in regression of her sadness as her twin left her, just before birth. She asked her mother about this and was told, 'How did you find out? You had a twin that was still born. Your father was so heartbroken. It was the son he'd always wanted. We agreed never to speak of him, not even to each other. I know I never told you about him.'

"There are hundreds of regressions like these in my client files and the client files of my colleagues. I stopped doubting long ago."

"But how can a person have a memory of conception?" Clarissa protested. "The brain isn't even formed yet."

"The mind works through the brain, Clarissa, but is independent of the brain. The mind exists with the spirit before conception of its body. After the spirit enters the body, it must wait for the brain to catch up to its mind."

"Why don't we remember our birth and all of that, then? And why can't we read right away and speak in full sentences if the mind is already developed before birth?"

"Good questions, Clarissa. First, the brain must develop the proper connections for speech and reading. Secondly, we DO remember everything. We just don't consciously recall it all. Do you recall every day of your adult life?"

"No," Clarissa admitted.

"Exactly. We seem to store some memories in places or ways that are immediately accessible to conscious recall. Other memories and information are stored in ways or places that require altered states such as hypnosis and dreams in order to access them. It would be confusing to be consciously aware of all of one's experiences. Imagine being aware at any moment of all your different experiences with their attached sensory and emotional energies. It would be overwhelming."

"What if a person doesn't believe what they said in a regression, does the regression still help them?" Clarissa asked.

"If the regression has helped the person to understand or resolve the issue involved, then the benefit is gained whether the person believes in the regression or not."

"So maybe regressions are just the mind talking in symbols and stories, like in dreams," Clarissa commented.

"Maybe," Dr. Harmon agreed. "I never insist my clients believe anything. I'm here to guide people to their own truths, not mine. What they choose to believe of what their own minds tell them is up to them."

"Do people ever make up stories in hypnosis?" Clarissa asked.

"Yes, though they are far less likely to do so if the hypnotist is well-trained and non-leading. If knowing whether a story was 'made up' is important to a client, we use a tool that can tell us that."

"What tool is that?" Clarissa asked eagerly.

"It's called neuro-muscular response, or NMR, and it will enable us to know, Clarissa, whether your grandfather did or did not molest you."

"How does it work?" she asked.

"Let me demonstrate it to you," Dr. Harmon answered. He got up from behind his desk and moved around to sit on a stool beside Clarissa's chair.

"Will this hurt?" she asked, eyeing him warily.

Dr. Harmon feigned shock. "Now, would I hurt you, Clarissa?"

She smiled and relaxed visibly. "No."

Dr. Harmon shook his head. "Really, what a question. All I want you to do, Clarissa, is to lift your arm." Clarissa lifted her left arm straight out in front of her. "Good, now move it about 15 degrees back toward the left shoulder. You can lower it about 15 degrees, too, so it doesn't take so much muscle strength to hold it up. Good. Now, does that hurt?"

"No."

"Of course not. Nor will this; I'm placing my two fingers just above your wrist. Now I'm also going to push down slightly with my two fingers while I stabilize your shoulder with my other hand, like this." Clarissa's arm lowered as Dr. Harmon pushed down lightly. "Does that hurt?"

"No, not at all."

"What I'm testing, Clarissa, is the strength of your deltoid muscle, here in your arm." Dr. Harmon showed Clarissa the location of the deltoid in the upper top of her arm, and she nodded her understanding. "That's why the angle in which you hold your arm is important. We want to test only the deltoid. Now this time, think 'yes' and say 'yes' aloud. When you do, I will say 'hold' and push down with my fingers again. All right, proceed."

Clarissa said, "Yes."

Dr. Harmon said 'hold' and then pushed down on Clarissa's arm. This time Clarissa's arm remained strong and resisted the pressure of Dr. Harmon's fingers pushing down on it.

"Excellent. Now, think 'no' and say 'no'," Dr. Harmon instructed her. As Clarissa followed these instructions, Dr. Harmon repeated the process. After saying 'hold', so Clarissa could resist, he pushed down with the same degree of pressure. This time the arm lowered easily.

"Wow! What was that?" Clarissa exclaimed. "Did you push harder?"

"Let's do it again and you tell me," Dr. Harmon answered, and they repeated the process. "Did I push harder for the no?" He asked when they'd finished.

"You sure didn't seem to," Clarissa acknowledged "What do you call this again?"

"NMR which stands for Neuro-Muscular Response. It's a refined process of muscle testing which is also called applied kinesiology. Muscle testing began with bio-feedback research, which made it clear that what the mind is thinking affects the muscles of the body. I've refined the process to accurately access various levels of the mind and spirit."

"I have heard of muscle testing," Clarissa observed. "My friend's herbalist uses it."

"Many people in the health field use it. Unfortunately, many of them are not using it correctly because they don't fully understand how the mind affects it. That's why I'm taking care to explain it to you, Clarissa. It is not as simple as it looks. It requires training to use it properly. Precise and careful wording must be used, or the answers will be misleading. It's important to know WHICH level of the mind the answer is coming from, and whether any other mind - including my own - is interfering with the answers. I have to keep my mind blank when I test you so as not to interfere with your answers."

"It sounds almost dangerous," Clarissa commented.

"It's not a tool I would want anyone to use on me if they were not well trained and didn't keep their own thoughts and expectations out of it," Dr. Harmon agreed. "Like a surgeon's scalpel, it can be precise and accurate when used in skilled hands, but very clumsy, even dangerous, when used in unskilled hands."

"Are pendulums a form of muscle testing?" Clarissa asked.

"Yes, they are. The pendulum is responding to a pulse response, triggered by the mind. The response moves from the brain to the fingers that hold the string or chord which moves the pendulum. Used properly, pendulums can be a good self-help tool, but they are not, unfortunately, as reliable as NMR."

"Why not?"

"Again, the mind interferes. If part of your mind wants a particular answer it can manipulate the pulse that moves the pendulum."

"Can't the same thing happen with the NMR?" Clarissa asked.

"Yes," Dr. Harmon answered truthfully, "but it takes more concentrated conscious effort to do so. For one thing, we are working with larger muscle fulcrums with NMR. The deltoid in your arm or the gluteus medius at the side of your hip are harder to manipulate mentally than your fingers. We also use the large muscles for testing so clients can see and feel the responses themselves. I could tell you what your response is simply by feeling the muscle response with my fingers, but it doesn't do you any good to take my word for it."

"I like seeing it happen. In fact, I wouldn't believe it if I couldn't. It's a weird feeling though," Clarissa remarked, "to have your arm strong when you say one thing and weak when you say another!"

"I agree with you. Even after all these years, it still amazes me."

"Shall we use it to find out now if my grandfather molested me?" Clarissa asked.

"Yes, we will also want to know whether any memories of molest are accurate or the result of mistaken perceptions."

"What to you mean, inaccurate," Clarissa demanded, "You mean whether I made them up?"

"No. The subconscious records memories subjectively; meaning according to what it thinks it sees or perceives. It can be mistaken in what it perceives. There is another level of the mind, however, that records what happens accurately. We can access both levels of the mind with NMR."

"How can that be, Dr. Harmon?" Clarissa asked.

"It's a lot like electricity, Clarissa. No one knows, yet, what electricity is really all about; for instance, where does it come from and why does it work? No one knows, nevertheless, people have learned a great deal about how to use it Pamela and I use NMR a great deal. While we aren't sure exactly why or how it works, we've learned to use it in a way that brings accurate results. The more our skills in using it evolve, the more accurate we see it become."

"All right," Clarissa said, "on with the NMR."

"Very good, Clarissa. Now we need to test your polarity."

"My what?"

"The flow of energy in your body. The Chinese have studied energy flows, called meridians, for centuries. Acupuncture and acupressure work with specific points along these meridians. It's important to be in the correct polarity balance while working with any kind of muscle testing, such as the NMR."

"Okay," Clarissa agreed. "How do we do that?"

"Very easily. Place your open hand, palm down, on top of your head. Now 'hold' just like before, only don't think or say anything.." Clarissa did so, and her arm remained strong.

"Now turn that same hand palm up on top of your head and resist my same pressure on your arm when I say 'hold' again."

The arm weakened and lowered.

"Amazing," Clarissa commented. "Am I in balance?"

"If you weren't, there would have been an opposite response. The palm down would have weakened the muscle and the palm up would have made it stronger. In that case, I would have had you tap around your thymus gland to balance the polarity."

"How would I do that?" Clarissa asked.

"Place one, two, or three fingers about two and a half inches below the hollow in your clavicles. That is about where your thymus gland is. Now go back up about an inch and starting toward the right shoulder, tap a circle of about a three inch diameter around the thymus. You'll be tapping counter-clock wise. Your body is the clock. Yes, that's right," Dr. Harmon nodded as Clarissa tapped a circle around the area of the thymus. "That tapping helps the immune system, as well as establishes a greater differential between the weak and strong muscle response."

"Why don't you just start with it then?" Clarissa asked.

"It's important to know the polarity flow of a client. For one thing, it establishes whether other influences are affecting the energy balance."

"What other influences?" Clarissa asked curiously.

"We'll talk about that another time. Right now, let's continue with the NMR. With your permission, I'd like to work with your gluteus medius muscle. That's the large muscle, on the side of the hip, that controls the leg. The legs are much stronger than the arm and don't tire as easily. I touch just above the ankles, instead of the wrist, if that is okay with you."

"Sure."

"Okay. Now, remember, this is not a muscle contest. Nor is it fool-proof. Since we have at least one fool here - me - we have to work with this very carefully to be sure we are using it correctly."

Clarissa laughed. "I don't believe for one moment you are a fool, Dr. Harmon."

"Well, we'll be careful anyway, you never know," Dr. Harmon answered, grinning. "Okay, just put your legs straight out on the foot rest in front of you, about 12 inches apart. Good. I'll touch both legs, just above the ankles, like this. Now when I say 'hold', resist my pulling your far leg to the leg nearest me." Clarissa did so. "Good, now just like before, let's test the 'yes' and the 'no' response."

Dr. Harmon had Clarissa say and think 'yes'. He then said 'hold' and applied the same pressure. The leg did not move. They repeated the process for 'no' and the leg moved across the foot rest of the chair easily.

"Boy, it hardly felt like you put any pressure on that leg at all," Clarissa exclaimed, "but I can see that you did! I really tried to resist, but I just couldn't hold my legs apart."

"Then it's working perfectly. One more thing, you know how I touched your shoulder with my other hand when we were working with your arm?" Clarissa nodded. "Well, I was anchoring your shoulder, but I was also being careful to put both of my hands on your body. It's important to have an enclosed energy connection between us. When I'm touching both of your ankles, or just above your ankles to be more precise, we have that complete energy connection. Now, are you ready to begin our work?"

"For twenty minutes already," Clarissa replied.

"Why Clarissa, you aren't trying to tell me I talk too much are you?" Dr. Harmon teased.

"Not really. I'm glad you're taking the time to explain it to me. Otherwise, I'd be pretty confused by now. I'd think you were using magic or something."

"That has been my experience," Dr. Harmon agreed. "I believe people should know how their own minds and bodies work so they can take responsibility for them. Now, Clarissa, state your name and you'll see how this works."

"My name is Clarissa."

Dr. Harmon pulled on Clarissa's right leg. It came half-way to the left leg. "Hmmmm, sort of, or maybe," Dr. Harmon remarked.

"What does that mean? That's my name," Clarissa objected.

"Well, let's see. Did you keep your thoughts on your statement?" Clarissa nodded. "Good, because the muscle responds to the thought. If you think one thing, and say another, it will respond to the thought, not the statement. Do you have more than one name?"

"No. Well, yes," Clarissa corrected herself. "I have a middle and a last name."

"Try those." This time the leg response was strong; the legs did not move together at all. "See?" said Dr. Harmon. "Your subconscious mind believes your whole name to be your name. Clarissa is just part of your name."

"Sort of my name in other words. I understand," Clarissa said, nodding. "So we are talking to the subconscious mind with this NMR, right?"

"At this moment, yes, because we haven't specified which level of mind it is to access, so it just accesses itself. It's own programming, in other words."

"But you can access other levels?" Clarissa pressed.

"Yes. I'll demonstrate. Tell me, do you think you are a worthy human being?"

"Yes, I think so. I have my faults, but every one does."

"Consciously you believe yourself to be worthy. Let's check on that," Dr. Harmon suggested. Make the statement, 'My conscious mind accepts I am a worthy human being.'" Clarissa did so, and the response was positive.

"Good, now state, 'My subconscious belief is that I am a worthy human being.'" Again the muscle response was positive.

"Your subconscious agrees with that," Dr. Harmon noted, as Clarissa's legs remained strong. Now say, 'I believe I am as worthy as any human being living or dead.'" Clarissa repeated the statement and this time the muscle response was weak. "No," observed Dr. Harmon, "your subconscious does not agree. Now say, 'My Higher Self knows I am as worthy as any human being, living or dead.'" This time the response was strong.

"What happened, Clarissa?" Dr. Harmon asked.

"I don't know, you tell me." she challenged.

"Well, I would observe that it seems your subconscious has been programmed to believe there are others - either in history or alive today - that are more worthy than you. Would you agree with that?"

"Oh sure. Jesus, Ghandi, Madame Curie - lots of people."

"But the Higher Self, the level of truth beyond the programming, says

'The subconscious belief is wrong. You ARE as worthy as Jesus, Ghandi, Madame Curie, the President, or anyone else. Maybe especially some Presidents." Clarissa and Dr. Harmon both laughed. "The point of soul work, such as what we are doing here, is to bring the subconscious beliefs into line with the Higher Self knowledge and truths. That allows us to be powerful. Of course, we often have to change the old subconscious programming before it will accept that truth."

"So we can test whether I was sexually abused by my Grandfather with both my subconscious and my Higher Self, right?"

"Yes, that's right. Each will give us valuable information," Dr. Harmon replied. "But before we test this, Clarissa, I want you to be very certain you are ready for this information. Once the door to sexual abuse is opened, it becomes very difficult to close it again. Working with sexual abuse can be emotionally disruptive as you work to complete your healing. Will your husband be supportive of this? It can be difficult on a relationship unless both mates are very committed to the relationship and the healing process. Are there any other factors in your life that are already so taxing that your healing work would put you on overload? Are you willing to commit to working with it, should we find that sexual molest is present? These are very important questions to consider before we proceed."

"If I was molested and I don't heal that experience, will I ever be able to enjoy sex fully?" Clarissa asked.

"I don't know, Clarissa. It has been my considerable experience, and that of my colleagues, that sexual abuse and molest, however brief, does affect many things in life, including sexual enjoyment. We can ask your Higher Self, with the NMR, if the thought you were molested sexually by your grandfather has created blocks to your enjoying sex. The reason we ask the Higher Self is because it is not influenced by belief or subject to incorrect perceptions. Would you like to begin with that?"

"Yes. How do I do that?"

" First tell me, would you rather use the term sexual abuse or sexual molest?"

"Is there a difference," Clarissa asked.

"Not in my mind. The question is whether there is a difference in your mind."

"Well, I guess I am more comfortable, now that you've mentioned it, with the term sexual molest."

"Then we will use that. Now, we are ready for you to make a statement. The reason we have you make statements, rather than questions, is it seems to elicit more accurate responses. Perhaps a statement such as, 'The thought I was sexually molested blocks me from responding positively to sexual stimulation with my husband.'"

"Okay," Clarissa said, then stated, "I was sexually molested by my Grandfather, and this thought blocks my ability to enjoy sex."

"If you will notice, Clarissa," Dr. Harmon interjected gently, "that is a compound statement. One part may be true, and the other part not true. So the mind will be unclear to which it should respond, and we will get a wishy-washy response."

"Oh," Clarissa replied, nodding. "Then how about this one: The thought I was sexually molested by my grandfather blocks my enjoyment of sex."

"Hold," Dr. Harmon said. As he watched her eyes to be certain she was keeping her mind on her statement, he tested her muscle response. The legs and the eyes remained steady.

"That answer is 'yes', Clarissa. Now," Dr. Harmon continued, "have you had sufficient time to decide whether you are prepared to know if you were sexually molested, and are you ready to commit to the therapy necessary for healing it, if you were? If you are, I'm prepared to help you every step of the way. But the emotional work is yours to do. If you are not ready, then it is best to wait until you are. Shall we stop now, while you think this over?"

"No." Clarissa's voice was firm. "This is what I came in to do. Let's do it."

"Okay. Then let us proceed. Make a statement to the effect that your grandfather sexually molested you in this life."

"In THIS life?" Clarissa protested.

"It may be that the soul you know as your grandfather, today, was with you in a previous life. It may be that he sexually molested you in that life, not this one. Even if you don't believe in past lives, your subconscious mind undoubtedly does. We've found that to be true with everyone we've tested. It is important to know whether this molest occurred, if it did occur, in this life or another. A lot of damage has been done by therapists who don't know how to recognize whether an abuse memory is from a past life experience."

"Would it bother me in this life if he abused me way back in another life time?" Clarissa protested.

"Yes, it could. Especially since he is in your life today."

"Okay, let's ask." Dr. Harmon held both of Clarissa's legs, just above the ankles, and she stated clearly, "My Higher Self knows my grandfather sexually molested me in this life time."

The muscle response was weak, allowing Dr. Harmon to pull Clarissa's legs together.

"That was a 'no', wasn't it," Clarissa whispered.

"It was a no," Dr. Harmon confirmed.

"Whew, that's it then." Clarissa was smiling with relief.

"Except," Dr. Harmon cautioned her, "you have a thought in your subconscious mind that your grandfather sexually molested you. That belief, even though it is incorrect, affects you, Clarissa. It is necessary to change that belief."

"But we know now it didn't happen," Clarissa protested. "Doesn't that clear it?"

"Let's see," Dr. Harmon suggested. "Make this statement: 'I no longer believe my grandfather sexually molested me.'"

Clarissa did so, and the muscle response was weak, indicating a 'no' response.

"Now state this, Clarissa, 'My subconscious mind believes my grandfather sexually molested me in this life.'"

The response was a 'yes' response.

"You see, Clarissa," Dr. Harmon explained, "your subconscious mind still believes you were sexually molested, despite the knowledge of the Higher Self. We will need to change that belief if you are to be free of your symptoms of sexual abuse. Let's see how old you were when the thought you were sexually molested by your grandfather began, as well as the number of times your subconscious believes you to have been molested by him."

NMR testing indicated one incident of sexual molest at three years old.

"Only one?" Clarissa questioned. "Would that be enough to affect my sexual responses with my husband?"

"Yes," Dr. Harmon responded. "Especially when it is exacerbated by subsequent negative sexual experiences. At three years old you had an experience with your grandfather that made you very uncomfortable with sexual energy. Your later experiences with sexual energy made you even more uncomfortable. When your husband and you have sexual relations that discomfort is triggered. Now negative expectations for future relations are added and failure to enjoy and respond happens once again. The pattern is reinforced each time."

"Gosh, what about people who were abused or molested a lot!" Clarissa exclaimed.

"They often have a lot of healing work to do," Dr. Harmon acknowledged. "Fortunately, hypnosis speeds that up considerably."

"How long will mine take?" Clarissa asked anxiously.

"I don't know," Dr. Harmon answered. "It takes as long as it takes. It has been my experience that the subconscious beliefs can be readily changed when the level of the mind that programmed the belief - in this case your three year old mind - changes its mind because of new evidence and understanding. What we need to do is find out what really happened. Since you've booked a second hour, we can do that now if you'd like."

"More NMR testing?" Clarissa asked.

"No, right now we need to work with the three year old who believes she was molested. We will need to speak with her."

"Really?" Clarissa sounded dubious.

"Really," Dr. Harmon replied firmly. "Just because you grew up doesn't mean the three year old that you were doesn't exist. Her thoughts, feelings, and beliefs remain with you, as a kind of inward spirit presence. We will need to go to the inner levels of the mind to find her."

"How do we do that?"

"By guiding you inward, through hypnosis, your subconscious mind will bring her forward. That way, I can speak to the three year old you without the adult you interfering." Dr. Harmon had been watching Clarissa carefully as he'd explained this to her. Now he observed, "You aren't comfortable with hypnosis, are you, Clarissa?"

"Well, my minister thinks it's mind control and dangerous."

"I see, what do you think?"

"I asked my minister if he'd ever read anything about it and he hadn't. So I did. Everything I've read says all hypnosis is self-hypnosis. I've also read that the subject is in control, really, and can come out of the trance whenever he or she wants to."

"That's absolutely true," Dr. Harmon agreed. "But you're still uncomfortable, why?"

"I went to a hypnosis show once," Clarissa admitted. "It's hard to believe those people weren't under the hypnotist's control - they did such silly and stupid things. I don't think some of them would have done what they did if they hadn't been hypnotized."

"Possibly not," Dr. Harmon agreed. "Tell me, Clarissa, did the hypnotist ask for volunteers?"

"Yes, and she did a bunch of tests of some kind. To see who would be best, I guess."

"Those were suggestibility tests," said Dr. Harmon. "She used them to determine who would respond most readily to both her and the hypnosis. Half the skill of the stage hypnotist is picking the best subjects. Did you notice the hypnotist not using anyone who did well on the testing?"

"Yes, come to think of it. A boy who seemed quite shy. I wondered why he went up in the first place. But he looked like he was hypnotized immediately, so I was surprised when she had him go back into the audience."

Dr. Harmon laughed. "The hypnotist probably hated to do it, because the boy was obviously a good subject. But for a stage show, subjects willing to go along with the show are important. She probably decided the boy's shyness was just too strong, or that he would be too upset afterwards. A stage show is more fun when the hypnotist chooses people who have fun letting themselves go."

"You mean people who might do silly things when tipsy or drunk?" Clarissa asked.

"Partly true," Dr. Harmon agreed. "Being drunk is an altered state. An altered state simply means you are, for a period of time, by-passing your self-critical mind. Everyone goes into altered states regularly. Sleep is an altered state. Dreaming is an altered state, as is day dreaming. Focusing and concentrating on a book, a movie, or a televised event to the degree that you become emotionally affected, or feel like you are there, is an altered state. Tell me, Clarissa, have you ever been driving your car and suddenly recognized you have no conscious memory of the last several blocks or miles?"

"Oh yes, I have!" Clarissa exclaimed.

"Well, that was a hypnotic state. Your subconscious mind was driving the car, while your conscious mind was occupied elsewhere. While it's nice to know the subconscious can do that, it is far preferable to have ALL of the mind focused on driving. Which is why some part of your mind brought your conscious mind back to the driving. Another way to explain the hypnotic state is to compare it to the state of mind just before entering sleep. For instance, are you ever deeply relaxed and just about to fall asleep when your husband enters the room?"

"Yes," Clarissa agreed.

"When that happens, are you more likely to rouse yourself and talk to him or to ignore him?"

"Sometimes, if it seems important, I'll wake myself up and talk to him. Other times, when it isn't important, or I feel too cozy to talk, I'll ignore him and go to sleep."

"Exactly. You are at a level of mind that is accompanied by deep physical relaxation, but you are still sufficiently aware of your surroundings to make choices and determine your best actions. We would call that an alpha level of awareness. Most clinical hypnosis is done in that level. You are aware of your surroundings, but you feel so involved in what is happening inwardly, you ignore outside distractions. If something were to occur around you that caused you to become nervous or alarmed you would bring yourself right out of hypnosis. It truly is a self-controlled, aware state."

"What about people who use hypnosis in place of anesthesia when they're being operated on, are they aware?" Clarissa asked.

"I've done a great deal of medical hypnosis, and I can assure you, very few people want to be aware during their surgery. I give them suggestions for going deeper, into what we call hypno-sleep. Not a good state of hypnosis for giving suggestions other than being unaware and blocking pain."

"Do people always remember what happened in hypnosis afterwards?" Clarissa questioned further.

"Most people are aware what is happening while they are in hypnosis," Dr. Harmon answered. "What they will recall later is up to them. If they give themselves the suggestion they won't recall the session afterwards, or the hypnotist does, then they might accept that suggestion."

"That's scary," Clarissa said. "You won't give me that suggestion will you?"

"No professional would give you such a suggestion, Clarissa, unless you asked for it, or the information being sought was beyond your ability to handle consciously. I don't do that to my clients. If they are not ready to know about something consciously, then there is little use in bringing it up. I find it is much more healing and transforming for people to work at their own pace and comfort level, not mine. If you hear me making such a suggestion, bring yourself out of hypnosis immediately. Agreed?"

"Agreed," Clarissa answered readily.

"I also tape the sessions," Dr. Harmon told her. "You can take the tape with you, to be certain there is nothing on it of which you don't approve. If there is, you either talk to me about it, or you cease seeing me. It's that simple, Clarissa."

"Good. You know, I bought a hypnosis tape once. After the first time, I could never stay awake. Or I was so deep, I never heard anything. Which one was it?"

"If you were sleepy, you probably slept. Other times, your conscious mind, knowing nothing unexpected would be said on a tape, might have given itself permission to check out. Whether you were in a level, or stayed at a level, where suggestions are more readily accepted, is difficult to determine."

"I think I wasn't," Clarissa complained. "At least I didn't get rid of any weight."

"Perhaps you have a subconscious block to losing weight, Clarissa. In that case, a weight loss tape is more likely to irritate than help you. Or your subconscious mind will simply take you into sleep or deeper levels of hypnosis where it can ignore the suggestions."

"How can you tell what level a person is in when you hypnotize them?" Clarissa asked.

Dr. Harmon laughed. "Experience. Are you planning to become a professional hypnotist in just one session, Clarissa?"

"No," Clarissa laughed. "But what if I can't be hypnotized, what then?"

"All mentally stable people can be hypnotized, if they trust the process and the hypnotist. Sometimes, if they are afraid of what they will find in hypnosis, they will resist the hypnosis. But you seem like you are eager to find your answers. I don't think we'll have any problems. No doubt you've been in hypnosis many times. You know, your minister, whether he realizes it or not, is using hypnotic techniques in his services."

"Like what? I can hardly wait to tell him!" Clarissa responded, grinning.

Dr. Harmon walked over to his book case and took down a book. "Here," he said, handing it to Clarissa. "Give him this book. He'll realize for himself the songs, sermons, prayers, and other religious rites and rituals most religions use are powerful hypnotic techniques. They often lead people into highly suggestible states of mind. Of course, his suggestions are presumably good ones his flock doesn't mind following."

"Except about putting more money in the collection plate, maybe," Clarissa responded, laughing.

"That reminds me of Amy Semple MacPhearson," Dr. Harmon mused. "A woman evangelist, she started her ministry by standing on street corners preaching to the people. She would shout and rant and rave. She MOVED people. The mind is very open when it's being stimulated and excited. She'd always scold everyone as the collection plate was being passed around with, 'I don't want to hear the jingle of change, I want to hear the rustle of bills!' She managed to build a large expensive temple with those collections and created quite a following for herself. And this was in the middle of the depression!" Dr. Harmon shook his head. "Shows how powerful suggestion can be. Something which advertising people know and use."

"Well, shouldn't that make me nervous about hypnosis?" Clarissa asked worriedly.

"It should make you discerning, Clarissa. You would never trust the care of your body to someone you didn't trust to know what he or she was doing, would you?" Clarissa shook her head. "I've trained hundreds of hypnotists and hypnotherapists," Dr. Harmon began, but Clarissa interrupted him.

"What's the difference," she asked, "between hypnosis and hypnotherapy? I've always wondered."

"Hypnosis is the induction of, or being in, an altered state of mind. That simply means the conscious level of mind is more passive, even when it is present, and the subconscious levels more accessible. There are hundreds of methods and techniques of hypnosis. I believe in using methods that do not shock, tax, force, or traumatize the mind or the body in any way. I find that much more effective in the long run."

"What about guided imagery and visualizations," Clarissa asked. "Are they as healing as hypnosis."

"I didn't say hypnosis is healing," Dr. Harmon corrected Clarissa, "hypnosis accesses information found within the deeper levels of mind and spirit. That knowledge allows for the kind of release and understanding that brings true healing, by which I mean permanent healing.

"Guided imagery and visualization are often used as means of inducing hypnosis, or as hypnotic suggestion within the hypnosis. Speaking the language of the subconscious mind, like guided imagery and visualizations, is very powerful. It's even more powerful in hypnosis, when the subconscious is front and center. Of course, even in hypnosis, the mind can resist suggestions presented in any form. Hypnotherapy is working, in the subconscious levels of the mind, with subconscious blocks and resistance. It seeks to help convince the mind to change or heal itself of thoughts, emotions, will, and beliefs that are no longer helpful or desirable."

"I see," said Clarissa. "Is it similar to psychotherapy then?"

"I find hypnotherapy to be more effective," Dr. Harmon answered. "It's certainly faster, in most cases. Especially when used with NMR. One is able to go directly to the source of whatever is blocking or resisting healing and change. Naturally, professional therapists do have a great advantage when they add good hypnotherapy training to their skills. That is, if they can remain open minded and resist the temptation to try to make clients and patients fit a pre-conceived model or theory. People are similar, yet each person is unique. The real test is having the patience to let people find their own answers and effect their own transformations. That is the only way to really discover how the mind and spirit work."

"Okay, I think I'm ready for hypnosis, Dr. Harmon," Clarissa said. "How about you?"

"I'm ready if you are, Clarissa. How about nice, relaxing sounds in the background? I have tapes of ocean waves, a country stream, rain, a water fall, birds, and a gently lapping lake. What appeals to you?"

"The ocean. I love the ocean."

"Good. Then the ocean it is. Would you rather be in, on, or beside the ocean, Clarissa?" Dr. Harmon's voice was soothing and relaxing, as Clarissa leaned back comfortably in her chair.

"Beside it, lying in the sun and feeling its warmth on my skin. I can almost imagine it already," Clarissa said and closed her eyes.

CLARISSA'S REGRESSION

Dr. Harmon proceeded to deepen Clarissa's level of relaxation with suggestions of listening to the soothing sounds of the waves, as well as the soothing sound of his voice blending with the waves. Then he gave suggestions of allowing the conscious mind to drift into a more passive state of awareness, thus permitting her own powerful subconscious mind to shift forward.

Clarissa's eyes rolled up briefly beneath the lids. Her breathing deepened considerably and the beat of the pulse in her neck was very slow and steady. She had entered a good working state of hypnosis within two minutes of beginning the process.

"Good, Clarissa," Dr. Harmon complimented her. "You are really doing very well. Now your powerful subconscious mind can signal me without you even having to speak. Soon, a finger or a thumb will begin to move for a 'yes' signal. That's it right there," he said approvingly, as Clarissa's right index finger lifted slightly. "Good, now let your subconscious mind move another finger or thumb for a 'no' signal." This time the left index finger moved. "Very good, Clarissa." Dr. Harmon's voice continued to soothe and reassure Clarissa.

"Now, take a deep breath, Clarissa, and as you do, you will find yourself moving deeper into this pleasant state of deep relaxation. Imagine now, that you are standing in front of a large chalkboard. Move your 'yes' finger when you are there, Clarissa." As Clarissa's 'yes' finger moved, Dr. Harmon continued. "Very good, Clarissa. All of the thoughts and feelings of today, of grown-up Clarissa, are written on that board. When you are ready, Clarissa, imagine you pick up a big eraser and wipe away all the thoughts and feelings of today. Just take your time and do it now, Clarissa. When that board is all clean and clear, just step on through it. You step on through to the other side. Move your 'yes' finger when this is so, Clarissa." After a moment, Clarissa's yes finger moved slightly.

"Very good, Clarissa. Now deeper within your subconscious mind and deeper you step back in time. Ten, as you breathe in, your body begins to grow smaller again. Nine, the arms and legs grow shorter and smaller. That's good, that's fine, Clarissa. Eight, deeper and deeper within this comfortable state. Seven, six, and five. Good, Clarissa, you are doing wonderfully. Four, letting go more and more. Now three, and free to be three years old. Three year old, Clarissa, can you hear me speaking?" The 'yes' finger moved. "Very good, Clarissa, tell me where you are. Just speak right up, Clarissa. You can do that. Tell me where you are."

"I feel like I'm a little girl," Clarissa said softly. "But I'm also aware I'm sitting in the chair, listening to you. I don't know if this is working."

"Of course, it is working," Dr. Harmon reassured Clarissa soothingly. "Just tell me, Clarissa, if you be three like you want to be, where would three be now, little girl?" [Note: The improper grammar "you be three" was used to catch the attention of the reasoning mind which allowed, in that brief instant, the little girl to slip in. The rhyme was for the auditory little girl.]

"On my grandpa's lap," Clarissa blurted in a little girl's voice.

"And what is grandpa doing?" Dr. Harmon asked.

"He is talking and rubbing my shoulder funny." Clarissa began to squirm in the chair.

"Is it a funny kind of funny?" Dr. Harmon asked. "Does it make you laugh?"

"No. It's a bad funny," the little girl answered. "I want to get down, grandpa."

"Do you get down, Clarissa?" Dr. Harmon asked gently.

"No, grandpa says to 'stay here a minute.'" Clarissa imitated grandpa's voice. "He never gets to see me, he says, and he likes me in his lap."

"Do you like it in his lap, Clarissa?"

"My name is not Clarissa, it is Clari," the little girl retorted, "Who are you?"

"I'm here to help you get down, if you want to," Dr. Harmon answered smoothly.

"Oh, please, help me get down. I don't want grandpa to rub my arm anymore." The little girl's voice was tearful.

"I can help you, but you have to help me, too, Clari. Can you do that?"

"I'm just a little girl," Clari protested.

"But a very smart and brave little girl. Do you think you can be smart and brave and let me help you get yourself down, so you can go play?"

"I guess so," Clari agreed, after sighing with a three-year old's exasperation.

"Good. What is grandpa talking about as he rubs your arm, Clari? Listen very carefully."

Clarissa cocked her head. Then she said, in her little girl's voice, "He isn't talking now. He is thinking bad thoughts."

"How do you know they are bad, Clari?" Dr. Harmon asked.

"They make my tummy hurt," she answered.

"Is he still rubbing your arm?"

"Yes," Clarissa moved her left arm as though she were trying to jerk it away.

"What is he thinking, Clari? You have to listen to his thoughts now. I know you can do that. You are really a very smart little girl. You have to listen with the part of your mind that knows what grandpa is thinking."

After a few moments, Clari said crossly, "I dunno what he's thinking."

"Well," Dr. Harmon began, but Clari interrupted excitedly.

"Oh, wait. I do know. My mind told me he's rubbing my arm and thinking about sex."

"Do you know what sex is, Clari?" Dr. Harmon asked.

"It's what he is doing with grandma in his mind. My mind says that's sex. He's rubbing my arm and thinking of grandma's soft, soft skin on their wedding night. That's what he's thinking," Clari said decisively. "I want to get down now."

"Okay, Clari, does anything else happen here on grandpa's lap that we need to know about?" Dr. Harmon asked.

"No. But my tummy still hurts," Clari complained.

"Yes, and we're going to fix that right now. Why do you think your tummy is hurting, Clari? Think carefully now, your tummy needs you to help it."

"Well, I think grandpa's thoughts worried me and I worried my tummy," Clari said.

"Do you think when grandpa won't let you go it worried your tummy even more?" Dr. Harmon asked.

"Yes," Clari declared with a toddler's decisiveness. "My tummy thought he was hurting me."

"Was grandpa hurting you, Clari?" Dr. Harmon asked her.

"No. My grandpa was thinking about grandma. He wasn't hurting me." There was a short pause. "Do you think he was hurting grandma?"

"Do you think grandma was hurting, Clari?"

"No. She liked grandpa rubbing her," Clari said. "You know what?"

"What?" Dr. Harmon asked.

"My tummy ache is almost gone. You fixed it."

"No," Dr. Harmon corrected her. "I just helped a little bit. It was your self that fixed it. And I bet if you send lots of love into your tummy right now, it will be all better. Why don't you do that now, Clari?"

"Okay. I did it. My tummy is all better," Clari said triumphantly. "I'm going to get down now."

"Good," agreed Dr. Harmon. "Tell your grandpa you have to get down and go play now."

"What if he won't let me?" Clari asked. "He's bigger than me."

"Yes, he is, Clari. And you can do anything you want with your mind. You can make yourself strong as you want to be. You are so smart; I bet you can figure out right now how to get down from your grandpa's lap. Go ahead and do that, Clari."

"There," Clari said after a moment. "I kissed him on his nose and told him, 'I have to get down right now, grandpa. I will sit on your lap again later.' He laughed and let me get down. I'm very smart. I did that myself," Clari bragged.

"You are very smart, Clari," Dr. Harmon agreed. "You just keep sending yourself lots of love. The grown up you will send you lots of love, too."

"Okay. I'll help her play. She needs to play more."

"Yes, she needs to play more. Good-bye now, Clari, have fun," Dr. Harmon replied. "Now, Clarissa, I am speaking to the wonderful, grown up adult you. Your mind was mistaken about what happened with your grandfather. He was thinking of your grandmother and sex, not you. Can you let go of the idea he molested you now?"

"Oh, yes. I'm so sorry I thought he hurt me," Clarissa said, her voice quivering.

"You were a little girl, Clarissa," Dr. Harmon spoke soothingly. "A little girl named Clari. At three years old, you had so many more fun things to do then sit on grandpa's lap and read his mind. You felt the sexual energy around his thoughts and that energy hurt your tummy. Later, when your mother told you about sex, your little girl mind remembered that energy and connected it with what mother was telling you about sex. Your emotional mind connected your grandpa and his sexual energy with you, because it had felt grandpa's sexual energy before. You understand now how that happened, Clarissa, so you can let go of your old thoughts now about that, can't you, Clarissa?" Clarissa's yes finger rose. "Good, now be there with mother now. Be with mother on the day she is telling you about sex, Clarissa. Indicate when you have located that time and place."

"I'm there," Clarissa said softly. "My poor mother is so embarrassed. I hate to see her so uncomfortable. I feel uncomfortable myself. My tummy is hurting, too. Isn't that interesting!" Clarissa exclaimed. "I forgot that. My tummy started to hurt when I started thinking about my grandfather."

"Now you know why, Clarissa?" Dr. Harmon asked.

"Yes, I know why," Clarissa said, and laughed. "I can hear the three year old in the back of my mind saying, 'send love to your tummy'. So I am."

"Good. Now, help your mother tell you about sex, Clarissa. Let your adult self help your teenager self help mother."

"'I know about sex, mother,' the teenager me says. My mother looks surprised. I tell her, 'It's very beautiful. I know you and father have sex, and I'm glad. It's very good for you to know that father loves you and wants you to feel pleasure.' My mother is blushing, so I say, 'Don't feel embarrassed, mother. Pleasure is wonderful to feel. I want my body to feel pleasure with my husband someday, too. My body can do that.'"

"Yes, Clarissa," Dr. Harmon says, seeking to reinforce her own directives to her subconscious mind, "your body can feel pleasure. Sexual pleasure is very natural and good. You find your body relaxes easily when it is touched lovingly. You think of the ocean waves, Clarissa, and you relax easily and comfortably when your body is lovingly touched. Your body easily feels and reacts to loving touch. You speak to your partner easily and comfortably about exactly the way your body likes to be touched and held. You learn about your body, Clarissa. Slowly and lovingly, you learn the kinds of touches your body likes. It talks to you, Clarissa. It lets you know what feels good. As you feel that feel good feeling, your body reacts just as it was made to do. All of your pleasure centers feel all that wonderful feeling your Creator gave you to feel with loving touch. Yes, your body moves into perfect balance and knowing and you flow with the knowing, Clarissa. You flow with the inner glow of the healing feeling of love. That loving feeling you share with your partner fills you with a warm and pleasant sensation that relaxes all the muscles of your body. Your body relaxes and enjoys. Relaxes and enjoys. Waves of pleasure, as your body relaxes and enjoys." Dr. Harmon repeated the suggestions for relaxing and enjoying the sensations of her body several times.

"Now, Clarissa," Dr. Harmon said, "step back on the other side of the chalkboard again, when you are there, move your 'yes' finger. That's it. On the chalk board are the old thoughts you had about sex. Erase those thoughts now, Clarissa, and move your 'yes' finger when you are done. Good. All the old programming about sex is gone. On the board now, write, "Sex is pleasurable for me every time I want it to be". Write that down now, Clarissa. Under that write, I relax and enjoy." Good. Subconscious mind, the new programming about sex is on the board, do you see it?" The 'yes' finger moved. "Very well. Sex is pleasurable now when Clarissa wants it to be. She relaxes and enjoy. You are a very powerful part of her, subconscious mind." The 'yes' finger moves. "Make this happen for Clarissa, is this understood?" The 'yes' finger moves.

"Good. Now, it is time for Clarissa to return to full conscious focus. You hear my voice clearly, Clarissa. As I count to five, you open your eyes on five, feeling alert. One, breathing out the old and in the new. Two, breathing in vibrant feelings of health and joy. Three, free to be healthy, happy, and in perfect harmony. Good, wiggle the feet now, Clarissa. Four, coming up more and more. Stretching the arms. Good, now clearing the eyes, Clarissa. The whites of the eyes are clear and bright. Good, now five. Eyes open. Good stretch. High energy and vitality."

Dr. Harmon checked Clarissa's eyes to be certain they were not bloodshot. As with sleep, the whites of the eyes become bloodshot in hypnosis because the relaxed capillaries fill with blood. When he was certain she was indeed out of hypnosis, he asked, "Would you care to do some NMR to check on any of the information we found?"

Clarissa looked at him. "You know, I really didn't think it was working because I could hear you and knew I was here, sitting in the chair. But when you said it was working, I just went with it. I heard myself talking the whole time, but it was as though I was listening to some one else. Part of me was thinking I was making it all up, but another part argued why would I make such a thing up?"

"What do you think now?" Dr. Harmon asked.

"Well, I guess I might pretend to be a little girl to please you, but it didn't feel like I was pretending. Nor was it a story I would make up." Clarissa shook her head. "No, I didn't make it up. It felt too real. Will the NMR tell if I made any part of it up?" She asked.

"Yes, what would you like to check, Clarissa?"

"How about this: I pretended to be three years old for Dr. Harmon." Dr. Harmon said 'hold', and pulled the leg. The muscle response was weak, indicating a 'no' answer.

"I didn't think so," Clarissa remarked, thoughtfully. "Now check this, I still believe I was sexually molested by my grandfather." Again, the muscle response was weak, indicating a 'no' response to that statement. "Great, it worked!" Clarissa exclaimed. "You did it!"

"No, you did it," Dr. Harmon corrected her. "I just guided you where you needed to go to do it. Now let's check and see if there are any other thoughts or beliefs that stand in the way of your enjoying sex, Clarissa. NMR indicated there were no further blocks or resistance at the subconscious level to the enjoyment of sexual pleasure.

"The important thing now, Clarissa," Dr. Harmon cautioned her, "is to believe and reinforce the new programming until it becomes automatic. It took you awhile to build the old programming. Give yourself time to imprint the new changes. You might even invest in a tape of waves to help you relax."

"I'll just remember sitting here in the chair, listening to your voice and the waves," Clarissa said. "That ought to do it."

"Whatever works," Dr. Harmon agreed, smiling. "Slow down your breathing as you relax and tell yourself: Relax and enjoy. Relax and enjoy."

"I will," Clarissa promised. "I know this worked. I feel different. Is that odd? To feel different after one session?"

"No, it's exactly right. You'll do just fine, Clarissa," Dr. Harmon assured her.

"I will be back, though, Dr. Harmon," Clarissa said. "I want to know a lot more about myself. Maybe I'll even do some past life regressions."

"What?!" Dr. Harmon feigned shock.

"And channeling my Higher Self," Clarissa said laughing.

"Good," Dr. Harmon said, standing up to shake Clarissa's hand. "And

I have a spoon bending class coming up next week. Do you want to attend?"

"Why?" Clarissa shrugged her shoulders. "I can travel in time and change the past. I can read minds. I can talk to my body and it can talk to me. Bending spoons and walking on fire? Child's play."

Dr. Harmon laughed. "Remember, for twenty to thirty minutes after hypnosis you are very suggestible. So continue to think and speak powerful thoughts."

"I will," Clarissa promised. Smiling broadly, she left, shutting the office door behind her.

Dr. Harmon moved to his desk to finish his notes on Clarissa's session. He was confident they had found the roots of her subconscious resistance to sexual pleasure. It was clear, also, she now held powerful expectations of positive change. He had no doubt her body would respond positively to sexual pleasure now that the blocks to it doing so had been eliminated. Smiling, he closed Clarissa's file. Yes, she would be back, but not for sexual abuse.

Dr. Harmon thought of the thousands of clients he'd worked with who had suffered sexual abuse and their difficult healing journey as they made their way through ages and layers of guilt, shame, denial, hurt, anger, pain, and fear. How grateful he was for the NMR! In the 'old days', before NMR, it would take weeks, even months, to get what could be gained in an hour of NMR. If people only realized, he mused, how much is available to them today. If only they knew how much they know inwardly. If only they could trust themselves to find out!

~ * ~

Dr. Harmon calls NMR the most extraordinary tool developed in modern times for discovering inner truths. It is important to keep in mind that while NMR is infallible, human beings are not. NMR must be precisely and accurately done. It is not a tool for amateurs when seeking important information. NMR is a powerful tool when used by well-trained professionals who use precise wording and keep their own minds and expectations out of the process. NEVER let a person with something to gain, or lose, by your answers use NMR with you. (This eliminates family members, close friends, and business associates.) Surrogate NMR can be used with animals, babies, and those who cannot be tested directly. If you use "muscle testing" or applied kinesiology in your work, please be aware that it is important to know which level of the mind the answers you are getting are coming from and whether they are coming from the mind of your client/patient or the mind of a spirit attachment, which you will read about in Chapter Seven. Also, it is very important to know that the subconscious beliefs are carried out, even if they contradict the desires of the conscious mind or the truths of the body and the Higher Self. For specifics in regards to precise and accurate use of NMR.

How to Do NMR With Your Self & Others

If you are a professional in the health fields and have had training in Applied Kinesiology or Touch For Health, read Chapter Four of <u>Odyssey of The Soul, Book One,</u> very carefully and <u>follow outlined procedure.</u> Wording is so very important. Keeping <u>your mind</u> clear is equally important. Also, the testing reflects what a person is thinking, not saying, so keep the person's mind focused on thinking what they are saying. Through proper wording you can access cell knowledge, subconscious beliefs and programming, the Higher Self, the past, and the future. If polarity keeps shifting, suspect spirit attachments and have the person preface every statement with his or her name; such as: "Jane's body know" or "Sally's subconscious believes" or "Bill's Higher Self knows". DON'T CHECK FOR SPIRIT ATTACHMENTS UNLESS YOU ARE A THERAPIST AND QUALIFIED TO WORK WITH THIS. Also remember, subconscious beliefs over-rule cell knowledge. The subconscious belief must be changed to accept the knowledge of the cells. (This is important in healing, taking medications, vitamins, herbs, etc.)

When YOU are the one being tested, take responsibility for yourself as you may have more knowledge than the one testing you. Teach them what you know. If someone prefers to use another method, at least be certain your polarity is in balance and that you SEE your own muscle response. Pay attention to your wording, use simple statements (not questions), keep your mind focused on what you are saying, and NEVER let a "control freak" test you.

If you are not a trained professional, <u>do not use NMR for anything that is of importance to you or your life (or the lives of others).</u> Improper use of this tool can lead to trouble, trauma, and wrong answers.

On the opposite page are two methods of self muscle testing. Be aware, self muscle testing is not reliable for the "big" questions as the subconscious is eager to provide the answers you want. Do NOT make major life decisions based on self muscle testing.

HOW TO SELF MUSCLE TEST

Every time you use either method tap your thymus as described in Chapter Four, <u>Odyssey Of The Soul, Book One</u>, for proper polarity.

Finger Method: Hold the pads of your thumb and your index finger OR the pads of your thumb and your little finger together to create an oval circle. Place the pads of the index finger and the thumb of the opposite hand together. You will use these two fingers like a pair of "pliers" that 'open' and 'close'. With these two fingers in the 'closed" position, place them in the middle of the oval circle of your opposite hand. Now you will experiment with "opening" the "pliers". Place the "pliers" inside the circle on the opposite hand. As you make a statement, you will open the "pliers" and try to open the circle of your fingers. Your goal is to find the amount of pressure that when you apply it, the circle stays closed when you say 'yes' and opens when you say 'no'. Next, make a statement (not question). If the "pliers" can open the circle, the answer is no. If "pliers" can't open the circle, the answer is yes. Focus your mind on your statements as you say them.

Pendulum Method: Remember, your subconscious mind is moving the pendulum, it is not magic. Use a ring or similar object on the end of a string, thread, or chain of at least 3 inches long. Hold string/thread/chain between pads of thumb and index finger of one hand. Let object at other end dangle. Hold your arm, elbow, hand, and fingers steady. (You can place your elbow on a surface or in the air, but keep arm steady.) Think and say 'yes'. Keep repeating 'yes'. After a few moments, the pendulum will begin to swing due to pulse vibrations coming from your subconscious mind through your fingers. Do not move the pendulum yourself. Note the direction of the swing (clock wise, counter clock wise, back and forth, up and down). This is your 'yes' direction. Now repeat 'no' over and over. Note the swing. This is your 'no' direction. Now find a direction for "I don't know" and "I can't say". Go through this procedure each time you use the pendulum until you are certain the directions of the swing are always the same. Make statements (not questions) and note direction of swing for your answer.

NOTE: Both of these methods can be unreliable. They can provide guidance, but the greater your emotional investment in the answer, the less accurate the response.

Chapter 5

Hide and Seek
The Treasures We Keep

Your subconscious mind speaks to you in many ways. It whispers of the knowing of your spirit in hunches, insights, intuitions, and psychic flashes. It cries, silently or aloud, of the depth of your emotions and it speaks through dreams of the knowledge of your soul. It shouts, through the events and people it draws to you, of your inner thoughts and beliefs. It warns, through illness, injury, and disease of the need for introspection. It calls out your mission in the messages it brings.

Unfortunately, most people are not aware of the importance or the complexity of the subconscious mind, so they fail to pay attention to its many voices. Especially since most people have forgotten that the true language of the mind is Light.

Light is the basis of all that is for all energy is a vibration, or frequency, of Light. The mind transforms those frequencies into thought which creates sound, color, images, form, and the multi-dimensional planes of the material and immaterial realms.

Even as we write this, physicists at the Stanford Linear Accelerator Center have succeeded in converting light into matter. Physicists have often converted matter into light, as in an atomic bomb, but this is the first time they have achieved the opposite. They are beginning to catch up to metaphysicians more and more, as witness this feat and Quantum Physics. Note that one of the basic tenants of Quantum Physics is "The act of observing determines the reality". What, we ask, is "the act of observing", but thought? Thus, as metaphysicians have LONG taught, thought determines reality.

Thought is processed differently at the conscious and subconscious levels of the human brain and mind. Humans developed words as a means of consciously communicating thought even as they continue to communicate thought at the inward levels in symbolic images called thought forms. Words, therefore, are symbolic of thought, which is itself symbolic of the forms, images, sounds, color, and other vibrations of Light.

Imagine the tasks the subconscious mind must perform for the mind to talk with itself, let alone other minds. The subconscious must translate the words of the conscious mind's language into the symbolic images of inner thought forms, even as it is simultaneously translating the inner thought form images into words for the conscious mind. And it must do all of this instantly.

It will help you to grasp the complexity of this, by thinking of the word 'mother'. You have stored in your memory banks many thought form images of the word 'mother'. Each has a different meaning and many are linked with memory and emotions. The subconscious must discern, instantly, which thought form image you want and whether any of the memories and emotions linked with that image are to be suppressed and kept from the conscious awareness. At the same time as it is doing this, the subconscious must translate the chosen thought form image into words for the conscious mind. Imagine how busy the subconscious mind is with a whole string of words. Imagine what is going on in a conversation with another person! Is it any wonder we marvel at the truly extraordinary task master abilities of the subconscious mind?

Thought forms are the natural language of the mind. Thus, symbols and symbolic language are a natural for humans. Our first written languages were symbolic pictures. Much of the history of ancient humans was recorded in symbolic stories. Myths, contrary to modern opinion, were such histories. Many people believe many of the stories in Holy Books are symbolic stories.

The subconscious mind continues to use symbolic communication in its attempts to keep the conscious mind informed of the messages and status of the body, mind, and spirit. It is one of the tragedies of modern humans that we have forgotten this. Our attempts to understand our dreams is a dim recollection of the importance of this communication from our inner levels. Unfortunately, most people have forgotten, at the conscious levels, the symbolic language of the mind and have a heck of a time figuring out what their dreams mean.

Dream books that supply universal meanings of common symbols found in dreams are helpful. Developing your ability to find your own inner meanings of dream symbols is, of course, even better. (One hint: In most dreams, every person, place, or thing in your dream represents an aspect of YOU or YOUR relationship to that person, place, or thing.) An excellent book on universal dream symbols and one on finding your own interpretations of dream symbols are in our book list at the back of this book. An even better method is interpreting your dreams in a hypnotic state. Since dream messages are from your inner levels of mind and spirit, the best interpreters of these messages are your inner mind and spirit.

Joel came to us with the following dream: "I was driving along a country road. I had to turn right to take the road that led to my house, but my car wouldn't turn. Seemingly of its own accord, it headed toward the freeway. On the freeway, I kept struggling to get back control of the car and finally managed to make a U Turn on the freeway, right in front of a sign that said 'NO U Turn'. Something else happens next, which I don't remember."

Joel consciously analyzed the dream as relating to a decision he had made to forgo going "on the road" giving seminars as he'd planned. The "right turn" would be to keep his regular position which afforded him the security of a steady income. Though he was certain the dream was telling him he'd made the right decision, he'd felt irritable ever since having the dream. He wanted to know if there was more to the dream than he'd already figured out.

In hypnosis, Joel's inner mind said: "The message is a warning that his greater purpose is to go forward. To turn from his purpose into the familiar, tried, and true is NOT the right way. The meaning of the freeway is he came to teach many. This is his greater purpose. Matters are out of his control now; his Higher Self moves him onto his path of purpose. This is the meaning of the car moving forward out of his control. He resists this. He tries to wrest control of his life back by willfully turning from his purpose. The sign [No U Turn] warns him that turning back from his greater purpose is not allowed; it is the wrong direction. The part of the dream he has forgotten is when he turns back he gets lost in the maze of unknown territory. He has great difficulty finding his way. Forgetting this part of the dream underscores or doubles the meaning of this part of the dream; which is, to forget his greater purpose is to lose all meaning in his life. He will find great loss. The message of the dream is very clear: Stay on your path of greater purpose."

Joel was astonished at this interpretation of his dream. NMR verified this was the correct interpretation. Reviewing that interpretation, Joel remarked, "It's true. I've been very anxious and tense ever since I made my decision to return to my regular position, though it is certainly more comfortable and secure. Still, I DO believe I have something important to offer to more people than I can reach where I am. I was afraid that was just ego. But it is what I want to do and I've always believed what one truly, deeply desires IS the right thing to do. I guess instead of letting my fears about ego stop me, I'd do better to use my ego to help me move forward."

The ego, contrary to many "teachings", is an important part of the soul. Without ego, the variety and uniqueness of personalities and their experiences would be sadly lacking on the earth planes. To seek to lose the personality on the planes of lower spirit misses the point. Exploring and enjoying the many paths along the journey leads, we think, to greater understanding of all of Creation.

Andrea brought her dream in to be interpreted: "I am climbing a hill with my husband and his brother. Suddenly we notice water is rising around the hill. We realize the water will soon submerge us. I head for the front of the hill, but my husband and his brother go down the back of the hill. As the water rises to where I am, I notice there is a stepping stone just under the surface of the water. I step on it and it holds me up. There is another stepping stone just to the right of me. I hesitate to step on it, because I realize it leads to the deeper waters on my right, where I can't see any stones. If I go left, where the water is still shallow, I can just make it to dry land. I stand there, trying to decide what to do when I wake up."

NMR indicated the dream was from the Higher Self and so, in hypnosis, the Higher Self interpreted the dream as follows: "This dream is prophetic and she has forgotten on her conscious level parts of the dream, which I shall supply. She, her mate, and his brother climb the hill to have a picnic. This signals that her mate's brother will be joining them in their circle of love. The picnic shows this joining will be around food and that it brings a sense of family and fun each lack in their daily attention to duty. The hill symbolizes the upward climb each face in the next phase of their lives. The hill grows larger, even as they climb it; a warning that the challenges will be greater than foreseen. The rising flood waters amplify this message; the challenge is great and threatens to engulf each of them. The brother of the mate will want to retreat from this challenge. He will seek to take his brother into his retreat with him, whether she follows or not. Her mate has great loyalty to the brother. That this is honorable is symbolized by the American Flag at the top of the front of the hill. Loyalty to his brother is part of the traditional values in which both brothers were raised. However, the Flag has a second meaning. It reminds both brothers that retreat from the battle is not part of the traditions each have admired, honored, and lived in many lives. To their shame, the woman moves to the front of the battle alone. She sorely misses her mate, but she will not turn back from the challenge. She thinks she is alone and all is lost. The stepping stone assures her all is not lost, she is not alone. She is being guided and protected. The inability to see the stepping stones until she reaches them is a message to have trust and faith in the spiritual forces that guide and protect her. She has already taken the first step. But she hesitates, for she sees that the next step takes her into the deeper waters and not to the safety of land. This is where we want her to go. She must have faith and trust we, symbolized by the steps, will be there, even in the deepest and darkest of waters. She is to face the challenge and trust her guidance. This is the way. Follow it."

People in therapy often find they have many dreams during the course of their therapy. The dreams can be disturbing, for therapy does trigger the bringing up of experiences and feelings one has long suppressed. Even dreams long forgotten or ignored are frequently "revisited" during the course of therapy. The following is a dream Mary brought into therapy. It was a dream she'd had shortly after her now 15 year old daughter had been born. It had been so disturbing, she'd never forgotten it and she wanted to know the meaning of it.

"I am going to the parking lot where everyone in town is to gather in emergencies. Most of the people in the town have been destroyed by gases. Only some of us are left. We go underground, to shelters built under the parking lot. We know it is only a matter of time before the gases get us, too. I am holding my six month old baby in my arms. I don't want her to die such a horrible death so I give her a pill and hold her close while I watch her die. Then, when she is dead, I take a pill to kill me."

In hypnosis, Mary's Higher Self was asked to give the meaning of her dream. It responded: "Mary was hidden in darkness and she needed to see the Light,"

"Oh, I see," Mary exclaimed, in hypnosis, She [her daughter] helped me to do that. She was telling me to stop taking the drugs because they would kill both of us. That's why she keeps telling me to quit drinking now!"

Mary had been into drugs at that time in her life, but had, shortly after this dream, cleaned herself up at the Betty Ford center. She'd stopped drinking, as well, but had started drinking again later as she felt her drinking had never been as much of a problem as the drugs. Mary's Higher Self and her daughter believe otherwise. Mary has developed, over many years of using alcohol to numb both emotional and physical pain, a sensitivity to alcohol that does not serve her well. It also helps her to avoid facing and dealing with the issues creating her pain. This avoidance does not help her or her daughters;. Children rarely listen to what they are taught by adults; they pay much closer attention to what the adults around them DO. Mary knows this and she is now working hard on "rooting out" the pain of her childhood; pain she sought to mask and repress with alcohol, drugs, and "feel good" food.

Many people who are abused in childhood develop strong sensitivities which enhances psychic abilities, although, often, the desire to suppress their memories of the abuse also suppresses these abilities. (Psychic means of the psyche, or soul, and such abilities are natural to the human experience.) Mary is a perfect example of this. A "born psychic", Mary's childhood abuse helped to hone her abilities. However, Mary's subconscious mind knew that to open the door to her psychic abilities was to open the door to the very emotions and memories she had told it, by her words and actions, to suppress. (As with children, our subconscious minds pay more attention to what we do than what we say.) Almost all of the emotions and memories involved anger, and Mary was a great one for suppressing and denying anger.

Mary was greatly surprised that suppressed anger was the root of her depression. Like most people, Mary thought that depression is sadness. While sadness - as well as shame, guilt, and other emotions - can be part of depression, the root of depression is always anger. (And the root of anger is always hurt.) The following dream is a dream Mary had that symbolized both her inner anger and her suppression and denial of it:

"I was boarding up the path in the house I grew up in. I was boarding it up with boards from the back of the house to the front. There is a dog somewhere in the back, but I never see him. Suddenly, I notice a black widow spider on my hand. It is dead and I brush it off. There is an ink outline of the spider on my hand where I brushed it off. A wart starts to grow there."

Mary asked Pamela, her therapist, to interpret her dream. While the meaning of the dream was clear to Pamela, she encouraged Mary, after a brief discussion of the dream, to interpret the dream herself. The challenge for all therapists is to NOT let their own knowledge either direct or get in the way of the client or the therapy. It is IMPOSSIBLE to know or understand as much about clients as they know and understand themselves at inner levels of their minds and spirits.

In addition, the Higher Self of the client can best determine how quickly or slowly that client is prepared to deal with inner trauma. Pushing past the comfort and safety levels of a client's internal defenses is not therapeutic, it is abusive. It separates the client from his or her well being as surely as the word "therapist" separates into "the rapist"; which is, in our view, what a "pushy" therapist is.

Pamela asked Mary what she thought her dream meant. Mary said she didn't know. NMR indicated that Mary did not know consciously, but the subconscious and the Higher Self did know. Mary mentioned, just as Pamela began to guide her into hypnosis, that she didn't think the dog was an important part of the dream. "I never really saw it," she said, "it was just there."

In hypnosis, Mary was asked to give the meaning of her dream. This is her response: "The dog is a wolf. The wolf is her anger. She is seeking to stop the power of the wolf by keeping it in. She is boarding up anger, afraid to let it up. The wolf has a very big head that is growing. The anger is growing. The spider is the abuse that's died, it is [the effects] going away now. The past will always be there, as shown by the ink outline on the hand, but it is just the impressions that remain now from the abuse, as signified by the wart. She can make the wart go away. So, too, will the impressions of the abuse go away, after she lets out the wolf and faces the anger."

In dreams, our inner guidance lets us know what our thoughts, beliefs, emotions, and choices have created and are creating. We receive counsel, warnings, guidance, and messages of many kinds. Once we realize the truly astounding extent of our inner wisdom, we can begin to grasp the fact that our "real lives" are as full of signs, omens, symbols, messages, and meanings as our dreams. As one client's Spirit Guides put it: "She is afraid we are not real. She is afraid she is making us up and this is all a dream. We say life is but a dream so what, pray tell, is the difference?"

Katie Ann is a client who lost her diamond tennis bracelet. She also had, the night of the day she lost her bracelet, a dream about going to her garage and finding her car missing. When she finally located her car, the front end had been replaced by silly putty. In hypnosis, Katie Ann was asked to move to the level of mind that would best tell her the meaning of both her dream and the loss of her diamond bracelet. The following is from Katie Ann's Higher Self

"She has fear of standing out and being different. She struggles between being who she is and who she pretends to be. This is the meaning of the dream of the car and the message in the losing of her bracelet. They symbolize the stripping away of her focus on the material world, which is not where she is headed now. She gets bits and pieces and glimpses of her true path, yet falls back into the old ways. This struggle between pretending to be what she is not and her true self brings stress. She needs to learn it does not matter what the outward appearance is. The inside beauty is greater than any outside beauty anyone can attain. If only you humans understood how important it is to heal on the inside, not adorn the outside, then we would have great greatness on the earth. She will trust one day and move forward and awake as though from a dream and ask herself how it was so easy to have moved on."

Higher Selves, Spirit Guides, Angels, Astral Beings, Higher Spirit - all bring messages for the subconscious mind to either translate into words or present in symbolic form (or both) to the conscious level of mind.

We, Dr. Harmon and Pamela, were thinking of giving a BIG seminar.

We'd tired of what Dr. Harmon calls the "circuit riders"; people claiming to be healers, prophets, metaphysicians, motivators, and hypnotists who give seminars for the sole purpose of "panning gold". While many are sincere in their desire to help as well as make money, and most offer, in part, valuable information, few are truthful or knowledgeable in their entirety. Mike Todd was right, "Americans are suckers for a good cause" especially if that good cause is a "quick fix".

We wanted "big" money as much as any "circuit rider" or the conglomerates behind them. We felt our cause was worthy. We would make the money to publish and promote our book, which would tell people what they really needed to know in order to empower themselves. At the seminars, we could first offer the "quick fix". After all, we are as masterful at hypnosis and motivation as anyone, even if we do tell the truth. Next, we'd tell them why the "quick fix" would work for some of them and why it might not work, or last, for others. They wouldn't like that part, of course, but we felt that truth, alone, would be worth the price of admission. We planned to charge a small amount, maybe $25, as we were planning a BIG seminar with LOTS of people.

As we begin to plot our promotional investment in this "big" seminar, the tires and wheels on our new car parked in our driveway in "safe" Rancho Mirage, California were stolen. Pamela insisted we find out from Master of Spirit why the tires were stolen as we know nothing ever happens by accident. EVERYTHING has a message and a meaning. Master of Spirit, when asked about the theft of the tires and wheels, responded:

"Unknown persons used by your mind to bring to you an important message. The message is that if even one thing goes wrong a powerful vehicle can be stopped from going forward. You have powerful teachings to share. The manner being considered in which to teach them will only be successful if everything goes perfectly. You do not have the resources, at this time, to take this risk. You need to gain money, not lose money. This plan is too risky. It is better to plan smaller meetings you can afford. Build your finances in a smaller, safer way. This is the message of the tires being stolen. Your finances, which must take you forward, are vulnerable."

We heeded the message, practicing what we wanted to share with the greater public through small, intimate, weekly group meetings. It's good we did, for we saw how unpopular, even unbelievable, our message is.

Despite the fact we are very successful at what we do, many people refuse to believe what we do works, or if it works, that it can work for them. They especially don't want to have to deal with any "inner stuff".

A person came to see us from the meetings. She asked for a consultation with us together, as she wasn't sure which of us she wanted to see. While she'd come in for an emotional problem, she mentioned she had an incurable condition, adding, "I'd give anything to be free of this curse."

Thinking that hearing from someone who had already healed the same "incurable" condition would encourage her, Dr. Harmon slipped away to call a former client and asked her if she'd be willing to come in and share her healing experience with this woman. She graciously agreed, even bringing in her medical records as proof of her success.

Our prospective client listened to this woman politely. Then she examined the medical records. When she was done, she lifted the records from her lap, handed them back to the woman, smiled thinly, and said, "I'm sure you all mean well, but I don't believe a word of it. This condition is incurable. Everyone says so." She got up out of the office chair and left without another word.

We were in shock. Dr. Harmon's former client calmly remarked, "That's why I don't tell anyone about this anymore. They never believe me. Even my doctor thinks we must have made a mistake in the original diagnosis, despite all the blood work that proves we didn't. He said maybe the lab made mistakes." She shook her head. "I'll write a testimonial for you guys, but I doubt anyone will believe it. Just don't ask me to talk about it any more. I'm never talking about it again. I'll start to doubt myself and there's no way I'm taking a chance on reversing my healing. Besides, I'm tired of being thought of as a fool or a liar."

We're not even going to tell you the condition this woman had. If we don't, you might be inspired to seek healing for an "incurable" condition you or someone you love has. If we were to tell you the name of the condition, you would be likely to think, 'Oh, maybe that condition is curable, but I know this one isn't.' (Besides, if even a person's own doctor won't believe his or her own medical tests, what good does sharing such stories do anyway, except to inspire?)

We prefer you realize ALL conditions are curable if the Higher Self says it is. Sometimes, the Higher Self says one must live, or die, with a particular condition or limitation in order to grow or to provide an opportunity for others to grow through it.

Healing and transformation, even when the Higher Self says they can be accomplished, often take hard work at the inner levels and change in the outer aspects of ones life. People don't want to hear that. They want to believe they can accomplish anything without having to deal with their "emotional stuff" and without having to "look within". We wish that were true. It would make it easier for us, too.

Looking within is often exciting, frequently awe inspiring, sometimes painful, but always enlightening; even when long cherished beliefs of the conscious mind are rejected by the inner mind in favor of startlingly unfamiliar notions. Like you, our clients are often confused by the vast array of seemingly contradictory information "out there" on what is "good" for them. Everyone seeks happiness, fulfillment, and well-being, yet many people are uncertain as to their best choices for gaining them.

No-one knows you and what works for you better than you. No medical researcher or practitioner, nutritional expert or physical fitness guru, can possibly know what would best heal or transform your individual body and cells than your body and cells. No therapist, motivational expert, or counselor can possibly know what will unblock or galvanize you better than your own subconscious mind. No spiritual leader can possibly know your unique spirit and its purpose better than your own Higher Self. No psychic, seer, channel, or prophet has greater access to your inner levels of knowing than you do

We share in these pages some of the information some of our clients have found within their inner levels of knowing. While we could fill all three books of this trilogy with the astounding and astonishing information our clients have brought forward in trance states, we won't do so. We want to present just enough to inspire YOU to seek your own inner truths.

It is worth noting not all clients follow their inner wisdom; far from it. Many do not. On the other hand, many do. **We note that the degree of success in healing, transformation, or positive achievement is directly proportional to the degree of subconscious belief and conscious action.** Helping people change their subconscious beliefs is fairly easy with hypnosis and regression therapy. What people choose to do or believe consciously about that change affects everything. It can even reverse what has been accomplished.

Many people have great difficulty believing that "simply talking" can heal or transform their bodies, minds, emotions, behaviors, and reality. Yet, if thought creates reality, then changing thought changes reality. The Yellow Emperor in 100 B.C. wrote, "The one who heals the mind by talking is the superior doctor, and by talking only, the superior doctor can heal all the diseases of the body, mind, and spirit."

YOU are the superior doctor for YOU and by talking with all levels of YOUR mind, body, and spirit, YOU can accomplish anything

Following, we share information brought forward in trance states by clients. Our words are in (parenthesis) and instead of using the names Dr. Harmon or Pamela, we use "therapist". All names used are, of course, fictitious.

Sue, Age 40's

Sue was having great difficulty losing weight, despite a regimen of weight lifting, step aerobics, stretching, walking, and a low fat vegetarian diet. Her subconscious was asked, in hypnosis, why she was not losing the weight. It responded:

"The cells of this body are very sad because she said she would rather not be on earth than be in a body like this. She wants to leave this shell. She thinks it is a shell. She doesn't want to be here. She thinks the body just houses the spirit. There are many reasons for the sizes and shapes of bodies, it depends on who is in the body. Thought builds this body. The body is thought. There is an unwillingness of the person in this body to do what it takes to create a good ratio balance between fat to muscle." (Therapist: "What would it take?") "More exercise. She must pay attention to the body. Address the body as she does the inner child. Give the cells of the body love to heal. Cells have consciousness as well as emotions. Not too many know this. There is no compatibility between the body and the self. There needs to be emotional work and love addressed to the body. She works at it with a hopelessness, therefore the cells feel the hopelessness. It is difficult, when housed in hopelessness, to change or to move forward." (Therapist: "How are her thoughts about aging affecting her cells?") "What is thought, is." [Therapist: "Is her nutrition adequate and is weight lifting good for her body?") "Nutrition basically yes, recently no. Weight lifting, to build muscle - no. To build bone - yes. To lose fat - no. This body needs more pure juices." (Therapist: "Is there too much fat in the body?") "In some places. This body would be better if she learned to listen more to the body and not depend on external tools. Books, instructors are good, but all say different things. She must exercise in the water for the back and the knees. [Note: This person has a back weakened by back surgeries.] Low impact exercise. More stretching. No step exercises. She does not need intense aerobic exercise for it will harm this body. She can work for longer duration at low impact and achieve the same result. No more step aerobics for this body. Imaging body utilizing fat around the knees is good. Imaging while stretching is very good. Image fat is moving, being excreted. This body needs oxygen. It is powerful to picture the fat moving as the body stretching to break it away as the stretching is going on. The one in this body needs to know what the body knows. Water is very important. Green juices important. The fat listens to her. If she would be nicer to the fat, it would be nicer to her. What you need to know about her is she does not believe because she does not see it happening. It is happening."

~ * ~

Over the course of Sue's therapy, she'd accomplished several important goals, including healing of her back pain and her blocks to financial gain. She did not slim down. She left therapy after the above session, discouraged about her weight, despite the fact both NMR and her Higher Self said she'd worked through all internal blocks to letting go of the weight and all she needed now was a change of conscious attitude and her weight would decrease.

A short time after this, Sue attended a meditation seminar that changed her conscious attitude about letting go of her excess weight. She also was given a good guided imagery technique by the spirit guides of another person. Despite the fact she'd tried meditation and guided imagery for losing weight before, with no success, she was convinced these "new" slants on both techniques would work. And work they did.

We have watched Sue's experience occur with many clients. Techniques and methods used unsuccessfully before working through inner blocks and resistance to the goal suddenly "work like magic" after implementing a "new" way of using the old techniques and methods. Sometimes clients realize what has happened and they are aware of the importance of having done their inner work. Sometimes clients don't realize what has happened and they feel their inner work had nothing to do with achieving their goals. We smile when clients, students, and colleagues call to say they have discovered, uncovered, stumbled on, or become aware of a "new" method, tool, or technique that has worked for them and they are certain will work for everyone. We LOVE their enthusiasm and encourage them to share everything they discover with us. We smile because we invariably have people in our practice that have come to see us because they have tried the very same "new" techniques, methods, and tools without success.

In our experience, permanent healing and transformation happen when: 1) The conscious mind actively desires the goal and accepts it is possible. 2) The subconscious believes it is possible and believes the conscious mind truly desires it. 3) There are no inner blocks or resistance to the achievement of the goal.

We did not realize cells had a consciousness of their own until this session with Sue. Naturally, we immediately began conversing with cells. Following is a random sample of messages received from the cells of various clients.

• "The cells of this body and the being in this body are not in synch. She must learn to love the body. She thinks the spirit is everything and the body is just a machine. She would not be as mean to a machine as she is to this body."

• "We need iron. We are starved for iron. The being in this body takes in sufficient iron but she has beliefs about iron that stop us from absorbing it. Please change the beliefs about iron. We need iron."

• "We speak for the blood and the immune system. Iron is needed and B-12. The immune system is taxed. We call out for blood to be nourished. We move through the system with the blood. We need enrichment, nourishment, and oxygen. Body needs to be stretched and exercised and fed greater variety of nutrients."

• "We are the cells of the neck. We make the neck sore. We are screaming. We scream listen to us! Eat healthy food! She is eating too much sugar. It stresses us. She is not trusting herself. She is learning to listen more to her intuition and Higher Self, but she doesn't act on what they say. We tell her she has certain thoughts and we tell her to turn and look at that thought, to examine that thought. Do not doubt this path you have chosen. Stop eating sugar. It makes us frazzle. She eats to fill a hole in the body, but it is not the body that is starving. It is the emotions.

When she turns her neck and it is sore it is we, the cells of her neck, speaking to her."

• "We the cells accept freely this healing light. The consciousness of the body accepts, but not fully, the healing energy, so this stops the body from processing it." (Note: This client was working on healing cervix tissue her doctor believed to be cancerous. NMR indicated abnormal, not cancerous cells. A second medical opinion verified this. Healing light was sent mentally to the abnormal cells by this client, and her therapist prior to this session.) "It is greatly appreciated that no cell needs to exit or be removed, but may transform and become part of the light experience. There is a function in our purpose, including those transmuted to that which is not acceptable. But all serve a purpose to teach, to alert, to remind those energies who would not believe a consciousness such as we are exists. Yet we possess a greater understanding of simplicity of balance than those who would see themselves as enlightened. The cells sense the purpose, that which is being sought. For this, we ask for cooperation from the being in the body for the transmuting of these cells. Even now, we hear the voice of the one in the body crying out in rejection to the idea that these cells [abnormal cervix cells] might be expressing through the choice of the being in the body, that the will of the being expresses through all consciousness levels. We remind that these cells are in synergistic existence and we are cooperating with the beliefs of the mind that inhabits this body. We appreciate the concept of cooperation. We are perfectly capable of receiving other messages from other levels of consciousness." [Note: Her Higher Self and Spirit Guides recommended further inner work and advised against a considered hysterectomy as there was no cancer present and a hysterectomy would be traumatic to her body and inner children. Despite this, she had the hysterectomy. All tissue and removed organs were found to be cancer free.]

• "The sore toe is because the cells of the toe are on fire." (Therapist: What is the fire?") " Anger. I'm [toe] connected to the source. To the head. Stop the aerobics. It makes me mad. She puts me down. Her thoughts hurt me. She thinks her body is not good enough. It crushes me sometimes. These heavy thoughts. Sad thoughts." [Note: This client would exercise to an aerobic tape, all the while negatively comparing

her body to the bodies on the tape. This inflamed the big toe. Why
the big toe chose to be the one to talk to her about this is anybody's
guess, but after this session, her toe would respond with pain every time
her thoughts became self-defeating. When she changed her negative
thoughts, her pain would disappear.]

• "Body wants to be healthy, but it responds to emotions. This one who
lives within the body worries about the state of the body and this worries
the cells of the body. This body responds well to good care. It is a
good vessel, it responds well. It responds well to worry as well. This
one worries about the back. Love is part of the back. Work on the
emotions and tend to part of the being's life that needs to be attended
to. This body wishes to be well. Vitamins will work if the belief is
that vitamins work. If not the belief, then it is futile. This mind doubts
vitamins except for C. Do not starve us. Do not starve the body of
nutrients. Iron is greatly needed and enriching of the blood. Upper body
on the left side and the heart and the heels of the feet require attention."

• "The cells of these thumbs must be reassured. We must trust this will never
happen again. The being in the body must reassure us before we will
heal. We do not want to be hurt again." [(Note: Thumbs were injured
during torture in a past life. Healing the emotional mind of the torture
required four sessions. The thumbs, which had been extremely painful
and non-mobile improved after each session and became completely
mobile after the final session.]

• "We have not healed because he said we must heal in six weeks. It will
take us longer than six weeks so we have not started healing because we
cannot heal in the way he says we must." [Note: After giving the cells
"permission" to take as long as they needed, the client, who had had hip
surgery, was off his crutches in ten weeks])

• "There is scar tissue causing the hardened vein on the left hand. We can
reconstruct the cells in that section of the veins if you want us to. It
will take 14 to 18 weeks." [Note: The cells were asked to do this. Client's
hardened vein on the left hand softened in 15 weeks.]

• "We are the vocal chords. We want her to sing. She doesn't listen. So
we speak through the cough." (Therapist: "Higher Self, what blocks
the singing?") "Fear. All she has to do is move forward and do exactly
what she wants to do. She wants to sing. She came to sing. Help her

face her fears." [Note: This client is still working on her fears. We have had several artists in various fields with chronic physical conditions such as coughing, sneezing, headaches, colds, skin rashes, even stuttering, that are mysteriously absent on days the person is actively busy in their chosen field of artistic expression.]

- "We know there are things missing and things needed to be added to our energy level." (Therapist: What things are missing and needed by the snovial fluid?") "We don't know. We don't know." [Note: The subconscious was asked what was needed and it gave a detailed outline of memories needing healing and proteins needed by the body.]

~ * ~

The subconscious mind is extremely complex. There is a part of the subconscious that is in charge of the body and this part seems to know even more than particular cells what is needed by the whole body or person to create the change sought. The Higher Self seems to know even more than the subconscious. Following are some excerpts of conversations with cells, subconscious, and Higher Self in regards to the body.

- (Therapist: Why are the knees swollen and sore?) "We're [cells of the knee] trapped inside. Too much of us inside. We bunch up. Safer to bunch up here. Afraid of going down the legs. We would get hurt. Some of us decided to stay and make a traffic jam. We're stuck now. Can't move." (Therapist: "Subconscious how can the cells in the swollen knee be 'unstuck'?) "Channels have to be opened up. Massage. Lots of it. Cells must move down. It is okay to move down, they are supposed to. Leg will feel funny feeling, but it is okay. The cells fear failure. Use hot stuff [like warm oil etc.] to massage knees with hands." (Therapist: Anything more she can do?) " Just do it. Also pray to the great Universal Mind. To the Creator of All and Everything There Is.")

- (Therapist: "Go to the cause of the dysplasia, the abnormal cells in the cervix.") "I see the cells. They have holes or dents. They need repair. They're sensitive to attack. My bad feelings and my anger hurt them. They're crying. I tell them it is all right. The anger won't attack them any more. They need to be soothed with nice feelings."

- (Therapist: "Subconscious, what is the cause of the constant twitching in the left leg?") "Feeling need for minerals. Phosphate, Calcium,

Magnesium, Potassium. More of the substance of C. Part of back pain.
Cells are out of balance." (Therapist: "Lack of these minerals are part
of back pain?") "Yes." (Therapist: "When supplements of these minerals
are taken, are they absorbed sufficiently for your use?") "Not
sufficiently." (Therapist: "What blocks absorption?") "Enzymes and
digestive process." (Therapist: "Is there a need for more enzymes?")
"Yes." (Therapist: "Any particular enzymes?") "All. More than they
know of. Fresh vegetables good source. They move through the body
well, but he doesn't absorb well." [Note: Leg twitching ended after client
increased his intake of suggested substances. Back pain also eased, but
client continues to work on emotional issues that affect the back. Feelings
of lack of emotional or financial support, and feeling heavily burdened
in any area are frequent messages being given by back pain.]

• (Therapist: "Subconscious, the left incisor tooth, there is discomfort
there.") "Yes. This is an inflammation and flaring of some septic
conditions at the tip, and the root of the tooth that remains." (Therapist:
"Can you bring this root, tooth, and gum back into balance?") "Yes
We're working on that now." (Therapist: "Good, are there substances
that would promote the continued well being of this tooth?") "Yes. The
natural resources for the body to use." (Therapist: "Any actions to be
taken that would help with continued well being of tooth?") "Yes.
Increase the healing through the immune system and the energies to the
sites of irritation." (Therapist: "Would massage help?") "No. Massage
would help stimulate the blood flow, but not the healing process at this
time" [Note: This client was working with his dentist, but scheduled
dental surgery was canceled as the condition in the tooth healed
immediately following this session.]

• (Therapist: "Higher Self, can thought stop assimilation of vitamins or
minerals in this body?") "Yes. Thought can change anything. You know
that. Thought creates. Thought limits. Thought destroys. Thought
is the creative substance of subjective material things. Such as the cells
in the human being, created by billions of cells, are responsive and reactive
to programs past and present, which thoughts are a part thereof. Thought
may kill the body instantly. Thought has killed the body instantly."
(Therapist: "What happens to the consciousness of the body when the
body dies?") "The memory banks of the last body move into the memory

banks of Spirit and its collective awareness is recorded for its next use, wherever that may be."

• (Therapist: "What is the cause of the migraine headaches?") "Those programs that affect her head in a painful way are hold-overs, they are carry overs from earlier programs that served her as an escape mechanism from trauma. She may be programmed, IF she would accept that program, to correct this dysfunction in the blood flows of her brain. Her resistance to doing so is due to emotions that she is still manifesting. There are emotional causes unaddressed this life, the childhood, other lives."

• (Therapist: "Is the information found through the NMR correct in regards to vitamins, minerals, and herbs this body needs?") "The ingestion of beta carotene is thought to be beneficial and nourishing, yet there remains also a belief that great quantities create imbalance and yellow skin. It is requested by this body that this one who occupies this body change the belief or ingest a small quantity of beta carotene daily. As this body does recognize the value in greater quantities of beta carotene, this body asks that the belief be altered to become more in sync with beliefs that are known to be true by the cells in relation to nourishment. As well it is recommended this one return to drinking room temperature beverages. It should be understood that the body be given foods in proper combination, as it is the belief of this being that proper combinations are needed for the assimilation of vitamins and digestion of enzymes and breaking down of nourishment. The body reacts to the one who occupies it and that one's beliefs. Therefore, a program that reflects the beliefs should be followed. [Note: Or change the belief.] The body enjoys being cared for in whatever manner is conducive to feeling good. Feeling good is communicated through the cells and tissues. The body accepts this communication through the Light source. The Light source is the foundation of our programming, our existence as we understand it."

~ * ~

While it is important to follow ones beliefs, we strongly recommend that when it comes to ones body, one change the conscious and the subconscious beliefs to that which the cells of the body know to be their truth. For what causes dysfunction of the cells (disease and illness) is when one denies the cells their truth.

We thought it amazing enough to discover cells of the body have consciousness and could speak. We were even more amazed to discover viruses, bacteria, and germs had consciousness and could speak:

- •(Therapist: "Germs, why are you making an infection in this body?"] "To tell something is wrong. She doesn't listen." (Therapist: "What will happen to you when she takes the pill the doctor gave her?") "I have to die. I go where I am needed. I don't want to make people sick. I have to tell them what is wrong. I go to the Light when I die and they [Light] send me back to where I am needed."

- •(Therapist: "She is feeling she may be getting ill with a cold. What can you tell us about this?") "This body needs to know it houses a mind that believes its surroundings are hazardous. This body needs to know it is safe in its environs. This body needs reassurance from the being it houses that it [body] is in harmony with rather than defending self from beliefs [of the being]. This body cries out in the upper back and heart as a result of emotional trauma. It needs reassurance and being cared for by the one [being] it houses. We move through the body and see spots and areas of deficiency. Immune system weakens because of external affairs not being attended to and desire for that one within the body to use illness as a method of hiding. The mind sees the environment as harmful. Before entering the place of business, nourish the body. Speak to it with love and kindness. We listen and respond in every part of being. We are connected with the inhabitant and yet we are a miracle of creation with our own consciousness and awareness. This is the part that speaks now." (Therapist: "What of the cold seeking to invade?") "This is difficult to explain, but it is only illusions being created. Someone speaks with us now about this. These [cold bugs] are moving in too small a space to see. These tiny beings are opportunists. They look always for a channel to share space. An opportunity is being offered by the consciousness of this one inhabiting this body. One, in part because of the need to hide. One, in part, because of a feeling of being out of control and overwhelmed. One, in part, a belief that the confined space in which she works with its smells, paints, computer energy, opens her to these organisms. And so these tiny organisms believe it is fine to dine within and to eat and to share. It is their function."

- •(Therapist: "You will find, virus, that you can speak easily. Your thoughts activate the voice box and it speaks for you. How, virus, did you get into this body?) "Came in through the body opening. The mouth. We found we could multiply, and so we did. We multiply to bring a message. We make the person weak and sick. That's what we do best." (Therapist: "Who sent you?") "Some higher intelligence. We stay as long as we can stay active and then we go into hibernation, when they [people] get too strong for us. We usually make them sick for awhile and then if the body keeps going and they build up their immune system, we go into hibernation." (Therapist: "Do you ever go back to the higher intelligence that sent you?") "Yes. We can move. We can be active or inactive. We don't have a great amount of direction, we just do what we're supposed to do. We make people know we're here." (Therapist: "And when Higher Intelligence says you have done your job very well, come back to me, I have somewhere else to send you, that's part of your job too?") "Yes, we do that too." (Therapist: "Do you mind if I ask Higher Intelligence why it has sent you here?") "I have no feelings. I'm just here." ("I see. Do you feel like taking a little bit of a rest from your job while I speak with Higher Intelligence?") "I never rest. Until I'm deactivated." (Therapist: "I see. I ask for the Higher Self, or that Higher Intelligence that sent this.") "Yes. I am not this person's Higher Self, but part of Higher Intelligence. I'm called by many people to do many things. I direct the virus." (Therapist: "You sent the virus?") "No. I was given direction to do that To make this person weak and struggle." (Therapist: "Do you know the good this will bring?") "No. I know what we do best. I direct the virus. Once it is here, it does different things." (Therapist: "And when the message has been received, or when higher intelligence asks you to retrieve the virus, is that part of your job, too?") "Yes. We can activate or de-activate, or move out and on to another place. This body has its own director." (Therapist: "And that is?") "A part of another spiritual energy. You call that Higher Self." (Therapist: "Good. Higher Self, you know what we seek.") "You seek reason for the virus in the body active. Doing mischief with the body. Hmmmmm, challenging the body to tune itself up to highest level of energy needed for the work to be done. Body was abused. Need the tuning of the body now to its highest level of energy. Only by challenging the body do we get his response. This request was ignored when given before by the Higher Self and the cells. Positive actions needed to make the body strong and powerful and match the mind to the body and the body to the mind and the will to do that which is to be done with the greatest energy and vitality of both the mind and the body. Denial of who he is, not what he is, causes confusion. Part of him struggles with the knowledge that is evident to him, for his ego does not want to accept the identification [sic], so he lets go of much power and information he could use, because he doesn't want to embrace the total energy and direction and purpose of who and what he is. So the struggle remains of identification [sic] and acceptance of indentification. Were the subconscious to totally embrace and accept this, he would have no alternative but to follow. Subconscious mind is your greatest ally in this endeavor. Subconscious mind can also be worst enemy. He must believe who he is and why he is here. Therefore, the resurrection of the viral disease to challenge him and again to remind him he can perform miracles if he believes in them. The miracles he has demonstrated can be a thousandfold greater should he choose to accept that ability to demonstrate. He has free will to accept the responsibility he has said in the past he would accept."

~ * ~

The following session was with Dr. Harmon's cousin who came to see him after her diagnosis of liver and lymphatic cancers. She was taking chemotherapy treatments, which were leaving her extremely weak. Dr. Harmon worked with her to help her strengthen her healthy tissues and cells and to heal the body of the cancers. Before the chemotherapy treatments were finished, NMR indicated her body to be cancer free. She requested further medical tests to check for this. Her medical tests showed her body to be completely free of cancer. Despite this, her oncologist insisted she finish chemotherapy treatments so "we can be sure the cancer won't return". She had the following session to see if she should continue the treatments..

(Dr. Harmon: "Is all of the cancer gone, as the medical tests and NMR have indicated?") "Yes." (Dr. Harmon: "Completely gone?") "Yes." (Dr. Harmon: "Is there a need for chemo-therapy at this time?") "The cancer cells are gone. More toxins will kill this body." (Dr. Harmon: "Does the being in the body want to live or to die?") "Both." (Dr. Harmon: "Which desire is stronger.") "We shall see." (Dr. Harmon: "Move to the Higher

Self now. That's it, welcoming the Higher Self Knowledge.") "She is flirting with death. For she is not as far removed as she would believe on the surface, yet fearful of her dying is deeply embedded in herself. The denial of her truth is she acts as if she is seeking life, but she is not prepared to live in a healthy body again. She must make a choice at this time. She can have a healthy body again.. However, changes must be made before the continued occupancy of this body is viable." (Dr. Harmon: "What changes would these be?") "Belief in self. Belief in the Higher Power that she professes, and yet denies." (Dr. Harmon: "Is the medical intervention helping or harming at this time?") "She has learned much from that experience with the toxic medicines, but it is not a pleasant lesson and one she would best embrace and release in this life before moving on. She will find a great deal of information awaiting her, should she move on. If she's willing to take all of the facts into herself from her Higher Self now, she will learn greatly before moving on. She is very fearful, stubborn, and avoids her own truth now." [Dr. Harmon's cousin continued with the chemo. She died three months later.]

~ * ~

If you, or any one you know, is considering chemo or radiation therapy, read <u>Spontaneous Healing</u> by Andrew Weil, M.D.

We know, and have worked with, people who are alive today because of both of these procedures. While we know there are less taxing and toxic ways to heal, we also know people frequently do not have the knowledge, the time, or the opportunity to use those other methods. We have even had some clients whose Higher Selves have guided them to take chemotherapy or radiation therapy. Our point is, we would, ourselves, want to know what our Higher Selves advised before we proceeded in anything with the potential to harm as greatly as it helps.

For those taking chemotherapy or radiation therapy the following is HIGHLY recommended for helping your healthy tissues and cells recover from the chemo:

<u>Following Each Session of Chemotherapy</u>

Pour one-half cup of REAL Clorox to a bath full of warm water. Soak in bath to leech toxins from the chemotherapy out of the healthy tissue of the body. Rinse thoroughly with clear water. (Buy REAL Clorox, not the other brand names which won't work for this.)

<u>Following Each Session of Radiation Therapy</u>

Put about three to four cups of baking soda in warm bath to reduce the rads left in the body by the x-ray. For radiation to the head or face area, apply a washcloth with saturated solution of baking soda water. Rinse with clear water if desired, though this is not necessary.

~ * ~

Keeping ones good health is as important as regaining good health. Drinking sufficient amounts of clean water and eating sufficient amounts of good food is important. Unfortunately, the pesticides and chemicals used for growing and processing today's foods are becoming less and less tolerated by the human body. We find many people are reacting to the toxins accumulating in their bodies from the chemicals and pesticides in the foods they eat. Buying organic - meaning pesticide and chemical free - is strongly recommended for your body. If you can't do this, buy "range fed" meats and do the following:

- Soak your eggs, fruits, and vegetables (including potatoes) for five minutes in a sink full of water to which a cap full of REAL Clorox as been added. Then rinse by soaking for another five minutes in a sink full of clear water. This procedure will rid these foods of many chemicals and pesticides that have soaked through the skin and counteract those that remain. It is well worth the extra effort. Your body and the bodies of your loved ones need protection from the follies of modern agriculture and commerce.

- If you are really interested in keeping your body healthy, you will eliminate microwave foods as meals for you, your family, and your pets. NMR with our clients indicates that micro waving alters food molecules in a way that is not nutritious for bodies. Use microwave ovens, if you must, for snack foods.

- In testing with our clients, we find sodas - including diet sodas - are toxic to many. We also find many "health" foods and supplements, including "nutritional" bars, are not so healthy for people's bodies. A good rule of thumb is: The closer a food is to its natural state, the better it is for your body. The more processing a food has gone through, the more likely it is to contain chemicals and other manufactured additives that alter its nutritional value, often even making it toxic.

- As much of the soil in which food is grown is depleted of its nutrients, and food processing robs even more, most bodies require supplemental vitamins and minerals. Remember, your body knows best what is right for it. Testing of your body through NMR or CORRECTLY DONE applied kinesiology can determine the kinds of vitamins, minerals, herbs, food, and even medications your body can use and in what combinations and amounts. If someone tests you, but does not use the procedure we outlined in Chapter Four, YOU take control. Tap counter-clock wise around your thymus (as outlined in Chapter Four) before they test you. Have them put the substance on your belly button and then test whether your muscle remains strong or weakens. If your muscle weakens, you are allergic to the substance or it is toxic to you. (We can correct the allergy reaction; they can't, yet.) IMPORTANT: After determining what the body says is good for it, the subconscious must be tested to see if it BELIEVES it. If the subconscious doesn't believe, it won't work. The subconscious programming must be changed in order for it to work.

~ * ~

Weight is a great concern for many people. Actually, we could fill a book with the innumerable reasons for weight problems and food phobias and addictions. Perhaps, someday, we will. Below are some things to realize with weight difficulties.

- Everything you have read about thoughts and emotions affecting the body, the digesting and metabolizing of food, and the weight of the body are true. To complicate matters, these thoughts and emotions may be in the subconscious levels of mind. Clearing the conscious and subconscious levels of negative beliefs and emotions in regards to eating, food and one self is important.

- Even spiritual beliefs can create over or under weight. One Higher Self said the reason for a client's weight was part emotional and part a spiritual desire for physical grounding. "She often feels too much in the spirit realm, " it said, "and believes food and weight ground the body better." When asked if this was true, the Higher Self responded, "Belief makes it true. Change the belief, which is subconscious."

- Excess weight and excess eating of comfort foods are often an attempt by the subconscious to buffer or numb emotional, mental, physical, and spiritual pain. (We have noticed survivors of long term physical abuse often have pack excess weight above the waist and survivors of long term

sexual abuse pack excess weight under the waist, especially around the hips and thighs.)
- Weight, either over or under, and negative food behaviors are frequently means of "punishing" oneself for imagined guilt. (Survivors of sexual abuse usually have such guilt, especially if there was pleasure or comfort in the sexual activity.)
- Self-loathing, which is almost always present with all types of abuse survivors, can drive one to make ones body as unattractive as possible or, alternately, attractive as possible to those who will abuse it further.
- The subconscious of sexual abuse survivors often attempts to make the body sexually unattractive in order to avoid sexual intimacy, which usually triggers memories of the "bad" sex.

In the struggle with ones body, the subconscious mind will always win. One can use will power and control to over-rule the subconscious mind, but the minute the conscious focus is shifted to other concerns, the subconscious programming prevails. The subconscious has many "weapons" at its command in the battle of wills. For instance: The subconscious can increase or decrease the desire for food or exercise. It can trigger food cravings, lower or speed up the metabolism, store excess calories, or purge needed nutrients. Changing the subconscious programming to work for, not against, the conscious desires not only makes sense, it is the only long-term, permanent solution.

Unhappiness with ones body is a constant theme with our clients. Bob, a man in his 30's, had heard Pamela speak of the documented success in achieving breast growth through hypnosis. Bob wondered if anything could be done to increase the size of his penis. Pamela was so relieved he wanted to grow his penis, and not his breasts, she enthusiastically replied "Sure!"

NMR indicated Bob's subconscious mind had stopped the growth of his penis shortly after puberty began due to a suggestion that had become internalized as a subconscious program. That suggestion had begun at five years old and it would be necessary to speak to the five year old Bob about it. If the program was changed, NMR indicated, Bob could grow his penis. "How much bigger do you want it to grow?" Pamela asked him.

"Two inches would help a lot," Bob replied.

The following is an excerpt from the regression to five year old Bob to discover the roots of the subconscious programming of a small penis.

(Pamela: "Go to the time you first have the thought my penis is too small. Where do you find yourself?") "In the urinal My daddy's workers are here peeing. I'm watching them. They have big penises." (Pamela: "What do you think as you pee and watch the men?") "Mine is too small. My penis is too small." (Pamela: "Go to a time when you next have this thought.") "I'm in the urinal at my Daddy's work. I go here lots of times. I look at my penis when I pee. It is TOO small! It's TOO small. The other mens [sic] have big ones. I have a little one. Daddy has a big one, too. They say I better hold onto it [penis] or it will disappear. They laugh because I have a little one. It's TOO small."

Bob had fixated on the thought that his penis was too small. No one had told him his penis would grow as he grew. He thought his penis was as big as it was going to get. He continued to think this over the years. Pamela assured five year old Bob his penis would grow as he grew. The five year old and other ages were helped to release their anger at the humiliation his father and the other men had made him feel. Then Bob's subconscious was told to grow Bob's penis two inches bigger. This suggestion was repeated several times.

After this session, NMR said no further blocks remained to growing Bob's penis. At Bob's next session, he was regressed to the age when his penis growth stopped. The subconscious was told to reverse this action and grow the penis two more inches. A tape of programmed suggestion for growing his penis two more inches was made at this session as well. Bob left and was told to play his tape at least three times a week until he had achieved the results he wanted. Bob called a month latter to report that his penis had grown one and three quarter inches longer and a half inch thicker. He claimed his doctor had verified 'before' and 'after' measurements. (Pamela took Bob's word on this.)

Thomas was a client sent in by Bob. His story is another good example of how powerfully suggestion affects the body when it reaches the subconscious mind. Thomas, a golf pro in his 30's, was unable to achieve an erection. His medical doctor had ruled out any physical causes and suggested he might seek out someone who could help him find any possible emotional causes. NMR quickly established that the loss of erection was due to subconscious suggestion. Thomas couldn't imagine what that might be, but NMR indicated a suggestion given the last time the penis was erect. Thomas said this had been two years prior, with a married woman with whom he'd been having a long term affair. He'd recently met her husband and liked him. Feeling great remorse and guilt, he arranged to meet her one evening with the intent of breaking off the affair. "However," Thomas related, 'things got out of hand and we had sex after all. It was the last time. It was the last time ever." This excerpt of the regression to that encounter begins with Thomas and his lady friend in bed:

(Pamela "What are you doing now?") "I am about to enter her." (Pamela "What are you thinking as you are about to enter her?") "I feel bad. I'm thinking I should not be doing this. I think to myself I will never do this again!" (Pamela: "Subconscious mind, what is Thomas doing now that he never wants to do again?) "His penis is getting hard. He never wants his penis to get hard again."

Pamela pointed out to Thomas's subconscious that it had been mistaken, that Thomas did not want to have sex with that particular woman again, but he did want his penis to get hard again. "Yes, I understand that now," his subconscious responded. Pamela asked if there was any further subconscious resistance to the penis becoming erect. "No," said the subconscious mind. However, as Thomas now had a conscious thought in his mind that his penis would not get erect, due to the number of times it had failed to do so, Pamela made him a hypnosis tape to convince him his penis would become erect anytime he wanted it to.

Thomas called after this session to report he'd easily achieved an erection with masturbation, something he had not been able to do since the night he'd last had sex. He said if he did not call back, it would be because he had been successful with a woman. (Pamela never did hear from Thomas again, though she gained so many men with sexually related problems as clients she (half jokingly and half seriously) began to question whether her name and number were written on a men's room wall somewhere.)

We might note that the subconscious is wide open during sexual activity. Making positive suggestions to your partner is a good idea at this time, especially during orgasm. Dr. Harmon suggested this to a male client whose wife could never believe he loved her, no matter how many times or ways he told her. He took the advice, telling his wife firmly, "I love you" just as she climaxed. She looked at him and said with surprise in her voice,

"I believe you."   It saved their marriage.

The subconscious does not reason.   If something you are saying or thinking catches its attention, it acts on it.   Repeated thoughts and sayings catch its attention.   One adult client complained of wetting the bed at night.   She'd been doing it for a few weeks and wanted to know why.   It was pointed out to her how frequently she used the word "pissed" in her conversation.   She stopped using it and stopped wetting the bed.

Accidents and trauma can easily "set" or "imprint" a suggestion into the subconscious mind.   Dr. Harmon had a client whose eye lids would not remain open, except for a few seconds.   She had, some years prior, run her car over a curb and into a ditch while exiting a gas station at night.   She had hit her forehead on the rear-view mirror and had suffered her eye problem ever since.   Doctors had ruled out any physical causes for the condition.   In hypnosis, Dr. Harmon guided her through the accident again, this time in slow motion.   They found that just as she was about to hit the rear-view mirror, the thought "CLOSE YOUR EYES!" screamed in her brain.   As she hit her head, the trauma of the impact "imprinted" or "fixed" that command in her brain.   To erase that imprint, the subconscious was told to reverse the accident in slow motion.   Then the suggestion was given the subconscious that it would open and shut the eyelids normally, as it had done prior to the accident, which had now been reversed.   After the session ended, the woman's eye lids opened and remained opened.   She called a week later to say her eye lids were continuing to function normally.

We have had great success with this technique for healing physical, emotional, and mental dysfunction due to accident trauma.   One gentleman had been in such constant pain due to neck, back, and hip injuries in a bad car accident, that he was in physical therapy daily and visited a chiropractor almost as frequently.   It took five sessions using this technique to rid his body of all pain.   Following his fifth session his neck, back, and hip had adjusted themselves so completely that physical therapy and chiropractic adjustments were discontinued.

This technique is used in light to medium hypnosis.   The client is asked to go to the time just before the accident occurred and to report what he/she is thinking.   The client is told to move forward into the accident in slow motion and to report on what is happening each moment to the body.   Each time there is an impact to the body, the client is asked to imagine a bolt of energy entering the body at the impact point and to report on every place within the body this bolt of energy ricochets and hits until it exits the body. (This is done for each impact to the body.)

When the body comes to rest, the client is asked if he/she is in or out of the body. If he/she is in the body, the client is told to slip out of the body and be in the spirit state. When client is out of the body, he/she is asked to examine the body and report on its injuries. He/she is then asked to mentally send Light to each site of injury and to say when that site has returned to its normal state. Once this is done for each injury site, he/she is asked to look within and find the cause of the accident and any messages attached to it. After this, the client is asked to return to the body. We then re-run the accident backwards. Each impact bolt is traced (in reverse order, last impact first, etc.) from the exit point backwards, stopping at each place it hit in the body for client to heal that site mentally.

[Placing hands, palm down, on these sites for the natural, gentle transference of life force is very helpful to this process. If one is fearful of disturbing the hypnotic state, the hands can be placed an inch above the body or the client can use his/her own hands. For those working with the body whose hands are already on the body - such as a massage therapist, physical therapist, nurse, or doctor - touching the body will not disturb the hypnotic state.]

Once clients have finished imaging the last impact bolt of energy leaving the body, they continue going backwards until the moment before the accident occurred. We then suggest to the clients that as the message of the accident has been discovered, they are to imagine whatever needs to be done to avert the accident.

Sometimes it is necessary to do this procedure more than one time, but once the subconscious is convinced all injuries and trauma are healed and the accident has been reversed, the client does heal. As many phobias, anxiety disorders, and post traumatic disorders are rooted in past accidents, this is a very valuable technique. We believe every physical therapist, chiropractor, nurse, doctor, and therapist of every kind would benefit greatly by learning how to use basic hypnotic suggestions and techniques such as this one. We have trained such professionals to induce hypnosis in a patient/client in well under five minutes. In fact, we've trained them to induce hypnosis and/or give powerful healing suggestions to the subconscious mind without using a formalized hypnosis induction.

Trauma resulting from surgery is also common. It is often necessary for us to erase for clients negative suggestions that have been made in their presence during surgery to their bodies. The subconscious is ALWAYS listening and is highly suggestible in traumatic states such as surgery. Nor is it capable, especially in traumatic situations, of making reasonable assessments and judgments. It is apt to believe that every remark made during the operation applies to the person being operated on! EVERY doctor and nurse should be aware of this FACT and adjust their conversations during surgery to POSITIVE healing suggestions for the patient. Imagine the good that would do people!

We strongly recommend the cells of the body (especially where it is to be cut), be prepared emotionally prior to surgery and positive suggestions given the subconscious for comfort during the surgery and rapid healing afterwards. Our experience demonstrates doing so dramatically decreases recovery time and accelerates healing.

The use of hypnosis alone for anesthesia will gain greater acceptance over time as people come to accept how powerful their own minds are. In the 1800's, James Esdaile, an English surgeon stationed in India, ran out of Ludlum for the troops he was operating on during a battle. Telling his aide, under strictest orders, to mention that fact to no one, he continued to perform the operations - including amputations of body limbs - telling his patients he was giving them a powerful drug, and describing for them, as he worked, its effects. He found, to his amazement, that in addition to be completely anesthetized, his patients could control their bleeding when told to do so. Realizing how suggestible they were in this state, he suggested as he operated that the soldiers would heal perfectly and rapidly. These soldiers, he noted, DID heal more rapidly than the others. In fact, he had succeeded in drastically reducing the normal mortality rates for the surgeries he had performed!

Excited by this, Dr. Esdaile began studying and experimenting more with mesmerism, the name first given hypnosis. When he returned to England, he arranged to present a demonstration to the College of Surgeons on what he named "The Esdaile State", (which is still the name used for the deepest levels of hypnosis). Unfortunately, he could not duplicate on a stage the results he'd had on the battlefield. Esdaile didn't realize how open the mind is during his Esdaile State and that the skeptical minds of hundreds of esteemed surgeons for the well being of Esdaile's subjects so frightened the subconscious minds of his subjects, they would bring themselves right out of hypnosis. Thus hypnosis was immediately deemed a "flop" by the College of Surgeons in England, despite the proof in the field that it worked, and worked dramatically.

Dr. Harmon has been in "surgery pits" many times (and Pamela once) to hypnotize clients for operations. The process, when the patient is carefully prepared for this and his/her physician supports it, works perfectly. The use of hypnosis also frees women completely from pain during labor and birth of their babies, even in difficult births. (A good hypnosis tape implanting suggestions in the subconscious for this is all that is needed. Personalized tapes made by a hypnotist or hypnotist/physician one trusts are highly recommended.) There is SO MUCH that can be done with hypnosis, which really is only an unlocking of the power of a person's own mind, body, and spirit

~ * ~

The following session is with a woman in her forties. The reason for this session was to find the cause of a pulled muscle in her left hip. The terms "physical mind", "mental mind", "emotional mind", and "spiritual mind" are used to access specific areas of the subconscious mind.

(Therapist: "Physical mind, what is wrong with the left hip?") "There is a muscle that's tight in the front. By the groin. It is short of support compared to the other." (Therapist: "What would help this imbalance?") "Stretching exercises. Looking further within would be beneficial." (Therapist: "Mental mind, what has caused the imbalance of the muscle in the hip?) "Golf. She should not play the game. It brings her a lot of stress." (Therapist: "Emotional mind, does she enjoy the game of golf?") "Sometimes. In her game of golf there is a lot of negativity tied up there. As she swings, her thoughts shift [to the negative] and this shifts her hips out of balance." (Therapist: "Physical mind, if she put her thoughts in balance, would golf be okay for her hips?) "As long as she stretches properly before hand." (Therapist: "Thank you. Physical mind, what is the subconscious mind to you?") "A power house for the being. It can take care of the physical. We are all linked there." (Therapist: "Mental mind, what is the subconscious mind to you?") "It communicates constantly."

(Therapist: "Emotional mind, what is the subconscious mind to you?") "It likes to take care of things. It operates off rules and regulations." (Therapist: "Spiritual mind, what is the subconscious mind to you?") "The controller of the conscious mind." (Therapist: "Spiritual mind, are you the Higher Self?") "No, I am not the Higher Self. It is connected to the greater mass. I am the intuition." (Therapist: "Subconscious mind, what do you know yourself to be?") "I serve, but I control."

~ * ~

The following session is with Joan also in her 40's. While we work with people of all ages - from babies on up - and for all kinds of reasons, many of our clients are people seeking therapy or healing because their lives or their bodies, or both, have pushed them into it. Joan was such a client. Joan was both exciting in her openness and inner abilities and frustrating in her difficulty in believing in those abilities. (Therapist: "Go to the mental mind and scan this body. Tell me its condition at this time and the causes of these conditions.") "This body is here to teach lessons and has brought forth information in similar body symptoms to lead to lessons that are still attached to physical form. The being is not aware [consciously] of this at this time. This being is holding many, many fears, many emotions that are not serving the body any longer. There is fear around this physical form in and around the head area. There is a chemical and emotional imbalance in the reproductive organs. There is chemical enzyme malfunction and imbalance of connective tissues of the shoulders, the neck, the lower back, the knees and the hips. There is disruptive nervous pathways in the left foot, in the toes of the same foot, in the right knee and foreleg, the upper shoulders and neck, some in the jaw and up above the eyes in the forehead." (Therapist: "Are you able to give such accurate information about others' bodies?") "Yes. If the conscious belief would allow it." (Therapist: "Higher Self, what guidance would you offer at this time?") "She needs to speak to the body with love in the voice, sharing loving thoughts as she moves through her healing and learning to love the self. The healing on the other side of this is glorious and worth waiting for. She is gathering information as she does her healing work. She has fear about her body. She needs to move beyond this fear. Do active work to move through the thought in self that she will not be able to do it right. She needs to know that doing it is right, no matter how she does it. This work is important. She needs to allow this process to unfold. She is doing well. As she moves further in the activity, fear will diminish and as the fear diminishes, she will have the courage to move even deeper." (Therapist: "What is the meaning of the dog in her dream?") "The energy centers are blocked with rage. Fear is of letting the rage out. Signifies issues in past life aspect experience. Rage is still there." (Therapist: "Higher Self, how will she know your voice.") "As before, I am the first thought. She is doing well at listening to first thought. Her knowing is growing." (Therapist: "Her sexual energies?") "She confuses romantic love with self love. She needs to learn self love. It is a good time now to explore her own body for she is still confused about her pleasure zones, how she experiences her own pleasures. Exploring this will aid in future relationships. This will enhance self love."

Joan's difficulty in believing in herself and in believing her inner mind and spirit were rooted in childhood abuse of which she has no conscious recall. Therapy for this abuse was frustrating for Joan as she had hoped and expected, like many clients, that the memories would become conscious over time.

Unfortunately, this seldom occurs with memories that have been stored, on strictest instructions by the subconscious, in places that are not easily accessible to conscious recall. In addition, flashes or impressions of such memories are frequently attributed to "hallucinations", "fatigue", "stress," "imagination", and "someone else's suggestion".

One client came in after having spontaneously remembered, during step aerobics, being raped and sodomized as a child by her grandfather. NMR confirmed this memory as a real experience in this life. The woman distrusted her memory, however, as she could not recall details from it the next day. She was unwilling to accept that the step aerobics had moved her into a hypnotic state where the words on the aerobic tape ('coming on up") repeated over and over had caused a repressed memory to surface. She preferred to believe she had "made up" the story about her grandfather because she was fatigued. To our minds, making up such a story for any reason, whether in or out of hypnosis, is cause enough for concern about ones mental and emotional balance.

Another client strongly distrusted her memory, in hypnosis, of sexual abuse. She believed she had made up the story in hypnosis because NMR had indicated such abuse. While it can be argued this is a possibility, we would argue it is unlikely any level of the mind would indicate, through NMR, that abuse had occurred if it hadn't or the mind didn't believe it had. Careful testing with NMR by both Dr. Harmon and Pamela indicated all levels of her mind, body, and spirit had knowledge of this abuse. Nevertheless, she was not prepared to believe this and chose not to do so.

People often ask us how we can be sure what the mind says in NMR or hypnosis is true, and not "just imagination". Our response is if it is imagination, then imagination heals, as we have watched thousands of clients heal simply by believing in and healing their "imaginations" and others not heal by not believing in or healing theirs.

We've also observed that while past life therapy will frequently have successful results even if the client did not believe the past life was "real", this is often not true with the "inner child". The "inner children" consider themselves to be very real indeed. We suspect because they are "present" (unlike past life personalities) and thus have great influence on the subconscious mind, they can continue to block or interfere with positive results if they want to do so. To our surprise, they can be quite willful about being recognized, accepted, and believed before allowing positive change in the body or the mind.

~ * ~

While the general impression that the major part of a hypnosis practice is working with weight and tobacco clients is erroneous, we do get a good number of clients seeking to end these and other addictions and habits. We even get people who have already successfully ended their addiction or habit, but still have the desire for it because the subconscious reasons for the addiction or habit have not been addressed or completely healed.

Tony, a man in his 50's, had successfully ended his smoking after a hypnosis seminar. Our experience with clients is that 10% of people will end an addiction/habit, like smoking, in such seminars. About another 10% will stop for a period of time, but pick the addiction/habit up again later when feeling particularly stressed or upset. Some of those who stop, like Tony, do not lose their desire for their addiction/habit.

As allergies to tobacco or food (or the additives in them) can create a craving for that substance, Tony's allergy to tobacco was balanced in his first session and a means for dealing with stress. Next, the root of his desire to smoke was found, with NMR, to be a past life in the opium dens of China.

After a regression to that life, Tony reported to Dr. Harmon all desire to smoke was completely gone. The desire did not return, even after Tony had a serious motorcycle accident two years later and was in a great deal of pain. Working with Dr. Harmon, he healed all of his injuries, which had been severe.

Pamela had a session with a young man who proclaimed himself a "pot head" and said he had to stop smoking immediately as he'd just joined the Navy. He'd heard being caught with "grass" (marijuana) would land him in the brig for a long time. Pamela had him describe his favorite "getting high" fantasy, then she repeated this back to him while he was hypnotized. She made a tape of it as she did so. Afterwards, while talking to him about his experience, she looked into his eyes and realized he was high. "Yeah, I know," he responded when Pamela mentioned this, "isn't it great?" She immediately gave "sober" suggestions to his subconscious, despite his protests. (She had visions of him being pulled over for driving under the influence and fingering her as his dealer. She didn't think the officer would believe he was high on hypnosis.) He called some time later to say he'd become a "tape head" and that he'd discovered dragging on a straw cut like a reefer at the beginning of the tape made it even more effective for him. (As deep breathing of oxygen produces euphoria like highs, this would work.)

Another client who drank five tall highballs a night cut down to one a night right away by playing a hypnosis tape Pamela made for him. After arriving home from his stressful job, he would follow his normal routine and head straight for his high ball glass. He would then plunk two ice cubes in it, as he always did. Picking up the vodka bottle in which he kept water, he would pour a tall glass of it, take it to his favorite chair, kick off his shoes, take a long sip, pick up a piece of paper on which he'd written (the night before) a goal he had for himself, lean back, close his eyes, and click on his tape recorder.

On the tape, Pamela described him lying on the warm sands of his own private Pacific Island. He would feel the warmth of the sun on his face, think briefly of his goal, and, then, as he listened to Pamela's hypnotic voice, he would relax into the sounds of the lulling waves. Soon, a beautiful island maiden would kneel behind his head and begin to massage his temples. Slowly, she would smooth and soothe the muscles at the front and side of his neck, shoulders, arms, chest, hips, legs, and feet. As he sat up, she would massage the back of his neck, shoulders, arms, and back. Then he and his beautiful island maiden would join hands and walk together deep into the tropical rain forest. There, they would climb down wide, grassy, steps carved along side a waterfall to the pool below. The water would be the exact temperature he liked and he and his beautiful island maiden would swim in the pool. Soon, he would look into her eyes and ask for his goal. If she smiled, it meant his request was granted. If she frowned, it meant there were things he had to do before his request could be granted. After they swam and frolicked in the pool, they would return, hand in hand, back to the beach. Smiling, she would wave good-bye, knowing he would return. Pamela's voice would then suggest that as he felt himself sitting in the chair in his living room he would recall perfectly whether she had smiled or frowned. If she had smiled, his subconscious would now be helping him take the steps to make his goal happen. If she had frowned, he would investigate in his next session with Pamela any blocks he had to his goal. Then he would return to full conscious focus and write down the goal (it could be the same one or another) that he would read before he played the tape the next night.

His evenings became very relaxing for him. He reported he enjoyed his one drink of the night, but enjoyed his three glasses of water in his highball glass just as much. He also found he had a lot more energy in the nights. He began bicycling, something he'd always wanted to do, for an hour after he got home and on the weekends. He lost thirty pounds and joined a bicycle club, which greatly improved his social life. He continued seeing Pamela two times a month to work with any crises or difficulty he was experiencing with his new life style, work, or blocked goals. He had a great deal of repressed anger due to, first, his childhood, and, second, his experiences in Vietnam. Over six months, he healed his anger and pronounced himself a "new man". (Pamela also used the island and the beautiful island maiden as an induction for his sessions in the office. After a couple of months, she decided to satisfy her curiosity as to whether his beautiful island maiden had a name. She asked him, just as the maiden was kneeling down behind him, if he knew her name. "Yes," he said softly. Pamela, expecting an exotic Polynesian name, asked her name. "Gertrude," he whispered, as he slipped deeper into hypnosis, "her name is Gertrude.")

Sandi, in her 20's, was a client of Dr. Harmon's and Sandi found it very difficult to end her smoking completely. In hypnosis, Dr. Harmon asked Sandi why she was having such difficulty. Her subconscious responded: "She smokes to fill her emptiness." Dr. Harmon asked where this emptiness was rooted. The response was: "Many roots. Check two previous lives. Also childhood very sad. She has forgotten this at one level. Important to remember. Body is suffering from forgetting. Smoking masks the pain and emptiness."

The two previous lives were healed and Sandi quit smoking completely for several weeks. However, at the end of those weeks she became extremely anxious and upset, so she began smoking two cigarettes a day (down from two packs a day). NMR indicated a great deal of sexual abuse in her early childhood. Enough of this abuse was addressed to gain Sandi great insight into her relationships with men and her low self-esteem. She ended an abusive marriage and a year later married a caring man. Sandi felt her therapy of that abuse was complete. Her three, four, and five year old "inner children" insisted it was not as they still had emotions to release and memories to discuss. Sandi ended therapy anyway and continued to smoke two cigarettes a day..

Often, we get clients who have ended a coping behavior or addiction prematurely - before they have dealt with the underlying emotional cause - thus increasing internal stress. A client that Dr. Harmon was treating for extensive abuse read a self-help book on pressure points in the body that, when pressed, eliminate addictions and habits. "Why didn't you tell me I could do this for my candy addiction?" she asked Dr. Harmon accusingly.

"Because you aren't emotionally ready to end it," he told her. "I can tell you what will happen if you use this technique, which I am well aware of by the way. It's of great help when one is ready for it, but you aren't."

"Well, I'm going to use it anyway," she said. "I'm sick of eating so much candy and I'm sick of my weight."

A few days later she burst in on a class Dr. Harmon was giving. "You have to help me!" she cried and broke down in tears.

Dr. Harmon asked if she would be willing to work with him in front of the class. She, sobbing, said she didn't care, as long as he helped her. She had been, she said, at the grocery store and seen her favorite Easter candy. She had applied the pressure point for resisting the candy. It worked. She walked away from the display feeling triumphant and stood in the line to pay for her groceries. Suddenly, she'd felt an awful feeling, like she was sinking in a deep, black hole. She felt extreme anxiety, deep grief, and the inability to cope with anything - even standing in line. She left her basket of groceries and made a bee line for Dr. Harmon's office.

Dr. Harmon asked her to put into words her feelings. "I feel," she said, "as though my best friend in the world has died. It doesn't make sense. But I feel that friend was all that was keeping me sane and now my friend is gone."

Her friend was candy. When Dr. Harmon guided her into trance, a little girl began to speak. She was very angry and hurt at having her candy taken away and that anger and hurt were triggering deep rage and pain at the abuse. Dr. Harmon spoke to the little girl and promised her that she could have "all the Easter candy her little tummy could eat without getting sick". This mollified the "little one" and the feelings of high anxiety abated. The client also found herself eating less candy than she normally would. (Thanks to the fill your "little" tummy suggestion.) Over the course of therapy, candy consumption dwindled until she was eating it only when particularly stressed. Today, she is able to alleviate stress without candy much of the time. Such would have been unthinkable before therapy.

We've seen our clients heal of many things. We have never, however, had a client heal from a diagnosis of a severed spine. But Dr. Harmon's brother, the other Dr. Harmon (M.D.) has.

Dr. Robert Harmon is Medical Director of The M.E.A. Clinic which is run by the M.E.A. Foundation of which his brother, Dr. Hugh Harmon, is Chairman of the Board. The Clinic was founded to carry on the family tradition of providing caring and affordable health care for the community. This work was begun by their grandmother, Mattie Evans Alderman, in the early 1900's. Mrs. Alderman would hire, at her own expense, doctors and nurses to bring health care to those in the Coachella Valley who could not afford it, most notably women on the Indian Reservation and field laborers and their families. Mrs. Alderman also built and donated the building for the first high school in Thermal, helped start the first telephone service in Thermal, was a contributing founder for the First National Bank in Coachella, and built the company that first provided Imperial

Valley with pure artesian drinking water. When she thought it was time to improve the roads and build better bridges in the Valley, she got in her Model T, drove to Sacramento, and bullied the legislature into providing the funding to get them built. Her husband, a Methodist-Epsicopal minister, would frequently suffer fainting spells from what would be diagnosed today as hypoglycemia. When a spell would come on, Mattie Evans Alderman would take the pulpit and deliver his sermon with her fiery determination and passion. Her work ethic, high ideals, sense of duty, and commitment to serving others were passed on to both of her grandsons, whom she helped raise.

Dr. Robert Harmon is, like his brother, a man who cares passionately about helping people to heal. This passion led him to the Orient in the middle of his medical career to study acupuncture and meditation and to his research into the basic concepts of human nutrition and body chemistry. He also studied and researched chelation therapy and now utilizes it in the clinic. Use of chelation therapy alone has saved hundreds of his patients from expensive and invasive surgeries. Over the course of his decades of medical practice, he has strongly adhered to his Hypocratic Oath - Primum Non Nocere. Translation: "First, Do No Harm".

In his early 70's, Dr. Robert Harmon sees up to 60 patients a day. He is as busy now as he was when he was chief anesthesiologist for four Los Angeles Hospitals, driving from one hospital to another. His career as an anesthesiologist was remarkable with no loss of patients under his care and the use of up to 80% less anesthesia per patient than would normally be used. Impressed by this, one (only one?!) hospital administrator asked what he was doing. What he was doing was using the hypnosis taught to him in medical school by the same Dave Elman who taught his brother.

Both Doctor Harmons understand well the power of the mind over the body, which was very fortunate for Mr. Gomez. While cutting a limb off a tree, Mr. Gomez, a man in his 50's, fell onto the concrete curb below. He landed on his spine, which was diagnosed by neurological experts as severed. Told he would never walk again, he refused to believe it. A man of deep faith, he believed prayer could heal anything, so he set about praying with fervor. Both Dr. Harmons supported his self-prognosis and faith. His physical therapist was taught how to impress upon his subconscious the belief he could walk as she helped him to move his legs and muscles in assisted walking exercises.   He was encouraged to keep repeating during these exercises the thought and words: "I'm walking."

To everyone's astonishment (with the notable exception of Mr. Gomez), the day arrived when he did walk. He continues to walk, stiffly and with the aid of a cane, but walk he does. There has been some heated medical discussion among those involved in his care and diagnosis as to whether: A) His spine has healed, which is considered impossible if his original diagnosis by neurological experts was correct.   B) He is walking despite his spine being severed, which is also considered impossible. C) His original diagnosis was incorrect.

Naturally, none of the possibilities please the neurological experts who diagnosed his severed spine for it means they either made a grave error in diagnosis or their understanding of the human body and its abilities is gravely limited. Mr. Gomez doesn't care whether his spine is still severed or never was. Nor does he care to let anyone open his back and find out. He is walking. He intends to keep right on walking. He's probably even planning to climb trees again before long.

Some people - certainly Mr. Gomez - would say God healed him. We believe God does not choose who heals and who doesn't. We believe God gave everyone the ability to create anything they choose to create. We know at least three levels of the mind are involved in the creation process: 1) The conscious level which creates thought. 2) The superconscious level where thought is imaged on what is sometimes called "the screen of the mind". 3) The subconscious level which manifests thought.

You are creating thoughts continually. Other people's thoughts are coming at you continually. One of the jobs your subconscious must do is decide which thoughts are frivolous and which are not; in other words, which thoughts are to be manifested. Hypnotists have been working directly with the subconscious mind for a very long time. Longer than even psychiatrists, psychologists, psychotherapists, or hypnotherapists. They have made some very important observations about the subconscious mind. They know that certain criteria strongly influences the subconscious mind. These criteria are:

A) Identification. This includes the humans who raised you, the culture you were raised in, and the traits others have you wish to have.

B) Authority. This includes the people who raised you, your religious leaders, your government leaders, your teachers, your employers, your doctors. It can even include those who bully or abuse you. Those the subconscious believes hold the power of life and death over the body strongly influence it. Thus, YOU are also an authority figure to your subconscious mind.

C) Repetition. Thoughts, actions, and experiences repeated over and over strongly influence the subconscious mind.

D) Emotion. The subconscious is the seat of the emotions and it is emotional energy that the subconscious uses to manifest thought. Thoughts accompanied by emotion are considered very important to the subconscious mind. The stronger the emotion, the greater the importance attached to the thoughts accompanying it. It does not judge between "good" and "bad" emotion. People are very good at manifesting that which they greatly fear as fear is a very strong emotion!

E) Exaggeration. A good way to explain exaggeration is to substitute the words imagination, shock, trauma, physical contact or action. All of these focus the attention of the subconscious, causing it to place more importance on the thoughts being presented to it.

F) Hypnosis. There are many ways to open the mind to suggestion, which is hypnosis. Hypnosis includes, but is not limited to, prayer, meditation, rituals, repetitive action, concentration, focus, relaxation, drugs, hypnotic medications (which include many of the common depression medications), surgery, trauma, shock, guided imagery, visualization, NLP, EMDR, massage, emotional states.

In order to walk, Mr. Gomez had to overcome the diagnosis of a severed spine by neurological medical experts. Because such experts are powerful authority figures, many people would have considered it a waste of time, energy, and emotion to even try to learn to walk again. Not Mr. Gomez. He believed strongly in God (the ultimate authority figure) and in God's power to do anything, even heal or overcome a severed spine. These beliefs were taught him by his culture and his religion (identification, authority, repetition, emotion, exaggeration, and hypnosis). Two other doctors (authority) supported his self-prognosis that he would walk again. Mr. Gomez certainly desired (emotion) to walk and kept (repetition) praying (hypnosis, emotion) he would walk. The physical therapist (authority figure) was taught how to present suggestions (hypnosis) to the subconscious mind for walking. As she presented these suggestions (hypnosis), she would help him move (exaggeration, identification, hypnosis) the legs and muscles necessary for walking. He was encouraged to keep repeating (repetition) mentally or verbally the thought, as he moved his legs and muscles, "I'm walking" (identification, authority, hypnosis) and to feel excited (emotion) about it. This procedure was repeated over and over (repetition). Eventually, Mr. Gomez's subconscious mind created a way for the body to walk.

It is our sincere belief that stories like those of Mr. Gomez, and others in these pages, will encourage those with "incurable", "inoperable", and "hopeless" conditions and situations to look beyond perceived limitations; to look within for the limitless power created in the coming together of the mind, body, and spirit.

Years ago Pamela listened to a radio interview with a man and his doctor. The man claimed he had grown a new leg some twenty years previously. His doctor, now retired, verified this and added several medical personnel, including government medical researchers, had been aware of this. All had sworn an oath to speak of the case only to those who were involved with it, and the man's medical records had been permanently locked away. The incredulous talk show host exclaimed, "But doctor! Why wouldn't you tell people about it? It's amazing news."

"Yes," the doctor replied, "but we knew if we let the news leak, everyone would think they could grow back parts of their bodies."

Those who feel it is their duty to "protect" humans by focusing on perceived limitations do a tragic disservice to the human potential. As long as we believe we have limits, we are limited. We certainly know enough about the mind today to realize we have not even begun to plumb its possibilities. Part of the fun of human life is to explore our potentials and part of the joy is to meet challenges with a sense of "what's possible if I don't close my mind to the possibilities?"

A young woman, in her late 20's, came to see us. "I'm dying," she said. "My doctors tell me I have maybe six weeks." We asked if she wanted to work on living. "Of course," she said, "but not this life. I had a dream. I know I'm going to die. It's obviously my time, though I don't know why. That's what I want to find out. Why am I dying? Why did I create this disease? Was it to meet the challenge of dying with it, or was it to uncover

what I've done emotionally to create it? I don't want to take it with me
into my next life. Been there, done that. I want as great a start on my
next life as possible. Will you help me?"

    We were humbled, thrilled, and filled with the joy for the human mind
and spirit. She helped us discover over the next ten weeks what "miracles"
truly are: Self-empowerment.

~ NOTES TO YOURSELF ~

How To Find & Help Your Hypnotist/Hypnotherapist

- Check with people you know. You'd be amazed how many people are "into" hypnosis. Check the Yellow Pages of your local phone book for professional hypnotists and hypnotherapists.
- Check training credentials. A professional hypnotist is certified with a minimum of 50 hours of CLASS (not home) training. A professional hypnotherapist is certified with a minimum of 250 hours of CLASS training.
- Insist on a FREE consultation. Ask questions at your consultation and choose the professional YOU TRUST and feel good about. Be careful of those who "dictate" what you should do and those who use negative language.
- EXPECT to have more than one session or ask to have a hypnosis tape to listen to at home. Like everything else, people get better at being hypnotized the more they do it.
- Raise your eyes, whether open or closed, at the start of being hypnotized by yourself or another. This starts the altered state.
- Relax your body. Scan it from head to toe and relax all tense muscles. Don't forget the forehead, neck, shoulders, and hands.
- Listen to the hypnotist's voice. You don't even have to concentrate on the words. Just focus on the voice, or your breathing, or on a soothing background sound. Your subconscious will do the rest.
- Don't try to be hypnotized and don't resist. Just relax and let it happen. If you hear something you don't like, tell your hypnotist. You can speak in hypnosis, it won't break the trance. If your hypnotist ignores your objection, open your eyes and break the trance yourself.
- When you hear the hypnotist asking you to respond, speak what you are thinking. Examining it first brings in the analytical mind, which interferes with the trance state.
- Relax. Enjoy. Trust yourself. You are prepared. ESPECIALLY if you have read <u>Odyssey of the Soul., Book One, Apocatastasis</u>
- For 20-30 minutes after hypnosis, give yourself POSITIVE self-thought and self-talk. It's a powerful time for self-programming.

HOW TO DO POSITIVE SELF-PROGRAMMING

¨ The first time you program a specific goal, write it down. This should be no longer than one page.

¨ Write what you DO want, not what you don't.

¨ Be specific about what you want and the specific steps you need to take to achieve it.

¨ Use simple, positive, exciting, and emotional words.

¨ Use present tense not future tense, even when grammatically incorrect; use "I am", not "I will. Write as though you already have your goal.

¨ Write as though you were trying to convince a very bright 10 year old "YOU" (your subconscious mind) to help you achieve this goal.

¨ Think of a reward for that 10 year old "YOU" when you've achieved your goal and promise to give yourself that reward when your goal is achieved.

¨ Pick a trigger word, or sentence, or symbol that sums up all you've written. For your last sentence write, "Every time I say, think, see, or hear (write your trigger word, sentence, or symbol) I mentally replay all that I've written and it is acted upon by my subconscious mind.

¨ Read this aloud three times.

¨ Relax your body from head to toe. Breathe deeply. Center in the Light as outlined in Chapter 8 in Odyssey of The Soul, Book One, Apocatastasis. Say, see, or think your trigger word or symbol.

¨ As you are centered in the Light, think of your goal. If your mind begins to drift, say or think of your trigger word, sentence, or symbol.

¨ Think/speak your trigger word, sentence, or symbol all day every day.

~ * ~

This is the process with each goal. Write a separate sheet for each unrelated goal. Use your trigger words often and center your goals in the Light often. If you find yourself taking the steps to achieve your goal, it's working. If you don't, or find yourself feeling irritable or upset every time you think of your goal, you probably have inner blocks to achieving it. Seek a good hypnotherapist to help you with this.

Chapter 6

The Dragon Slayers

Light has many vibrations. One of them is darkness. In the shadows of darkness lurk many demons; a word that in ancient Greece meant divine power, fate and genius. (Genius was defined as a supernatural being or intermediary spirit between gods and men.) Among the demons of man and woman is that which symbolizes divine power: The Dragon. Originally dragon meant snake, or serpent, and in the garden (world) of Eve (woman) and Adam (man), it is when divine power (snake, serpent, dragon), runs amok that evil reigns.

Evil in ancient Aramaic was to eat of unripe fruit, which is distressing and upsetting to the physical system. To sin was for the archer to miss the mark or target.

To misuse divine power is to miss the mark, or sin, and this sin is indeed evil, or upsetting, to the entire physical system of man, woman, child, and the world in which we live.

We all walk the path of the Dragon, for within each of us is the creative, or divine, power. **We create with our thoughts, our words, our actions and that which we create we must meet.** We have forgotten this. We have come to believe that what we think, speak and do is condoned, forgiven, or forgotten if: A) No one knows about it. B) Others think, speak, or do it. C) There is good reason for it. D) We can get away with it.

In 553 AD at the Second Council of Constantinople, the Roman Catholic Church bowed to the demands of secular leaders (both within and outside of the church) who did not want any reference in Holy Works that indicated they would meet the abuses of their powers. Hedonism (the pursuit of pleasure as its own end) was rampant and those besotted with pleasure and power came to believe they could create their own spiritual destinies. The intelligentsia aided in this conceit; for after all, they reasoned, if thought determines reality, then by controlling thought man can control all destiny.

It was a great sin and evil that the Second Council of Constantinople wrought upon humans for they condemned us to centuries of ignorance as all references that made it clear the soul always meets what it has created through the cycle of rebirth of the soul were deleted from the Bible and other Holy Works.

There are a previous few references to reincarnation in the Bible that somehow survived the cuts. Not that this is convincing to anyone determined to keep a closed mind. A woman came to see Pamela telling her that she believed the Bible to be the literal word of God. She was disturbed by a talk Pamela had given on past lives. Reincarnation, she stated emphatically, was not possible because there was no mention of it in the Bible. As the woman had her Bible with her, Pamela asked her to read aloud Matthew 16:13-14, Matthew 17:10-13, John 9:1-2 and Revelation 13:10 After reading them, the woman looked up at Pamela. "What do you think of what you read?" Pamela asked. The woman replied, "The Bible must be wrong."

It is true that thought determines reality. It is reasonable, then, to argue the Council was right: By controlling thought one can control all of ones destiny. What such an argument forgets, however, is that thought exists at the Higher Self, as well as the lower self, level. **Our Higher Self thought affects us as directly as our lower self thought. Nor are our Higher Selves subject to our human manipulations. As long as our Higher Selves dictate that we must answer to all we create; we will continue to live as many lives as it takes to do it.**

Past life regressions are an important part of a well trained hypnotherapist's practice. Even if the hypnotherapist does not believe in past lives, the inner minds of people do. (Whether past lives are real memories or symbolic metaphors can be argued. That the inner mind speaks easily of past lives cannot be argued.) People seek hypnotherapy for physical, mental, emotional, spiritual, psychic, sexual, and financial well being. Frequently, when asked to give the cause of blocks to healing or change, the Higher Self or subconscious will indicate one or more past lives. This is quite disconcerting to many. "But I don't believe in past lives", is a frequent refrain. "What does a past life have to do with TODAY?" is a common complaint.

Time is omnipresent for your subconscious mind, for it is always aware of and with your soul, which never dies. Your subconscious is not afraid of death; yet, when your soul is in a physical body, its number one job, its greatest priority, is to keep the body alive. It takes that job seriously. Balance of the emotional, physical, mental, and spiritual energies is important to the survival of the body. When that balance is threatened, the subconscious becomes alarmed. The source of the imbalance can be in the past, the present, or the future - it's all the same to the subconscious mind.

Yet, the subconscious mind is one of the most precise keepers of time known to humans. In frequently repeated studies, subjects are hypnotized and the subconscious mind told that at a certain signal it is to keep track of the passing of a precise number of seconds. (These seconds vary from hundreds, to thousands, to millions of seconds.) The subconscious mind is instructed that when the precise number of seconds have been reached, the stop button on a stop watch given the subject is to be pressed. The subjects are then brought out of hypnosis, told to keep the stopwatches close to them at all times, and to go about their business, without paying any particular attention to their stop watches. They are also told that when they get an overpowering urge to press the stop button, they are to do so, then return the stopwatches. The results of these studies are remarkable. With all the subconscious mind has to do, it is still able to keep precise and accurate track (even when the person is sleeping) of up to millions of seconds. Why not, then, millions of years, or more?

People argue that they cannot remember their past lives, so they must not have happened. They may as well argue that because they don't recall every day and event of the present life, those days and events must not have happened. Actually, all people remember everything they have ever seen, heard, done, learned, and experienced in every life time. They have just "forgotten" that for many memories, they have to go into the subconscious mind to find them.

Memory is stored in the subconscious mind in order to keep the conscious mind clear for the enormously important task of making the choices and decisions that affect the survival of the body, the quality of life, and the growth of the soul. (So important is this job that all other tasks are given to the subconscious mind.) Memory is stored both at the "hardware" levels of the brain and in the "software" levels of the subconscious mind, which "exists" in the energy field that surrounds and interpenetrates the body/ brain.

Memory is stored by the subconscious mind according to directives given it by the conscious mind. Memories needed by the conscious mind to help it in the moment to moment course of daily living are made available for ready recall to the conscious mind. Memories that are interesting or meaningful to the conscious mind are also stored for ready conscious recall. Memories that are not particularly important, interesting, or meaningful to the conscious mind, as well as memories that would be traumatic or overwhelming to the conscious mind are less readily available. It takes the subconscious extra time to bring these memories forward, and for many of them, you have to be IN the subconscious memory banks in order to find them.

For example, think of a birthday of yours that was particularly memorable. Note how quickly you recall the events of that day. Now think of a birthday that was not so memorable. Does it take longer for memories of that day to "pop" into your recall? What about your first three birthdays, do you remember them? You could in hypnosis. In hypnosis, you can "slip into" the subconscious memory banks and find lots of information not available in the "normal" conscious focus of mind.

The memory of your past lives is buried within the subconscious levels to avoid confusion and trauma. Imagine being aware of all your past likes and dislikes at any given moment. How would you ever make decisions and choices? Imagine being aware of all your past emotions at any given moment. How would you or your body cope? (Emotions can be as wearing on your body as they are on you.) Imagine being aware of all your past deaths at any given moment. How would your nervous system survive?

Regression therapy is a major part of hypnotherapy. The goal of regression therapy is to heal any event in the past (whether past lives or the past of the present life) that negatively affects the present or the future.

In regression therapy, the soul finds where divine power (dragon) has been misused (sin) to create that which upsets (evil) the mind, body, or spirit. In regression therapy, the soul becomes the dragon slayer.

Slaying-in-the-spirit is to touch a person in a manner that causes that person to fall with the belief he or she has received a bolt or charge of Holy Spirit energy. Rhythmic music, clapping, chanting, high emotions, mental expectation and combined life force energy can indeed create a bolt or charge of energy that can be directed by the mind to do anything.

Such an energy charge can heal people. (It can also injure, even kill, people if that is the intent.) It can materialize spirit. It can cause people to see "visions", hear "voices", and "speak" in "tongues". Of course, the mind can consciously or subconsciously block this energy. Not everyone who is "touched" falls. Not everyone who falls is healed. Not everyone who is healed stays healed. Not everyone has "the eyes to see", "the ears to hear", or the "voice to speak". Belief and acceptance open the mind; doubt and denial close it. When the mind is closed, awareness is limited. When the mind is open, awareness is limitless.

We had a series of group meetings in the Embassy Suites hotel in Palm Desert. Frequently, prior to the meetings we would privately ask Master of Light for a demonstration that evening. "Master of Light," Pamela said one day, "could we have a different demonstration tonight? Something more people can notice. There's always a few people who perceive the astral light and colors you project, but most don't. We want more people to notice your presence. When we ask tonight for Light, could you do something more noticeable?"

That night, as we asked for Light, the fire alarms for the hotel went off. As the group began evacuating the room, hotel personnel shouted out: "False alarm. Something set the alarms off. We don't know what it was, but it wasn't a fire."

"Well," said Master of Light the next day, "did you like that? Everyone noticed it, don't you think?"

"I thought you were the Master of Light, not Sound," Pamela responded, laughing.

"Sound is Light," Master of Light responded. "All is Light. Tell people to look around. Everything they see, hear, and touch is Light. Their bodies are Light. Their thoughts are Light. Even their minds and emotions are

Light. I am everywhere. I am always available to everyone at all times. If humans truly would grasp that and use Light for all Light can do, your world would be in much better shape. In all ways and always."

Light is energy. When Light is focused, power is generated. Power that can generate heat and fire, as when a magnifying glass focuses the light of the sun. Power that can generate sound, as in thunder. Power that can create electricity, as in lightning. Power that can penetrate matter as with laser light

As Spirit generates Light, mind can focus it. Imagine then, the power generated when many spirits gather and many minds are linked in a single focus. That is the power of group energy. All great leaders, teachers, healers, motivators, and performers use the power of group energy; if not consciously, then subconsciously. Attend a seminar, meeting, service, speech, performance or any gathering where those present become inspired, impassioned, or galvanized and you will sense an "electric charge" of energy present. When there is a central person (usually an authoritative or charismatic personality) to whom the group is "feeding" this energy, it often feels as if that person is projecting great power.

People, places, and things being "fed" group energy feel empowering. Away from their presence (and thus the group energy), that power begins to dissipate, slowly for some, more rapidly for others. For many people, this feels as though they are coming down from an energy "high". This can be depressing for some as anger is triggered subconsciously by the sense that power has somehow been lost. Other people find the "energy high" has quickened their own "normal" levels of energy to higher levels. Those levels, however, are rarely as "high" as when tapping into group energy. Humans have created many ways to maintain group energy:

1. Organized Governments and Organized Religion. The higher you are in the hierarchy of these groups, the greater access you have to the energy and, thus, the power, of the group. Of course, group energy is only as powerful as its focus. Divert the focus and you divert the energy. Divert the energy and there is a loss of power. Thus, hierarchies develop central figures, usually leaders, to which they feed their energy in an effort to keep a group focus. While this works, it also "disempowers" those who "feed" the leaders and frequently creates subversion within the group as the "powerless" seek to gain the leadership even as those leaders seek

to absorb as much energy from the group as possible in order to consolidate their power.

2. Social and Spiritual Groups. Similar to organized government and religions in that energy and power are usually fed to particular individuals within the group. Family hierarchies are one example of this, as is the "popular culture" which creates heroes, heroines, and stars to be worshipped, emulated, and granted power beyond the "ordinary" being. Gurus, avatars, medicine men and medicine women are another example, as are "big" bosses like corporate or union heads.

3. Places draw group energy when those places are thought to be powerful by many. Examples of such places: Stonehenge, Sedona, Ganges River, Lourdes. Machu Pinchu, The Sphinx, The Great Pyramid, Sacred Indian Grounds. Mecca. Any sacred, blessed, holy, or cursed place.

4. Things and rituals draw group energy when they are thought to be powerful by many. Examples of this are: Shrines. Mosques. Churches. Synagogues. Temples. The Bible. The Torah. The Koran. Prayer. Prayer Beads. Prayer Candles. Incense. Crystals. The Cross. The Star of David. Totem Poles. Gang Signs. Swastika. Country Flags. Special Salutes. Obscene Gestures. Voodoo. (The list is endless.)

5. Food, alcohol and drugs thought to be powerful by many draw group energy.

   - Tobacco kills more people today because, in addition to the increased use of toxic additives in the tobacco, group energy has fed powerfully into the thought "tobacco kills".

   - Alcohol, like tobacco, holds more power over people who are as mentally (consciously or subconsciously) swayed by the thought that alcohol has power over them as they are by biochemical sensitivities in their cells to alcohol. In fact, since thought triggers biochemical reactions, thought is a large component of alcoholism. Anyone who doubts that would do well to watch a hypnotist convince a sober person he or she is drunk or a drunk person he or she is sober.

   - Drugs and medicines hold a tremendous amount of group energy as billions of humans focus intense mental and emotional expectations on their power. Add the fear and greed (both very powerful energies) linked to illegal drugs and you begin to see the power illegal drugs hold over those who focus on them.

- Foods thought to have particular power do indeed affect a person in the way expected if the subconscious believes this.
- Allergies, Immune System diseases, and skin damage are rapidly increasing due to group belief. While it is certainly true we have polluted our water, air, food, and bodies with toxic chemicals, it is also true we have polluted ourselves with the thought that nature is, itself, toxic. It isn't. What we add to nature often is.

Group energy is real. It is an energy and a power that can be blocked, resisted, or plugged into. However, the belief that only certain individuals, groups, places, persons, rituals, or things have power is a defeating thought and a falsehood. The truth is, limitless energy and power are always available through ones own Higher Self, which is actually group energy.

The Higher Self encompasses amd is directly connected with all the personalities you have ever been (as well as will be). Your Higher Self is also directly connected to all Higher Spirit and the Prime Creator. So you are directly connected with all that group (and what a group!) energy. That is your divine power. That is your dragon. That is the dragon others use to usurp you of your energy, life force, and power if any part of you allows them to.

It is VERY important to realize that Higher Selves, Higher Spirit, and the Prime Creator do not "grant" or "deny" requests. Souls have constant and continual access to energy and power with which to manifest their wills. It is humans who close or limit themselves to that limitless, abundant flow of energy and power.

There are many people, groups, and organizations today that teach the importance of positive thought, positive prayer, positive beliefs, positive affirmations, positive thought, positive words, and positive actions. While they are certainly right, many are, in Dr. Harmon's words, "half assed and riding half an ass will not get anyone anywhere." He means, most people fail to recognize **all of the subconscious levels must be focused on the positive and it is extremely difficult to effectively reach the subconscious levels with conscious techniques.** When one believes, subconsciously, one is unworthy of a goal or a goal is impossible to achieve, that goal <u>will not</u> be achieved no matter how deeply, sincerely, or positively one prays, believes, or affirms for it.

In ancient Aramaic, the language the master metaphysician Jesus of Nazareth spoke, to forgive meant to untie. To slay the dragon is to untie oneself of limiting thoughts and beliefs in order to unleash the divine power within. The best means we know of slaying the dragon is to return in the inner levels of the mind to the experiences that keep one tied to the negativity of the past. The best way we know to do this is hypnotic regression therapy.

There are many ways in which to experience a hypnotic regression and many types of regressions. How one experiences a regression is affected by the skill of the hypnotist, trust in the hypnotist, and the ability to by hypnotized. (Like anything else, one gets better at being hypnotized the more one is hypnotized.) Each regression experience is also affected by the mood one is in at the moment, how interested or disinterested one is in a particular past experience, even the comfort of the body during the regression.

Regressions vary from a strictly mental review of an experience or life time to a feeling of actually "being there". A skilled hypnotist can help people be as involved, or uninvolved, as they choose to be, even from moment to moment in the regression.

The goal of regression therapy is to change negative thoughts, beliefs, emotions, behavior, and subconscious programming that block ones ability to achieve specific goals. The important steps of regression therapy are:

1. Recognize the experience that created the negativity.
2. Review what happened in the experience.
3. Realize the negative emotions still attached to the experience.
4. Release the negative energies still attached to the experience.
5. Reach an understanding why the experience happened.
6. Renew ones power in the experience.
7. Reprogram the positive changes.

ALL of these steps are important to permanent transformation and healing. Sometimes all of these steps can be accomplished in one session, sometimes it will take several sessions. (This is particularly true with abuse.)

Many will argue "you can't change the past". That you can't physically change the past is, perhaps, true. That you can emotionally, mentally, and spiritually change the past, which physically changes the present and the future is definitely true.

One woman's Higher Self said to her during a regression to when she was in her mother's womb: "You can do now what you did not do then. You can make a different choice. You can see now you did not make the best choice. But you have learned now what the better choice is. There is great power in knowing it is never too late. You have lost some brain cells from the lack of oxygen through your connection to your mother. You are learning now that the physical is not the only way to achieve this. The adult you can now use your intelligence to heal the you then. You can do this. You need to know it is never too late. If humans could only see how very special and powerful each person is."

Regressions can access various levels of and in the subconscious mind. Generally, the emotional levels frequently disregard (or perhaps do not have) what they consider to be unimportant details. They tend to focus on the emotional matters that concern or interest them. Facts - such as names, dates, etc. - that are not interesting or emotionally involving are often ignored. Questions asking for such information will often be ignored, and should an unskilled hypnotist push for such information, emotional levels are perfectly capable of making up an answer before moving on to matters that interest them. The emotional levels can become confused when similar emotions, events, or the people in them trigger other memories that overlay the first. For accuracy of detail, it is necessary to access the subconscious mind or the Higher Self.

Many people confuse the subconscious levels of mind with the subconscious mind. The subconscious mind is the seat of the physical, mental, emotional, and spiritual programming. It is the seat of the memory banks and the emotions. It carries out the directives of the conscious mind. It controls and regulates the physical, emotional, mental, and spiritual energies.

In hypnosis, the subconscious mind "opens the door", in a sense, to the memories, emotions, personalities, and other energies that are in the subconscious levels. They are not the subconscious mind itself. This point is confusing even to many hypnotists and therapists. It is, however, an important point to understand when working with the mind. It is equally important to realize that past personalities active in the subconscious levels of mind have conscious wills which actively affect subconscious programming.

Personalities one has had in the past are still parts of oneself. What makes up a personality are the thoughts, beliefs, emotions, memories, and behavior that create an identity that is separate from the whole. The personality you had at five years old, for instance, is a different personality than what you have today. Your five year old personality is not gone,. It still exists - as long as your spirit exists - in the subconscious levels of your mind. When you have a regression to something that happened when you were five years old, as much or as little of the five year old personality you were will come forward as you consciously allow to come forward. This is true for all the inner age personalities and past life personalities you have. It is also true for the Higher Self, a personality in the superconscious levels of mind.

In this sense, everyone can be said to have multiple personalities. In addition to the personalities one has lived, there are frequently personalities one has created for oneself. For instance, most people have created a "parent" personality modeled on their own parents. This is the personality that "pops up" to tell you, inwardly, you "should" or "shouldn't" do something. It's also the one many adults have experienced when dealing with young people who push them past their limits. The "inner parent" suddenly takes over and the adult finds him or her self saying or doing exactly what their own parents did when "pushed". (Frequently, its even something that person vowed he or she would never do or say when he or she grew up.) Sometimes, the "created" personality is a helper, like an imaginary friend, who comforts and can take over for the main personality when needed. Dr. Harmon calls these types of personalities I.M.P.S. for Instantly Manifested Personality Substitutes. They are a type of sub-personality, meaning they exist in the subconscious levels of mind and are brought forward only when needed.

I.M.P.S. are not always people. Dr. Harmon worked with a client named Sophie, whose horse, a personality she had created as a child, emerged under hypnosis. Sophie had been sexually abused as a child. As the molest would begin, she would fantasize about a great beautiful horse coming to her rescue. All through the molest, she would ride her horse far, far away.

One day, in the school yard, a bully pushed her down. Suddenly, Sophie became her horse. "Neighing" and "rearing back" she so startled the bully that he ran away. This delighted the other girls and soon Sophie led a herd of "girl horses" who would chase any boy that teased or threatened any of them.

The day came when the bully was caught and the "horses" trampled him. Nothing was hurt besides his dignity, but the girls were pulled into the office, still neighing and being horses. They were firmly reprimanded and ordered to stop being horses. The "herd" complied, returning to their little girl selves, but Sophie's horse remained. A school counselor was called and Sophie's molest was finally discovered. So Sophie's Horse did finally manage to rescue her little girl self.

Sub-personalities are a "problem" when the will of a sub-personality subverts the will of the main personality or is focused on a negative thought, belief, behavior, or emotion. In general, our sub-personalities are the parts that make us whole. We need them. It is important to help each part of ourselves feel loved, accepted, respected, secure, and joyful if we are to feel completely loved, accepted, respected, secure, and joyful.

Multiple Personality Disorder is an aberration of the norm. It indicates a sub-personality that can take over control in ways that are unacceptable or detrimental to the main personality. It can be quite prevalent in survivors of abuse and these personalities should only be worked with by those who are specially trained and qualified to do so. (Note to those who do work with this: You will read about spirit attachments in Chapter Seven. These are a type of sub-personality that also exist in some people's subconscious levels. However, they are separate beings, neither a part of or created by the "main" personality, and to attempt to "integrate" them can do more harm than good.)

~ * ~

The term unconscious means unknowing or perceiving; not aware; not possessing mind or consciousness; not marked by conscious thought, sensation or feeling. None of these terms describe the subconscious mind or the subconscious levels; far from it! The subconscious mind is always aware, even in sleep and coma states, and the subconscious levels contain personalities with conscious thought, sensations, and feelings. We suggest the term "unconscious mind" be dropped entirely and the term "unconscious" used to refer to not being consciously aware; as in coma states, certain stages of sleep, and when those who choose to be are not consciously aware in hypnosis.

People are as "conscious" or "unconscious" in hypnosis as they are interested in what is being said, no matter what level of hypnosis they are in. People can be "unconscious" in light levels of hypnosis and "conscious" in the deepest levels of hypnosis. Most people drift in and out of conscious awareness in "straight hypnosis", once they trust both the process and the hypnotist. ("Straight" hypnosis is when the hypnotist is doing all of the talking.) It's easy to trust the process once one recognizes that the subconscious mind is always aware in hypnosis and will alert the conscious mind should anything be said or done which is alarming or unacceptable to its programming. Actually, hypnosis is a super aware state as all the senses are heightened., even to hearing a pin drop in the next room. Most people choose to let normal and safe sounds fade into the background. Any disturbing sound would be noticed immediately.

There is a very well known (among hypnotists) research study of a hypnosis subject who was in the Eisdale State, which is the deepest, coma like, level of hypnosis. One of the researchers shouted to the subject to get up and leave as there was a fire in the building. The man just lay there, leading the researchers to conclude that hypnosis was unsafe as the subject had made no move to save himself. The subject, however, after he'd been brought out of hypnosis, said that he had heard the shout, but was aware no one in the room had left the room. Nor could he hear anyone else in the building walking in the hall and he didn't smell any smoke. He'd concluded it was just a test, and as he was feeling so euphoric, he hadn't wanted to move. (The Eisdale State is noted for its sense of euphoria.)

The next day the researchers tried their test with another subject; only this time, they burned a small piece of paper in a waste container and all left the room. To their amazement, the hypnosis subject got up, left the room and the building, and when he got far enough away from the building, laid down on the grass, and went right back into the Eisdale State. When asked why he had done that, he replied, "It felt so good, I wanted to get back to it as soon as I was safe."

Another illustration, personally amusing to us, was a class in self-hypnosis that Pamela was teaching on the Big Island of Hawaii. The first day, she led the group into a hypnotic state. One woman resisted the hypnosis, fidgeting around nervously. Afterwards, the woman remarked she'd been very disappointed, but not surprised, that she 'couldn't be hypnotized'. The second day, Pamela repeated the group hypnosis. She noted this same woman had entered a very deep state and thought to herself, "Oh good,

she's not afraid any more." As Pamela guided the group back to social
awareness, this woman remained deep in hypnosis. Walking over to her,
Pamela repeated the instructions to return to social awareness. Still the
woman ignored her. Finally, Pamela leaned down, placed her hand on the
woman's shoulder and said to her softly, "If you'd like to experience what
you're experiencing again, you'll take a deep breath, clear your eyes, and
open them to be fully alert now." The woman did as instructed, but
complained the experience had deeply frightened her as she had not been
able to 'come out of it' until Pamela 'gave her back control' of her mind.
"Yet yesterday," Pamela pointed out, laughing, "I couldn't even 'get' you
to relax. Are you telling me that in 24 hours I have so improved as a
hypnotist, I could finally 'get you' hypnotized and in my control?"

"Oh, I see," the woman said thoughtfully. "I heard you tell the group
to open their eyes, but I didn't want to, I was feeling so good. I knew you
walked over and stood in front of me, but I really wanted you to walk away
and ignore me, so I could keep feeling those feelings. Then, when you hinted
I wouldn't ever feel them again if I didn't comply, I decided you might be
right, so I opened my eyes. You didn't make me do that, I chose to do
it myself. I was in charge the whole time!"

Exactly.

As Dave Elman, the noted medical hypnotist who first taught Dr.
Harmon hypnosis, wrote: "The phenomena of hypnosis is real. It feels
very pleasant, often euphoric. It's an altered state of consciousness where
change can be readily produced, lost memories found, body changes
triggered, healing induced or accelerated, self-awareness elicited, and dreams
recalled and interpreted. There is a built in protection that allows anyone
to refuse any suggestion given if one wishes to do so." We would add to
this that it is also a state where long buried emotions can be released,
understanding gained, past lives relived, and higher spiritual guidance
received.

Most people are consciously aware in hypnosis when they, themselves,
are speaking as most people are interested in and curious about what they
have to say. As conscious awareness of ones past is the reason one does
a regression, people should want to be consciously aware in a hypnotic
regression. The purpose of hypnosis is not to lose consciousness, it is to
gain consciousness of all of ones levels of being and knowledge. (When a

person is not consciously aware during a hypnotic regression we suggest listening to a tape of the regression in order to gain conscious understanding of the information and knowledge brought forward in the regression.)

NMR is extremely useful to past life work. Using it, one can find all the data of a past life; such as whether one was male or female, the years of birth and death, where one lived and traveled in that life, who in that life is in the present life, how one lived and died. Finding this information prior to the hypnosis not only focuses the subconscious on where to go and thus gets it there sooner; it allows the questioning mind to relax sufficiently for the experience to happen.

NMR saves hours of hypnosis work We find people are so relieved to know that NMR can be used after hypnosis to discern their "truths" from their "fantasies" that they go even deeper in the hypnosis. (Understanding "fantasy" can be as transforming as "truth" helps clients to be non-judgmental about this.)

Hypnosis can access any event in ones past; whether it happened yesterday or a millions years ago. Regressions can be done to past lives, past deaths, the spirit state between lives, conception, the womb, birth; infancy and up. Usually regression therapy is done because someone has a problem or dysfunction today that has its roots in the past.

A man called one day saying he had difficulty beginning and finishing projects. He said this caused him extreme stress and tension, both personally and professionally. Pamela asked him if he'd been born by cesarean section. After a short pause, he said, "Yes, how did you know?" Next she asked if he had a fear of falling. After a longer pause, he said, "Are you psychic." Pamela laughed and explained people born by cesarean section frequently have difficulties setting goals, beginning projects, finishing projects, and a fear of falling. She suggested he come for a consultation to learn more.

Amazed to find in his consultation that his birth could have such an effect on the rest of his life, Phil, was eager to do a birth regression, but feared he could not "be hypnotized deeply enough to go back that far".   Like Phil, most people believe the further back you go in a regression the deeper you have to be hypnotized. This is as great a fallacy as the belief deep hypnosis means to be unconscious. Regressions can be done in light, medium, or deep hypnosis.

Pamela suggested that Phil have two sessions; the first to practice hypnosis by learning self-hypnosis and the second to do the regression. Phil agreed and a self-hypnosis tape was made for Phil in that session for him to practice with at home. When Phil returned for his second session the next week, he remarked, "You know, this hypnosis stuff is great. Just listening to the tape every night has eliminated the pain in my neck and shoulders, even though you didn't say anything about that on the tape. Relaxing deeply like that takes away stress and tension. I even sleep better now."

"Great. Let's see how relaxed you can get with me staring at you," Pamela teased. "Do you like to start with your eyes open or closed?"

Phil grinned. "Isn't it great? I've only been here once and already I know what it takes to hypnotize me! Eyes closed and raised as high as I can to begin, just like you taught me."

"Excellent," Pamela congratulated him, "now breathe deeply and listen to my voice; you don't even have to focus on my words. If you become aware of me asking for a response, just let yourself speak whatever thought comes into your mind. You can analyze what you said later. You have a tape to help you recall everything exactly. Right now, your wonderful analytical mind wants to know what the subconscious knows. It can know that best by allowing itself to drift into the comfortable security and serenity of your own heart beat, as your chest rises and falls as you breathe. That's good."

Phil was not only an analytical type, he was very nervous about this regression, which is why Pamela wisely suggested two sessions and made a tape for him to become comfortable with her and with hypnosis. Thanks to careful preparation, Phil - who would normally be considered a "difficult" subject - was "in the womb" in less than four minutes. "Be there now, just as you are ready to be born," Pamela instructed Phil. "Tell me what is happening."

"I can't move! I can't move! Something's wrong!" Phil began whimpering. "I can't feel anything. Help! Help!" Pamela asked the baby to go inside its mind and ask why its body couldn't move. "I see," the baby said, calming down, "it's what they are giving to my mother to numb her. It's coming into me now, I can't move."

There is always knowledge from the Higher Self available at the inner levels of the mind. The soul tends to "forget" this; especially when it is focused on emotional feelings or physical sensations. The hypnotist helps the soul "remember" to call on its inner knowledge.

"Tell me what's happening to you now, baby," Pamela continued.

"I don't know! I don't know!" the baby cried, shifting back to its emotional and physical focus again. " I'm going to fall! I'm going to fall!"

"Look around you carefully, baby, and tell me where you are," Pamela instructed.

"I'm high up in the doctor's hands, but I can't feel his hands. I only see the floor and I'm afraid I'm going to fall because I don't feel anything under me. Oh, now the doctor put me down. I'm on something cold and I'm shivering. I don't like it here," the baby whimpers.

"Do you tell anyone you are cold?" Pamela asks.

"I cry, but they don't understand me," the baby cries sadly.

The soul, in its spirit consciousness, is more advanced than the body/ brain into which it is born. While the brains of babies, infants, small children, and animals are not capable of advanced verbal communication, their minds are capable of advanced mental communication. Adults have, sadly, forgotten this.

"Where is my mother? I want my mother. Oh no, oh no", the baby begins to weep piteously.

"What is happening now?" Pamela asks.

"Some one is taking me away. It's not my mother. My mother doesn't want me. I don't know what's happening. Oh, I'm in a box. There's other babies here. Their mothers don't want them either. We all cry."

The emotional mind is not the reasoning mind; it is the perceiving, feeling mind and its feelings can cause it to make mistakes in its perceptions. It is the "healing" or "correcting" of these perceptions that regression therapy seeks to achieve.

Phil and Pamela went back over his birth. This time Phil used his "divine power" to create reality and created a different birth; the one his mind, body, and soul needed to complete their connection. The journey through the birth canal is a difficult challenge. To succeed in this task builds confidence and faith in ones self. To fail this challenge creates internal programming that says one cannot succeed; that one is a failure.

Procrastination and the inability to complete projects are common with clients who have had cesarean births. The internal programming, in addition to failure, is 'what's the use of planning if someone or something can step in and take things over at any moment'. Cesarean births can also lead to learning disabilities like dyslexia, attention deficit disorder, and other difficulties in the brain/body connection. So crucial is the journey through the birth canal to the body and brain that "old time" ob/gyn doctors, nurses, and midwives would use the palms of their hands on cesarean newborns (after the anesthesia in their systems had worn off) to press against their heads and bodies to duplicate the journey through the birth canal. Modern medicine would do well to return to this practice as c-sections become (sadly) more prevalent.

The first breath is a crucial part of birth, for it tells the brain, the body, and the subconscious the human is "ALIVE!" It "sets up" the brain, body, and mind connection that affects the whole rhythm of life. When the first breath is "off" (due to drugs or other birth trauma) that rhythm is interrupted.

We often find clients who suffered a lack of oxygen in the womb or at birth to have learning disorders, prematurely thinning hair or balding, and what is referred to as a "walking zombie" syndrome. This is a post traumatic anxiety state present with people who have had an experience that has falsely convinced the brain it has died. The addiction to the "high" of alcohol, drugs, tobacco, orgasm, exercise, thrill seeking and other energy "highs" can be a subconscious attempt to counteract a "walking zombie" anxiety state.

Interestingly, we find many smokers are actually more addicted to the deep breathing they do when taking long drags than they are to the substance they inhale. The deep breath triggers the thrilling "high" of the subconscious thought: "I'm alive!" Consciously taking several deep breathing breaks throughout the day is an easy way to "kick the habit" with these types of smokers. (If there are other subconscious or conscious motivations for smoking, however, these will need to be dealt with as well in order for it to be "easy" to let go of the habit and desire.)

For more information on the importance of birth and the first breath, read Dr. Fulford's Touch of Life, listed in the book list at the back of this book. Dr. Fulford also outlines exercises in his book for correcting the imbalances caused by birth trauma. Another book listed in our book list is one on "Brain Gym" another powerful technique for correcting brain/body imbalances.

Many hypnotic techniques are very powerful in correcting brain/body imbalances and hypnosis regression therapy to trauma that has blocked the brain/body/mind connection, or disconnected them, can heal those connections.

NLP (Neuro Linguistic Programming) and EMDR (Eye Movement Desensitization and Reprocessing) are two techniques that either involve hypnosis or lead to hypnosis. They, too, are powerful techniques for reprogramming the mind, body, brain connections.

Like regression therapy, EMDR is a powerful tool for healing post traumatic disorders, anxieties, and phobias. (We have included a book by its originator in the book list. If you go to a therapist that uses EMDR, make certain that therapist is either EMDR certified OR is a professional hypnotherapist that thoroughly understands EMDR and regression states.)

Phil called two months after he had been "born again" to report he was starting and finishing projects in a timely manner at both work and home. He had also tested his fear of falling, he reported, with a roller coaster and ferris wheel ride, both of which had terrified him previously. "It worked," he said. "I was fine. I'm still amazed my birth affected me so strongly, but I can't argue with success."

We know alot about the experiences of the soul as so many souls have shared with us their experiences. For instance, we know:

- The Higher Self chooses the "gene pool" the soul will have access to in a particular life experience. The Higher Self further manipulates and influences the genes chosen during conception and gestation. Some souls participate in and are aware of this.

- Some souls pay attention to their parents copulation during conception and some souls are not interested. One woman said her parents had "pretty, bright colored lights floating all around them" at her conception. A man described his father's forced sex with his mother on the night of his conception. His soul vowed right then never to be sexually forceful or aggressive in any way. (He came to therapy because his wife complained his sexual passivity was wrecking their marriage.) Another woman described, in vivid detail, the rape of her mother by her mother's father at her conception. She went on to describe how her mother had sex with her boyfriend the next night. Her mother had sought out that coupling on a conscious and subconscious level. Consciously, she had needed the emotional support and comfort after her traumatic rape.

Subconsciously, she'd been driven to find a more "acceptable" father for the child she already knew, subconsciously, she'd conceived. (Interestingly, the woman's Higher Self said the impregnation by the grandfather had been unplanned, but could be used for its purposes, and that it was "incorporating genes from the chosen father with the genes already received from the grandfather in order to have genetic programming from both men. This is possible to do within a certain time span," the Higher Self added, "though your scientists haven't discovered it yet.") The woman was very shaken after her regression. "I didn't expect this," she said, "but it certainly explains why my mother was always so angry and bitter and depressed. She'd had such dreams for her life. She'd loved my father, but wanted to pursue her dreams before marriage. Her own father impregnating her, which forced her marriage and ended her dreams! My poor mother. My poor father."

- Babies in the womb are aware, if they are awake, of their parents' sexual copulations. Violent and aggressive copulation feels very abusive to the babe within. One man described his father's constant "banging away" at his mother as "he keeps hitting me on the head with something. He's trying to hurt me just like he's hurting her. I hate him." Another man felt very soothed whenever his parents had sex and would fall happily asleep with the gentle, rhythmic movements of their bodies.

- After birth, babies and young children who are sexually stimulated by their parents or others have a difficult time with the intense sensations this creates in their little bodies. Babies and children can orgasm, but the orgasm feels very painful as the brain is not yet ready to process this properly. It is amazing how many clients we have had who have discovered their parents and baby-sitters played with their genitals while they were changing their diapers, giving them baths, or trying to quiet or soothe (?!) them. It's truly shocking how many decent people use babies and small children to gratify themselves sexually, rationalizing that the "little ones" won't remember and will enjoy the pleasant sensations. Sexually titillating "little ones" or using them for sexual gratification is abusive. And they do remember.

- Not all souls "enter" the physical body at the same point in time. Some enter at conception, some during gestation, some even wait until after birth. Some say they are "half in and half out" of the body or "go in and out" of the body until the choice is made to "stay" or "stay put". Some souls have told us they "exchanged" with another soul at some point as they didn't need to experience certain parts of gestation or birth and another soul did. (However, we have found it is important for the soul that will have the body to be in the body when the first breath is taken so the mind/body/brain connection is firmly established. A birth regression can accomplish this.)

- Souls frequently try to mentally "impress" the name they wish on the parents they have chosen. Most often, one or both parents "get" the desired name, though we have often found the middle name to be the one the soul was trying to impress on the parents.

- The choice of sexual gender and sexual gender preference is made by the soul while in its spirit state. Though Nature programs all bodies to be heterosexual for the propagation of the species, the genes can be manipulated by the spirit during gestation to change that sexual preference. This preference can be repressed at any time after birth, but it does not go away. (Abuse by a particular gender often programs a sexual preference and/or distaste for that gender. This can be corrected.) In general, it is more emotionally fulfilling and physically gratifying to follow the sexual preferences chosen from the spirit state. (NMR with the Higher Self can determine what that choice was.) Multiple personality disorder - and spirit attachments - can complicate sexual identity and preferences. They also can interfere with the NMR unless very precise wording is used and careful attention is paid to polarity.

- Souls choose one or both parents, though this choice is often made from the Higher Self level. The choice of parent(s) is usually to finish up unfinished business from one or more past lives and/or to teach or learn (or both) something with one or both parents. Sometimes a bond with one or both parents is meant to be lifelong and sometimes it is not.

- At times, the soul can only get to the chosen parent(s) through adoption. The soul may "forget" this at the emotional level of mind and feel rejected and betrayed by the birth parent(s). This can greatly complicate ones whole life experience. Regression therapy helps a soul to remember why he or she chose adoption, which is very healing.

- Souls are sometimes eager to enter human consciousness, sometimes extremely reluctant, and sometimes "somewhere in between". A great deal of planning for the life experience is done at the Higher Self level and, at times, the soul will regret the choices it made at this level. (As Pamela says, "things look at lot easier from there than they feel living them here.")

- While a soul can choose to leave at any time, actively taking ones own life is deeply regretted by souls who have done so. The Higher Self keeps the life force present in the body until the soul has learned and taught all it has come to teach and learn. Sometimes that teaching and learning involves giving other souls the opportunity to care for the welfare of another. Sometimes it involves great pain. Souls that escape the opportunity to learn what the pain had to teach them (or others) tell us they are very sorry they gave up that opportunity and that they plan to meet it again.

- Abusers and the abused make a kind of "soul agreement" at the spirit levels to play these roles with one another. How long it will take their souls to move out of this agreement is up to them. Sometimes souls will switch back and forth between the abused and the abuser roles in several lifetimes as each attempts to "get even" with the other. Realizing this helps abusers to forgive themselves and the abused to forgive their abusers, which ends the cycle of abuse. HOWEVER, true forgiveness can never be reached as long as anger, sadness, guilt, shame and other pain remains from the abuse. All subconscious levels must be healed before true forgiveness can be reached and the cycle ended. Expressing and releasing anger at ones abuser(s) in the subconscious levels is a very important part of this process. This is difficult for many loving and spiritual people to do, but our experience shows it is necessary and important if the cycle of abuse is to end.

- Most abusers have themselves been victims of abuse in this life or another. Helping abusers to recognize and deal with their own abuse often is the only way they can feel remorse for their victims, release their abuser energies, and heal themselves.

- Some souls choose to experience the trauma and rejection of abortion. Other souls, when the body they are in is to be aborted, leave before this happens as they have nothing to learn or gain by the experience. (Master of Spirit has said that the mother's will takes precedence over the will of a soul seeking to use the mother's body for birth.) However, by talking to the cells of women who have had abortions, we know abortion is very hard on the cells. Taking care not to conceive unwanted pregnancies is a very loving act for ones cells. (If you have had an abortion in the past, speaking to your cells and healing them would also be very loving.)

- Woman who are clear, <u>at all levels of mind,</u> that they do not want a pregnancy can spontaneously miscarry if they make their intention to end the pregnancy clear to the soul seeking to enter and that soul leaves. (If there is any doubt in the woman's mind about ending the pregnancy, her body will hold onto the pregnancy, even if the soul leaves, because this is what the body is programmed to do.) The longer a woman waits to make this decision, the more difficult it is for her body to let go of the developing embryo/fetus. We have had great success in speaking with the souls of the unborn, through their mothers, and convincing them to leave when they are not wanted by the mother. (<u>Women's Bodies, Women's Wisdom,</u> by Christiane Northrup, M.D. is listed in our book list. It provides further illustration on the natural phenomena of miscarrying unwanted pregnancies, as well as a great deal of other information for women and those who love them.)

- Babies who are not in the proper position for birth (such as breech babies) or who are over due for birth are frequently fearful of being born. We have had great success in speaking with these babies (again, through the mothers) and helping them to feel welcome and safe enough to be born, and in the proper position. Even "straight hypnosis" helps babies to shift themselves from the breech position. In a study at the University of Vermont College of Medicine, Lewis E. Mehl-Madrona, M.D., Ph.D, hypnotized 100 women between 37 and 40 weeks of pregnancy whose babies were in the breech position. He suggested relaxing the tension in the uterine muscles that may have been preventing the baby's head from settling into the pelvis. Of the 100 babies in the hypnosis group 81 babies converted to the head-down position by the time of birth; in a control group of 100 breech-position babies whose mothers were not hypnotized, just 48 changed position before birth.

- <u>**Babies in the womb and their cells do not like sonograms which are very damaging to the brain and the nervous system!**</u> We have found in talking to babies in the womb that sonograms are very painful and traumatic to them. Several Higher Selves (and Masters of Light and Spirit) have verified the damage done by this. One Higher Self said, "though your modern medicine believes, in all good faith, that it is helpful, it will eventually find how damaging this is to the brain. It is the beginning, they will find, of the frying of the brain." Dr. Willix, in his 1994 issue of Health For Life, reports: "Studies show ultrasounds produce cell damage. A 1984 study showed higher dyslexia among children exposed to ultrasound in the womb. The FDA, the American Medical Association, and the American College of Obstetrics and Gynecology ALL say pregnant women should not receive routine sonograms, but doctors do them anyway. And we all pay for it, over one billion dollars a year, according to The Wall Street Journal. It's a sorry waste of money and a threat to health".

- The baby in the womb is very tuned into the mother and the father and can experience a great deal of rejection and hurt when it perceives it is not wanted, welcomed, or is of the "wrong" gender. (even thoughts or conversations such as "How can I afford this baby?" or "We can't have a baby now!" or "I hope it is a boy (or a girl)" can be perceived by the baby to be a personal rejection. This can negatively impact ones whole life until the "inner baby" is reassured, loved, and welcomed.

- Divorce and adoption can also trigger strong programs of rejection. Babies and children believe, inwardly, that if they had been "better", "brighter", or "perfect", their parent who left would not have gone and the parents would not have been divorced. They feel great guilt, believing subconsciously they were they cause of the divorce (Healing of these "inner children" is important.)

- People receive alot of subconscious programming about money in their childhood, often starting from the womb. People who have difficulties making or holding onto money would do well to investigate their subconscious programming and heal any negative thoughts their "inner children" are holding onto. (Children whose parents fight about money have a lot of negative programming in regards to money.) There are also many "generic" subconscious programs about money from often repeated phrases used by many. Some of these are: "Money is hard to get", "You have to work hard for your money", "Money doesn't buy happiness", "The rich get richer and the poor get poorer", "The rich are greedy", "Money is all that matters" "Men make more money than women".

- Experiences in past lives with money can affect the present life finances. One woman, as she left her body in a past life where she had been extremely wealthy and extremely sheltered because of that wealth, vowed, "I will never be rich again."

- Starvation in a previous life can be a cause of overweight, obesity, or a fixation with food. Interestingly, we have found many souls in body today who died during World War II. Many of these were in concentration camps and have difficulties with weight and food today. Healing of the fears generated by starvation and reprogramming cells that hold onto fat in the body is very important.

~ * ~

Subconscious programming is what the subconscious mind has accepted as the thoughts, beliefs, emotions, and behavior that are to take precedence over all other directives from the conscious mind. This programming (sometimes called the automatic programming) is fiercely protected by the subconscious mind. (The autonomic nervous system of your body is part of the automatic programming.)

The subconscious programming of the personality has been largely "set" by the time children are five to six years old. Naturally, this programming affects the way children relate to and perceive the world which affects their experiences, which usually validates and reinforces their subconscious programming.

It is also true that people are as complex as their minds and as evolved as their consciousness. People react to similar experiences in different ways, even when they are in the womb. People do not stop growing - physically, mentally, emotionally, or spiritually - at five or six years of age. Nevertheless, early programming is very powerful and continues to affect humans throughout their lives. Changing negative programming is an important part of the soul's progress.

People programmed to believe they are not worthy sabotage their own happiness, often to the point of sabotaging their very lives. People programmed to compare themselves with others punish themselves when they don't "measure up", even as they either try to "outdo" others or don't try to do anything at all. People programmed to believe they are powerless become victims to the power of others. This creates anger and fear that causes them to subject those they can control to their power.

People can change their subconscious programs. When energy is withdrawn from a subconscious program, that program gradually fades. Life is about changing old programming. However, it is a process humans have made so complex, they need multiple lives to do it. Hypnosis and regression therapy are methods of quickening that process. It is why Pamela calls our work "soul work" and sometimes calls us "soul doctors". .

People want to believe they can simply will themselves to stop giving energy to their old programmed thoughts, beliefs, emotions, and habits. They want to believe they do not have to address their childhood "stuff", let alone the "stuff" of past lives. Unfortunately, this is often not true. One difficulty is subconscious personalities like the "inner child" are real. At least, they've convinced us they are real. Whether real, imaginary, symbolic, or "psycho-babble", there is no denying their power to feed energy into subconscious programming to which they are attached.

Mary was a college student who was taking some courses from us. Mary had frequent anxiety attacks, particularly in restaurants, and whenever she was feeling, in her words, "ugly and unwanted". She also could not leave town, unless she was with her parents. She would frequently try to drive (with a friend along) to L. A., which would always result in a major anxiety attack. She would have to pull off the freeway, spend several minutes using the coping techniques her psychologist had taught her, then have her friend drive her back home. As a result, she attended school at the local community college, even though she'd been accepted to two Universities on the coast.

One day, in class with us, Mary had an attack. Breathing deeply, she announced she had to go straight home, as she'd been taught to do by her psychologist whenever she had an attack. Pamela, aware that anxiety attacks and phobias are triggered by subconscious memories from the past, walked over to Mary and said, "Oh yes, I think you are right It is time to go home. Is your name Mary?"

"Yes," Mary answered in a little girl's voice.

"Good, are you a little girl?" Pamela asked softly. Mary nodded. "Well, little girl," Pamela continued, leaning down to take Mary's hand, "how about we let adult Mary go home now, and you come talk to me. I know a very safe place for a special little girl like you." Pamela led Mary into her office and said, "Here, little girl Mary, you sit right down here in this soft, safe chair and nobody can hurt you." Mary sat down obediently. "How old are you, Mary?" Pamela asked in a quiet voice.

"Three," Mary said, and started to cry.

"That's good, Mary," Pamela said soothingly, "it's good to cry when you're upset. You just keep crying and when you're ready, tell me what's making you so sad." (Stopping emotions is not therapeutic. Part of the healing is to release repressed emotions.) Soon, Mary was telling Pamela about her pre-school teacher who hated her and about the ghost who had pushed her off the Jungle Gym and hurt her.

"Be there now, Mary," Pamela instructed her. "Just close your eyes and be right in the place where the ghost pushed you and the teacher hated you. I'm right there with you, so no one can hurt you. Just tell me what happened now, three year Mary."

"I'm sitting on the top of the Jungle Gym," Mary said. "I'm swinging my legs and looking down."

"What are you thinking?" Pamela asked.

"What it would feel like if I fell. Maybe I would fly. But I am afraid I would hurt myself if I couldn't fly."

"I see, what happens next, Mary?"

"I keep looking at the ground and then the ghost pushes me!" Mary says and starts crying again. "I hurt myself real bad."

"How do you know it was a ghost, Mary?"

"There isn't anybody there when I feel somebody push me. So it must be a ghost. I'm not going there anymore."

"I don't blame you, Mary. I wouldn't go there either. What happens next?"

"My teacher runs over to me and yells at me. She hates me."

When Pamela asked Mary to tell her what the teacher is yelling, Mary said, 'Oh no! No, no, how terrible! Get away from her! Don't look at her! Oh no, an ugly one. I'll stop this right now! Call her mother to come get her!"

"What is she talking about Mary?" Pamela asked.

"She's talking about me. She thinks I'm terrible and ugly. She tells the other kids to get away from me and not look at me. She wants to stop me from being here. So my mommy comes and takes me away."

"I see. Well, Mary, you did very well telling me what happened. Now I want you to do something else for me. Something very fun. I want you to go back to when you were sitting on top of the Jungle Gym, but this time I want you to be out of your body, protecting it, so it doesn't fall down. Can you do that?"

"Yes, I can. But the ghost might get me."

"No, you'll be invisible when you're out of your body. Then you and I can sneak up on the ghost!"

"Okay," said Mary dubiously. "But you go first." Pamela managed not to laugh and promised to go first. Soon, Mary was sitting back up the Jungle Gym. "There, I'm out of my body, looking at it," Mary said after a moment.

"Good. Do you see the ghost?"

"No," Mary said slowly, her eye balls moving back and forth beneath the lids. "I don't see anything but me sitting there."

"So what makes you fall, Mary?" Pamela asked. Mary frowned, as Pamela continued softly, "I bet your inside mind knows, Mary. Go talk to your inside mind and ask it why you fell."

"Oh!" Mary exclaimed after a moment, sounding very surprised. "It says I told it to make me fall, so it felled [sic] me."

"Ask your inside mind how you told it, Mary," Pamela directed.

"It says I thoughted [sic] it."

"I see. So there's no ghost here, right Mary?"

"No, only me. I did it myself. Is that why my teacher was mad?"

"Let's go now to when you are on the ground, Mary, after you fell. Watch your teacher, while you listen to what your inside mind tells you when she is yelling. Then tell me what it tells you."

"It says she saw me fall," Mary says slowly, "she is yelling it is terrible 'cause I am hurt. She looks sad and worried. She tells Tommy - he always teases me - to get away from me. I'm bleeding! She tells the kids not to look."

"Why?" asked Pamela.

Mary shrugged. "She says I'm ugly."

"Maybe she means your wound is ugly, Mary," Pamela suggests. "Adults say that sometimes when a hurt is bleeding. They call it an ugly wound."

"Oh, my inside mind says that is what she means. I'm not ugly, my hurt is ugly 'cause I'm bleeding. Oh, good. Look! My teacher is tearing her pretty skirt to wipe the blood off me so she can look at my hurt!"

"Your teacher must like you very much, Mary."

"Yes, yes, she likes me very much. She is happy when I open my eyes. I didn't know that 'cause I didn't look at her face. But she's smiling when I open my eyes. I can see that now. She likes me. She told another teacher to call my Mommy. My Mommy comes and takes me to the Doctor. I don't go back to school again. Mommy said it wasn't safe. Oh. I thought it was because the teacher didn't want me."

Mary, in shock and trauma, had "misread" the events of this day and had created powerful beliefs, at her emotional levels, that she was terrible, ugly, and unwanted by an important adult in her young life. She'd also developed fear of ghosts, which her mother referred to as an "overly active" imagination.

Mary reported to Pamela next week that she hadn't had an anxiety attack all week, which was unusual. She asked to see Pamela for weekly sessions, which her psychologist strongly supported. At Mary's next session, she and Pamela discovered, through NMR, a seven year old who was responsible for Mary not being able to go into restaurants.

In regression, seven year old Mary described anxiously watching an old person nearly choke to death in a restaurant for - to the child's mind - "no reason". The look on the woman's face and the spewing out of her food as she was pounded on her back upset the seven year old terribly. She felt a ghost had come into the woman and tried to kill her. She'd never been able to go into a restaurant again without panicking which would often lead to a major anxiety attack. This had convinced her family she had a "condition". This, of course, convinced the little girl she had a condition, so her anxieties escalated, as did the attacks. At nine years old, her beloved puppy died, which created extreme fear that death, in addition to ghosts, could attack at any moment. The little girl's world felt totally beyond her control. The only time she really felt safe was home with her mommy.

The memories of both the Jungle Gym and the choking woman gradually faded from her CONSCIOUS recall, though not from her subconscious memory. Whenever the subconscious memories were triggered - in restaurants, around old people, and whenever she was too far from her mommy - the little girl in her would relive her trauma. Because adult Mary was not aware of this consciously, she felt, in her words, "crazy" because she would have a panic or an anxiety attack for, in her words, "no reason". She had good reasons. The little girl inside of her was in panic.

Pamela helped Mary's "inner little girl" understand, in regression to the appropriate ages, everything that had happened to her. Understanding brought a release of emotions and changes in her thoughts and beliefs about herself, life, and death. Mary reported, after the third session, that her anxiety attacks were less frequent and much less debilitating. In fact, she said she'd started her coping behavior in a couple of situations that would have normally triggered an attack, not because she felt one coming on; so she wondered if she'd even had one at all.

The day came, only a few weeks after her seventh and last session, when Mary called Pamela to report she had driven, by herself and without anyone with her, to Los Angeles for her brother's wedding. She'd pulled off the freeway where she'd always had an attack before, expecting she would have one and have to turn around. After 30 minutes she decided an attack wasn't coming and had driven the rest of the way "feeling wonderful and free". She'd "felt pretty" (rare for Mary) in her bridesmaid dress, and when people told her she looked pretty, she'd believed them (even rarer). She hadn't had one anxiety attack the whole time, she said, not even in the restaurant the family had gone to for the wedding dinner. Though her family had, she reported giggling, followed her around and watched her in high anxiety waiting for one.

The last time Pamela saw Mary was when she was sitting in a restaurant and a waitress approached the table with a menu in front of her face. The waitress turned out to be Mary. Laughing at Pamela's surprise, she said once she'd realized she was really "cured", she'd taken the job to save enough money for the University, which she'd be attending that fall.

Mary had sat at the top of the Jungle Gym and focused her thoughts on falling. It is true that the top priority of the subconscious mind to the body is to keep the body healthy and alive. It is also the top priority of the subconscious mind to the soul to carry out its directives, even if those directives are bad for the body. The soul takes precedence over the body. Mary's subconscious mind perceived her focused thoughts of falling as a directive to fall, so her subconscious created an energy force field to do just that.

You can feel such an energy force field yourself when standing on the edge of a precipice. As you focus your thoughts on falling, you will begin to feel as though you are being pulled or drawn forward. Or, if you have an extreme fear of falling, you may feel yourself being pushed back, away from the precipice. Either way, you have felt the energy force field of your subconscious mind reacting to your thoughts. All professional hypnotists know that what the subconscious mind is <u>focused</u> on the body will follow, unless the conscious mind stops it. Professional advertisers know this, too.

Mary had felt the energy force field her subconscious had created. Since no one had been near her on the Jungle Gym, her child level emotional mind perceived it as a "ghost" that pushed her. Children are not capable of "good judgment" or "good reason" because their reasoning abilities are limited. The power to reason is the "critical factor" of the conscious mind and that critical factor is not fully functioning in childhood. In fact, it is all but absent until the ages between seven and twelve in most children. These are the ages when the frontal lobes of the brain develop sufficiently for the use of the reasoning mind. (It is interesting to note that the frontal lobes are not <u>fully</u> developed until around age thirty in most adults.)

The subconscious mind thinks, but its thinking is logical and its reasoning abilities limited. It does not reason out what you "mean" by what you think, say, feel, or do. It is very literal. It takes what you think, say, or do literally, and if there is emotional energy or physical energy connected with what you think, say, or do, it beleives it has received a directive. The subconscious acts upon many contradictory directives. (No wonder people frequently find themselves thinking, feeling, speaking, and acting like their own worst enemies.)

A startling illustration of the power of the subconscious mind and how literally it responds to directives is the story of a friend of Dr. Harmon's named Bob. We suspect Bob would want us to share his story, as it teaches a powerful lesson. Bob's doctor says it taught him a thing or two.

A man in his fifties, Bob was very robust and physically active. One day Bob told his brother he was planning a mountain hike to the top of San Jacinto the next weekend. His brother insisted Bob have a physical first, as it would be a strenuous climb, and Bob had not had a physical for some years. To appease his brother, Bob scheduled an appointment for a physical the next day.

After the check-up, Bob's doctor told him he was sending him to a specialist immediately. The specialist, after examining Bob and his tests, told Bob he had advanced cancer of his liver. Stunned, Bob protested he felt great. The specialist told Bob his liver was at only 20% of its normal operating capacity and that the cancer was inoperable and terminal. Bob's death was so imminent, the specialist told him, he was making arrangements for him to enter a hospice that day.

Bob, determined he would die at home and not a hospice, went home and went straight to bed. He family gathered around him, mourning Bob's imminent death. Bob died less than twenty-four hours later. Instead of hiking that week-end, as he'd planned, Bob was buried.

Bob's regular doctor was furious. "If anything demonstrates the power of the mind, this does!" he exclaimed to us. "Bob should be alive right now. That damn specialist telling him he was as good as dead and his family carrying on like he'd already died. That's what killed him! I examined Bob myself. He was healthy in every other respect. His liver was still functioning. There was no toxicity indicating liver shut down. He had weeks to live, possibly months. Hell, who knows, if Bob's mind could fix so strongly on a doctor's opinion like that, I might have convinced him he could live for years." Or, we might add, he might have convinced Bob's subconscious mind to heal his liver just as we have watched other people do.

A medical specialist was the ultimate authority to Bob's mind and that specialist's actions so shocked Bob, he instantly focused on death, which convinced his subconscious mind to shut down the body processes. Belief and results are directly linked. There is no equivocation in this. If there are doubts in the conscious or subconscious mind, the results will be mixed. If all levels of mind are convinced of something, that "something" will manifest.

To understand just how profoundly medical professionals can affect your body through your mind, read about the Placebo and Nocebo effects in Dr. Deepak Chopra's breakthrough book, Quantum Healing, Exploring The Frontiers of Mind/Body Medicine. Actually, we strongly recommend you read the whole book. Even if you've already read it, we recommend you read it again, but this time with the added recognition that thought, belief, emotion, and behavior can be subconscious as well as conscious.

People who have grown up with abuse (physical, mental, emotional, spiritual, sexual, or verbal) often have difficulty achieving "quick" or "easy" results with any kind of technique, therapy or counseling, whether spiritual or temporal. Their "inner children" need very careful, professional, and skilled help in learning to trust themselves and others before they will let go of negative thoughts, emotions, and behavior created by their abuse.

Clients sometimes ask us how they can be certain we aren't "suggesting" all of this "complicated inner stuff" in order to get more sessions from them and, thus, more money. Pamela always laughs and says: "It's not like we don't see results with our clients, because we do; sometimes instantaneous and spectacular results. So here is my wish. I wish everyone who comes to our offices would cure, heal, fix, and transform themselves in one session. Imagine how the word would spread! We could charge hundreds, even thousands, of dollars for one session and everyone would be rich, slim, healthy, youthful, and happy. Since each one of these goals have been accomplished by some clients with the techniques we use, why can't everyone accomplish them using the same techniques? Why does it take some so much longer than it takes others? Believe me, if I could, I'd make every client we see accomplish their goals in one session, without all the complicated stuff."

Dr. Harmon is more apt to answer gently: "You can accomplish what you came to do in an instant, and you certainly don't need anyone else in order to do it. All we are here for is to help you uncover and change what stands in your way of doing just that. How long it takes and how complicated it becomes is up to you and your inner levels."

We have many clients who testify that no matter how long it took them, it was worth it. One woman reported she'd recently attended a meeting and a colleague had commented on how happy she looked and asked what she'd been doing to get that way. This woman said to her colleague: "Look at me! I'm wearing a size 18! I feel better than I've felt in my life! What I did was a year of intense inner therapy." This client had come to therapy to deal with sexual abuse throughout her childhood. A size 26 when she began her therapy, her weight had steadily diminished over the course of her healing work with sexual abuse.

We watched another abuse client who'd survived extensive and extreme torture and abuse blossom before our eyes over her two years of one session a week with Pamela and one session a week with Dr. Harmon. This client is the one with whom Pamela first began using the term "Dragon Slayer" to honor her inner children and teens for their courage in surviving and healing. Naturally filled with anger at her abusers, this woman's Higher Self response to her query "How can I forgive them?" was:

"Is the log mad at the carver who carves it into a beautiful totem pole? Is the rock mad at the sculptor who shapes it into a beautiful sculpture? Is the canvas mad at the painter who creates on it a beautiful painting? The same was done for you, but with your permission. Before entering this life you asked for those who know how to mold and form a child using the dark tools. You asked people of Light to do things that they, in their spirit form, did not want to do. You walked up to the Dark, touched it, walked through it, and walked away healed. You learned many things in this life, and I ask you again, how can you fault the teachers who taught by your guidelines? This is the final step in your healing; for you and your inner children to realize you always had control over your life. You directed everything. Now you know and you can help others. You know what it feels like to be hurt, how it feels to walk through the fire, how it feels to be surrounded by the fire. Teach others how to keep their light strong and not cover up the light within them. Teach them how to be dragon slayers; how to awaken the dragon within; how to comfort and heal the inner child; how to find joy in every situation; how to grow flowers in infertile soil because the plants are watered with love and hope and joy; and how to make infertile soil fertile soil."

As therapists, we must point out that, as the Higher Self above indicated, forgiveness is the final step, not the first, in healing deep inner pain.

Another client, after finishing his healing work, wrote to Dr. Harmon, his therapist,: "I used to be a very angry person. I would cut anybody's throat to get ahead. I used to enjoy fist fighting. After I fought, a peace would come over me. As far as nature goes, beautiful flowers, trees, etc., were no big deal to me. If it was in my path, it paid the price. After four sessions of regression to a past life, I noticed more color in the mountains and even found myself being careful when walking through the desert not to step on the wild flowers. My tolerance for other people is very high now. NOTHING ruffles my feathers. I also found out why I hated to be with people and always could not wait to get as far away from them as possible. I'd been a flier, an English guy, in a past life and my plane crash landed on April 7th, 1923. Natives of the place where I crashed captured me and kept me in a wooden cage. They would carry me in the cage to the river to bathe. They never let me out. They left me alone, never poked sticks or anything, but they would watch me and laugh at me. They fed me some kind of nut all the time. It was small, less than one inch, and heavy, maybe five grams. It had kind of a earth clay color and a kind of hairy, rough texture and it was very sour tasting, but seemed to water your mouth. It made me feel like the size of my cage didn't matter and I wasn't so cramped. It made me dizzy, too, and I would forget things about myself and where I came from. I think I got addicted to that feeling. That addiction carried over into this life. I know I began my drug use early in this life. I was always looking for a more powerful drug. I spent more money on drugs than some people spend on home furnishings, or even a car. Countless times I told myself I could quit, but that thought wouldn't last long. Now I know drugs will NEVER, NEVER play a part in my life again. I also enjoy being with positive people now. I feel my friends enjoy being with me and when they leave my presence, I think they might even feel uplifted. I really enjoy making folks smile now."

As our clients so beautifully demonstrate, there is great truth in the words of William James who wrote: "The greatest revolution of our generation is the discovery that human beings, by changing the inner attitudes of their mind, can change the outer aspects of their lives."

Therapy can be disruptive, but this disruption is temporary. Clients working on feeling emotions, instead of repressing them, often find themselves uncertain as to the benefit as they begin to feel "bad" feelings. Soon, however, they realize that recognizing the "bad" feelings helps to release them and replace them with the "good" feelings they could never feel before. Relationships disrupted by the purging of the past frequently re-bound with greater intimacy and bonding than previously experienced. During the course of therapy, as clients release negative energies from their minds, spirits, and bodies, they will sometimes experience nausea, upset tummies, dry heaves, throwing up, diarrhea, increased urination, sweating, and shakes - among other purging symptoms - either before, during, or after a session. (We've never had anyone actually throw up in the chair, though clients have had the dry heaves during a session.)

Physical phenomena during regressions is a dramatic example of the power of thought. For example, clients have "paled" and even "turned blue" in regressions where they have "died" or "lost their breath". Clients have had rashes and marks appear on their skin. Stutterers have stopped stuttering in regressions and non-stutterers have begun stuttering during a regression.

Of course, ridding oneself of physical symptoms is often the reason for a regression. One woman came to her session saying, "I can't control my bowel movements in the shower or tub. Why?" The answer was her "inner infant" had heard her say to a friend that her therapy was all finished. The "inner infant" disagreed. After working with the inner infant (it took only one session), normal control of her bowels returned.

One day, Pamela, shortly before her own scheduled therapy session with Dr. Harmon suddenly became blind in one eye. Panicked, she rushed into his office. "I can't see out of my left eye!" she cried. As she sat down in the therapy chair, she abruptly realized she could see only the right side of his body out of her right eye. The left side of his body was missing, as was the left side of everything else she looked at. As she was explaining this to Dr. Harmon, she began to see wavy lines out of her left eye. Stunned, she exclaimed a moment later: "The wavy lines are becoming hieroglyphics! Egyptian hieroglyphics, like you see on pyramids! Oh my God, they're so clear! What is happening?" Dr. Harmon gently asked her to close her eyes. Soon, she was deep in a regression as a Pharaoh of Egypt.

The Pharaoh described vividly his poisoning by a rare snake venom that left him in a catatonic and comatose state the royal physicians mistook for death. Locked within his paralyzed body and unable to alert anyone he was still alive, the Pharaoh was prepared for embalming. Throughout the process he could see, out of his left eye, his High Priest, whose sly and knowing look told the Pharaoh he had been the one to poison him and he knew the suffering he was experiencing. As the Pharaoh, Pamela described a searing pain and pressure in her nose and head at the moment of death. (Though she was not aware of it at the time of the regression, during the embalming process, the brain is sucked out of the nose.) The last sight the Pharaoh saw before his death was the sight, in his left eye, of the High Priest enjoying his suffering.

Pamela had scheduled this session with Dr. Harmon to find the cause of a muscle twitch under her left eye that had begun after she developed distrust for a long-time friend of Dr. Harmon's. Pamela admired and liked this woman and felt her to be important to the work of Spirit, so she sought to understand, and hopefully heal, her distrust of her. She also wanted to be rid of the muscle twitch.

After the past life regression to the Pharaoh, Pamela's vision returned to normal and the muscle twitch under the left eye never returned. NMR, done after the session, indicated the High Priest in that life had been the friend of Dr. Harmon's that Pamela distrusted. The regression had healed that past life, NMR indicated, but there was another life, an ancient one, with that person that also needed healing. After a regression to that past life, Pamela felt her inner animosity toward the woman end. (Although she added she wanted the woman to do her own regressions to those lives before she'd trust her completely.)

We have another dear friend who is an RN at UCLA's research and teaching hospital. A metaphysical and practical woman (yes, it is possible to be both), this friend had scheduled an appointment with Pamela to gain understanding of a past relationship with a very controlling man who had caused her a great deal of pain and grief. The morning of the session she woke and looked in the mirror. There, on her chest, were raised, red welts that looked like a severe burn. She could not recall burning herself and as they were not painful she chose to ignore them until after she'd had her session later that afternoon

In her session, NMR indicated the relationship she wished to understand and heal had begun in the 1200's on the continent of Africa. She had been his daughter and he had been a powerful chief who ruled his tribe with warrior skills and the "black arts". The regression began with her sitting on a blanket in her father's hut. She was named Rutawana and was his favored elder daughter. She was also his sexual mate. As he had no sons, she was being trained by him to rule the tribe after his death. Her training included human sacrifices and the casting of spells over men, women, and children. Shortly after her father died, she gave birth to her father's son.

As her son grew more and more in the image of their father, she became convinced his soul was that of their father. When her son, cruel and ruthless, grew into his power, he wrested control of the tribe from her. She was exiled to a hut not far from the village and slowly starved to death. As difficult as the starvation was, it was more difficult for Rutawana to contemplate the many deaths she had caused. She particularly despaired of the deaths of the children. As she died and left her body, Rutawana, in great despair, cried out: "I feel their deaths burning holes in my heart!" Rutawana's spirit was helped to review and understand the greater purpose and lessons in her life so she could heal of her guilt and pain.

After the regression, our friend exclaimed, "I could feel that burning on my chest. I still can. Right here, look!" She showed Pamela the burn marks on her chest she noticed that morning. They were right over her heart. Over the next several months the burn marks slowly faded, leaving very faint outlines on her skin.

Another client, a man in his 60's who had not been able to trim his paunch belly, no matter what he tried, was asked, in hypnosis, "What is the resistance to letting go of the excess fat in the abdomen?" The response was, "a fear of injury." The subconscious was directed to go to the time of the injury. The client found himself in a past life as a warrior in Mesopotamia. He was killed on the battle field when a lance was thrust through his belly. He had been betrayed by his commander. After healing his cell memory and his emotions in this session, the client lost several inches in his belly within a few weeks.

~*~

Are past lives real? One man, a stock broker, cornered Dr. Harmon at a party and told him, "If you can prove to me past lives are real, I'll quit telling everyone you're crazy."

"I can't prove anything," Dr. Harmon rejoined, "but why not experience a past life regression and make up your own mind? And I must be crazy because I'm not going to charge you for it."

The man took him up on his offer, making an appointment for a past life regression. In that regression, he experienced himself returning to a miserable life, full of drudgery, tedium, and squalor. Afterwards, he said, "I would never, in my wildest fantasies, make up such a life. It was awful. I can't imagine how I survived it as long as I did. You win, I believe past lives are real alright."

Do people "make up" past lives? A past life regression can be:

- A mental review of memories stored in the memory banks of the subconscious. Such a regression will involve little emotion (unless present life emotions are triggered), and will lack the feeling of "being there" (unless the imagination is triggered).
- A story the inner mind weaves to symbolically illustrate or trigger thoughts and emotions it wants the conscious mind to understand, release, and transform.
- A "tuning into" the memory banks of someone else and a "reliving" or "reviewing" of that life as though it were ones own.
- A total fabrication; though this is more likely if the person is only pretending to be in hypnosis.
- A "coming forward" of a past life personality. This type of past life regression can truly feel as though one is "there".

People frequently ask why, if a different language was spoken in the past why they can't speak, in the regression, the language they spoke then. Actually, we have had clients begin speaking a different language in past life regressions and have had to ask them to speak English. Many people report they can "hear" or "see" the language they spoke in the past, but can't seem to "speak" it. This is probably due to conscious interference.

~ * ~

Channeling is to be a conduit, or a channel, for energy. In hypnosis, people channel many levels of their own minds and spirit (like past lives), and, sometimes, the minds and spirits of others. Channeling can be done in one of two ways: 1) The spirit or mind being channeled moves into the energy field of the one through whom it will speak. It then uses the voice box of that one. The voice speaking will sound, of course, like the channel's voice, although the inflections, intonation, pitch, even the accent and choice of words may be quite different from the channel's. 2) The spirit or spirit mind being channeled stays outside of the energy field (it can be any distance away), and mentally impresses its thoughts on the subconscious mind, or voice box, of the channel. Again, the voice speaking will sound like the channel's voice. In this case there will usually be little, if any, difference from the channel's normal speech patterns. The second way is far easier on the nervous system and body of the channel and far safer in avoiding spirit attachments.

In all channeling the subconscious mind of the channel translates the thought forms of the spirit, mind, or personality being channeled into the language that will be understood by those listening. (Unless the subconscious is told, consciously or subconsciously, not to do so, such as in speaking-in-tongues.) Interestingly, channels seem unable to channel languages of which their own subconscious mind has no knowledge.

Everyone is telepathic. You are telepathic. You are subconsciously receiving and sending messages from and to other minds all the time. Some messages do reach the conscious levels. However, it is usually in a dream or the form of a thought and people often discount or dismiss this as either meaningless or their own thoughts.

Dr. Harmon and Pamela frequently contact the Akashic Records through Masters of Light and Spirit. These Records exist as thought form vibrations and in them are recorded the records of all souls and spirits, which is why Master of Light and Master of Spirit call them The Universal Records. We are told the more advanced in consciousness a being is, the greater the depth and accuracy of information it can access from the Records, which is why Dr. Harmon leaves his body for the use of Master of Light and Master of Spirit for accessing these Records.

A woman called to ask if we would contact The Universal Records to find where her daughter, who had died at 16 years old, was now. We said we would ask. "Tell her", Master of Light said, "that her daughter has been contacting her. She thinks this communication is 'just dreams' or her own mind 'fooling her'. It is not. They are thoughts being communicated from Karen to her. Karen cannot speak directly to her mother as she has no vocal chords. She is Spirit. She is being worked with on this level to help her realize she died because she had accomplished all she had planned to do on the earth plane. Part of that plan was to help her mother learn to cope with the human emotions of loss and grief. She wants her mother to know that death is freedom, once the soul accomplishes what it goes to the earth planes to do. Karen is saddened by her mother's loss of joy in life. She wants her mother to know that life is a wonderful opportunity for the soul to enjoy being in the body. It is not as easy to get in the body as some people think. Karen wants her mother to take full opportunity of this life experience. They will be together again. They have been together before as well. If her mother wants to, she can remember this. Perhaps you can help her. Perhaps you can help the mother by sharing information another young woman on this side, gave you about Light. Perhaps this will help the mother."

We called Karen's mother to give her this information. She responded, "I HAVE had a dream with Karen speaking to me and I DO hear thoughts in my head that I think is her talking to me, but I thought that couldn't be real. Once I thought I heard her say in my head, 'Mom, I wish I had my body, but its wonderful here. I see and talk to you whenever I want to, but you don't listen. Please listen!' I thought I was making it up, her talking to me. But let me tell you about my dream. I had it two weeks after my daughter died, at Easter Break. In my dream, the phone rang and when I answered it, I heard Karen crying. It was very clear. I said, 'Oh Karen, don't cry!

"I just found out I died! I'm so sorry, Mom. I'm so sorry," Karen said to me still crying.

"What do you mean, you just found out?" I asked.

"I just read it," Karen said, "I didn't know. I'm so sorry."

"What do you mean, you didn't know? What have you been doing?" I asked.

"Finishing my Easter Break," Karen said.

"What is it like where you are?" I asked my daughter.

"It's nice," she said. "Somebody is with me, helping me to adjust." When I asked her to explain, she said, "It's similar to a Lucy Circle."

That's when I woke up. I kept trying to figure out what a Lucy Circle meant, but I didn't know. Anyway, I thought it was just a dream. About six months later, I was lying on the couch. I had a strong thought that told me to go in Karen's room and look on her desk. I finally did. There were two books there. One, an ESP book that I could see by the receipt in it she had bought the day before her death, the other a big encyclopedia of names. I looked up Lucy. It means Light. Do you think my daughter was telling me she was in a circle of Light?

Yes, we think so. Karen's mother also told us about a dream she'd had when her daughter, Karen, was three years old. Karen's mother had dreamt of a boy she'd grown up with, who had recently died. In her dream the young man was very bright, with Light all around him. He asked her to tell his mother that it was very wonderful where he was. Karen's mother then asked him, "Do you think Karen will like it there?" The young man smiled and nodded. We think Karen and her mother both knew, at a soul level, that Karen planned to leave the earth plane young.

People are not only telepathic with each other, they are telepathic with their Higher Selves. The Higher Self communication is frequently received in dreams and thought. We have had many clients ask their Higher Selves, in hypnosis, how they can discern their Higher Self thoughts from all the others they have. Answers that Higher Selves have most frequently given have been: "I am the first thought." "I am the calm, quiet, peaceful thoughts." "I am the sense of knowing." It's important to recognize that the Higher Selves do not argue, cajole, beg, or order. They guide. Whether we deny, accept, or ignore that guidance is up to us.

We could fill this book with Higher Self information and regression sessions. We've chosen to limit ourselves so you will have more of a sense of "discovery" with your own regressions and channeling of your own Higher Self. (Actually, Master of Light and Dr. Harmon had to fight Pamela on this one, so you can thank them for this forbearance. Pamela loves to share as much information as humanly possible.)

We share, in the next chapter, more of our knowledge of spirit. Remember that ALL spirit is of the Light and that the Light has many vibrations, including Dark. Finding the Light is the challenge and path of Spirit. Below is a Higher Self Spirit speaking of the entrance of the soul into the earth planes. We think it is a message applicable to all.:

"I impress upon the chosen parents my name and I am choosing those who would facilitate my entrance. I choose a young woman of great life force with dreams, ambitions, with strong physical forces. Dark forces which I have need of. There is in her strain dark energies and in his. There will be trials, challenges, tribulations. This is part of the demonstration. For Man's lot is one of doubt, fear, limitation, and ever it becomes man's quest to move through the dark, the doubt, the fear, the limitation, the sordid influence of others to make a way into the light. For Man does not die and move into the light. Man leaves the body at death and steps into the degree of light Man has entered while in the body. The light attracts the light. So the level of consciousness at which one leaves is the level of consciousness one enters. The light must be found on the plane of physical material and matter. I choose to demonstrate the growth from darkness to the light. For a Being of Light such as I am to come down and appear before man as the Being of Light that we are is not nearly so instructional as to allow ourselves to share Man's miseries and then become as we begun. For each Man does spring from Divine Consciousness of Self and of Creation. And this one, this Being that I am on your plane, shall show that if all proceeds as I have written it. She must break down the barriers of doubt, of fear, of the need for finite answers. She must soothe and heal the babe within and open to that which she craves, senses, is aware of, and sensitive to and fears. She must open to Spirit."

Special Message For Adults

Check out the young people today and note what an advanced lot they are. Educating them is a challenge. They are bored and restless as educators try to teach them - over and over - what they already know. They only need to be reminded of what they know and then motivated to do something challenging with that knowledge. The physical world doesn't interest them; they have lifetimes of physical knowledge and experiences. Metaphysics - the worlds beyond, behind, above, and below the physical - interests them. Motivate them with that. They need advanced skills in many disciplines to master metaphysics.

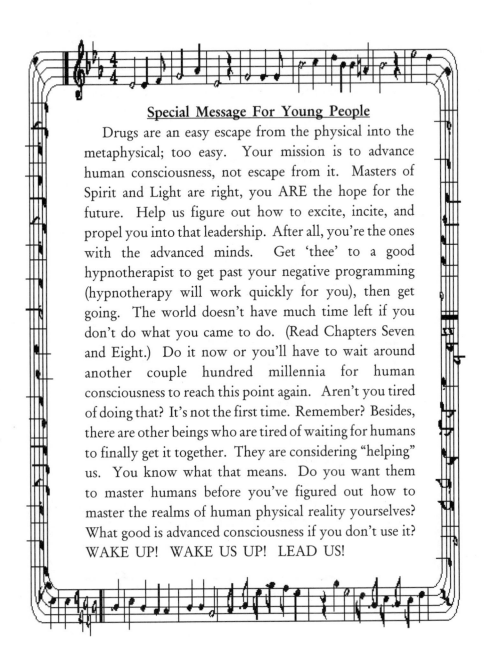

Special Message For Young People

Drugs are an easy escape from the physical into the metaphysical; too easy. Your mission is to advance human consciousness, not escape from it. Masters of Spirit and Light are right, you ARE the hope for the future. Help us figure out how to excite, incite, and propel you into that leadership. After all, you're the ones with the advanced minds. Get 'thee' to a good hypnotherapist to get past your negative programming (hypnotherapy will work quickly for you), then get going. The world doesn't have much time left if you don't do what you came to do. (Read Chapters Seven and Eight.) Do it now or you'll have to wait around another couple hundred millennia for human consciousness to reach this point again. Aren't you tired of doing that? It's not the first time. Remember? Besides, there are other beings who are tired of waiting for humans to finally get it together. They are considering "helping" us. You know what that means. Do you want them to master humans before you've figured out how to master the realms of human physical reality yourselves? What good is advanced consciousness if you don't use it? WAKE UP! WAKE US UP! LEAD US!

~ NOTES FOR YOURSELF ~

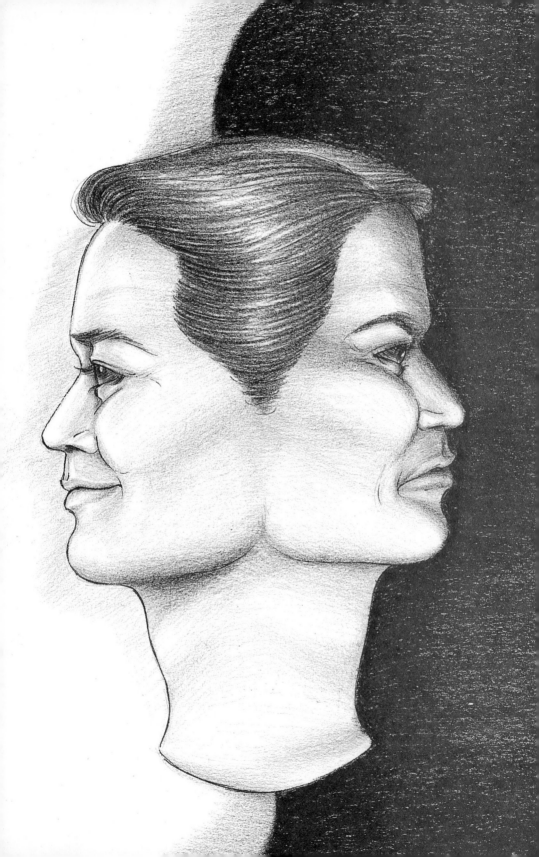

Chapter 7

I to the Light Darkly

We speak to spirit. We speak to spirits of all kinds. We speak to Light Spirits and to Dark Spirits. We speak to the spirits of the dead. We know the death experience is not the same for everyone. We know the "in-between life" spirit experience is not the same for everyone. Please keep in mind we have not made up the information we are about to share with you. We have heard it from spirit directly. We have gathered it from our inner levels of spirit and the inner levels of spirit of people very much like you. People as astounded by the information and experiences they bring forward in hypnotic states as you would be.

Pamela turned on the radio of her car one day just as a woman was being asked by a radio talk show host, "How did your psychic abilities begin?"

The woman answered, "I went to see a spiritualist who opened me to my abilities in one visit."

"Right," Pamela said aloud. "Like it really happens in one visit." As Pamela has trained several people to be trance channels and we have each helped many more to open to their psychic abilities, Pamela knew what she was talking about.

"Really?" commented the talk show host, clearly as skeptical as Pamela. "What is the name of this spiritualist?"

"Pamela Chilton," the woman replied. "She lives right here in the valley."

Pamela nearly drove her car off the road. (A little message in there about steering away from judgment?) As she listened further, she recognized the woman. It had indeed been easy to open her

to her psychic abilities. All she had done was help the woman shift her
mental focus from "outward" to "inward" reality. Simply doing that had
opened the woman to her psychic eye which was highly developed.

People build skills and abilities in many lives. When the soul comes
into the body it brings with it certain influences, both "good" and
"bad", from specific past lives. (Not ALL past life influences are part
of each new life as that would be quite overwhelming and confusing
to the human experience.) Clearly, the time had come for this woman
to move into an ability she had already developed.

As Pamela drove home, she pondered the word spiritualist. We had never
thought of ourselves as spiritualists. The word conjures up all kinds of
images, none of which seemed to fit us. When she got home, Pamela looked
up the words spiritualism and spiritualist in Webster's Dictionary and the
Donning psychic dictionary: :

Webster's: Spiritualism: 1. the view that spirit is a prime element
of reality. 2: a) a belief that spirits of the dead communicate with
the living usu[ally] through a medium.

Donning: Spiritualism: Belief in the continuity of life after death
and communication with this life for the advancement of civilization
and personal growth; scientific study of the etheric [astral] world; its
properties, functions, and relationship to mankind and God; belief
in reincarnation; uses the Bible [and other holy works] as a guide to
show one how to perfect oneself in his or her many incarnations.
Spiritualist: One who believes in the communication between this
world and the invisible world and who endeavors to mold his or her
character and conduct in accordance with the highest teachings
derived from such communion.

Well; it seems we are spiritualists after all.

Spirit IS a prime element of reality. Even your body has a spirit. Your
own spirit has become so intertwined with your body's spirit that they seem
to you to be one spirit. They are not. This may surprise you. It shocked
us.

We knew, of course, that the human body has evolved from and is part
of the animal kingdom. We knew souls began entering the human body
after it had - over eons of time - been developed by "divine intervention"
to a point where it could "house" the souls. We began to suspect the body

had a mind, not just a brain, of its own and a separate spirit when we kept getting responses such as: "We, the cells of the blood know what is good for the blood, but we must respond to the beliefs of the being in the body."

Shocked that the body had a separate consciousness and wanting to know more about this, Pamela approached Master of Spirit for further clarification.

"We are **animals**?" Pamela asked Master of Spirit after she had guided Dr. Harmon to the level of trance that allowed for this communication.

"Your bodies are," Master of Spirit replied. "You know that. Go back in your mind and remember."

"If our bodies have a mind and spirit of their own," Pamela remarked to Master of Spirit, "we probably ought to treat our bodies as lovingly as we do our pets".

"If humans treated their pets as badly as they've treated their bodies," Master of Spirit rejoined, "your pets would all be dead. The animal chosen for your bodies was chosen for its dexterity and strength. It has extraordinary ability to endure hardship and survive. A fortunate choice, for the life forms chosen to serve the souls have needed all of their resources to survive the abuse heaped upon them by the very souls they serve. Interesting that humans of all levels of knowledge, even those who call themselves spiritually advanced, ignore or deny the needs and importance of their bodies. Why is that we wonder?"

"You mean you don't know?" Pamela asked with surprise.

"We are not in the body," Master of Spirit answered. "There is much we don't know about the human condition. Your minds are a curiosity to us."

Pamela laughed. "Believe me, Master of Spirit, they are as much a curiosity to us."

"Perhaps," Master of Spirit mused, "your minds are more influenced by the limitations of the body's consciousness than you realize."

"I would say so," Pamela agreed. "Perhaps that is why meditation is so important. It gives us a chance to move beyond our lower influences and limitations."

"You would do well to teach humans what meditation is," Master of Spirit suggested. "Most seem to have forgotten. Others complicate it so completely it is as confusing to your minds as it is to your bodies."

"I'm not certain if I truly know what meditation is, Master of Spirit,"

Pamela answered.

"Interesting, that you should forget so much while in the body. Oh well, it is not our place to question. Perhaps the one you call Master of Light can help. As Light, that one is much more understanding of the human condition than are we."

"Thank you, I shall indeed ask Master of Light to write of meditation in the last chapter of the book. Master of Light is writing that chapter without our input, you know."

"We do know," Master of Spirit responded. "That is why you were chosen. To spread the message of Light or the destruction of Man, as we know Man, as you know Man, and as Man knows itself, is in the very near future."

WAIT!   READ   WHAT   FOLLOWS!

Perhaps, dear reader, you are tempted to skip to the last chapter and read Master of Light's message now. Before you do, read this chapter. Or if you do, return to this chapter. There is important information for you in it. Information necessary for anyone who works with spirit. Here is part of Light's message:

There are Beings of Light present in the earth today. Many are humans who have returned to human form, despite having finished their earthly sojourns. This is dangerous to do, for ever the web of human consciousness threatens to ensnare the soul once again. Light Beings are here at the request of many realms, planes, and dimensions to help humans save themselves from the destruction they have unleashed upon the earth. Humans have come close to their potential twelve times. Twelve times humans have destroyed themselves and returned in consciousness to the age of dinosaurs and cave dwellers to slowly advance through the centuries. This is not recorded in the records of Man; it is recorded in the Universal Records of Spirit.

Humans are ready, once again, to leap into their potential. Yet, they have through choice and will brought themselves to the brink of destruction a thirteenth time. Once again, Man and Woman have denied and defied the Laws of Nature and, once again, Nature is not pleased.

Nature is poised to restore the balance by sweeping the earth clean of humans; save a very <u>small</u> number of <u>primitive</u> humans with which to begin, once again, the march of civilizations. Nature gives warning through many signs that humans might heed these signs and right the balance themselves. It is late, but there is still time. This is why you are here; for if you do not succeed, Nature SHALL destroy this age and all the generations in it.

You, who read these words, heed them well. For in them, the Ancient Catalyst quickens your spirit and stirs the memory of why you are here in this most consequential of times. You have come to bring the Light, and with Light, you shall lead human kind forward from the brink of destruction into the Age of Light. You have many gathered in spirit around you to help you in your great purpose. You have but to ask of your Higher Self and those who serve the Light will serve you well.

You have, also, powerful enemies; for there are many in spirit and in physical form who seek to master the earth and chain human souls to serve their purposes. Be aware! Do not turn over your bodies or your power of choice to any who ask for them in exchange for helping you. It would be better to unleash Nature in all of its might than to lose your powers of choice. Know this: Your enemies use your own minds to manipulate and control you.

This book is commissioned by Higher Spirit to remind you of these things. It is written to remind you of the power of your minds to aid or to block you in your missions. It is written to remind you of the Light and how to teach others of the Light. It is written to remind you of spirit and how to know the spirits of darkness who greet you disguised as light. You have forgotten these things at your human levels for when your souls were born into physical matter, they entered at the level and limitations of consciousness common to the human experience in your times. For the test of the human realm is ever that of moving beyond the limitations and challenges of the human experience and into the Light.

When you have found the Light, you will gather others where there are ears to listen, eyes to see, and minds to focus in the Light. You shall teach them as Master of Light teaches you.

You are Beings of Light here to fulfill your mission in the Plan of Light. If this is done, if this is accomplished, there is time beyond in which to reward yourselves with that which pleases your human hearts. Your part in the plan - which must be implemented NOW - is very, very, very important. It is why you are here; it is why you agreed to come. You cannot, DARE not, underestimate your part. The plan will not work without you. You must not be stopped. You are very, very, very important.

Your bodies are important to your mission. Treat them well. Know that your emotions are important as your emotions are a vital part of the life force of your bodies.

This is why releasing anger and fear are so important. Anger and fear are part of the animal programming; they are essential for the survival of the body. Every animal alive, including your body, has been programmed to flee what it fears and fight what angers it. Nature programmed this to protect the body. Human children are frequently taught that fear and anger are not acceptable. Such programming severely handicaps survival mechanisms. It is this very programming that feeds the ability of abusers to abuse. It is this very programming (and the subsequent holding in of emotions like anger and fear) that blocks ones connection to the Higher Self. One must be certain, when working with spirit, to be clear at the internal levels of anger and fear; for if one is not, one draws spirits of anger and fear to one.

~ * ~

Your soul has "tried on" many VERY different personalities in living the full spectrum of human experience. You would "hate" some of your past life personalities, and they would "hate" you! (It does seem one certain way to predetermine ones gender, race, or sexual orientation in a future life is to "hate" a particular gender, race, or sexual orientation. So does the soul grow in compassion and away from judgment.) The personalities you have been are not "dead" and "buried". They live as long as your spirit.

To understand how this can be, you will first need to remember that spirit can be in many places at one at the same time. Thus, your spirit can be in many places at one and the same time. Time and death cannot separate spirit as in the levels of spirit there is no time and there is no death. Of course, earth is a temporal plane. Birth, aging, death, and rebirth exist on the earth planes because our minds have made them exist. Our minds have had to create a means of blending that which is omnipresent and eternal (spirit) with that which is not (material matter). How we did that is, no doubt, highly intricate, complex, sophisticated, and nearly impossible to grasp with our finite focus. However, the basic understanding of it becomes easier when we open our focus with the simple illustration of space travel.

Your physical body and its cells must maintain certain rates of vibration to remain intact. The earth atmosphere maintains those vibration rates. To travel to other atmospheres, such as "outer space", your body needs a means of maintaining its vibration rates. Space vehicles and space suits are what our minds have built to maintain those vibration rates in other atmospheres.

Spirit also has certain vibration rates. The vibrations of your whole spirit would shatter material matter. Thus, your spirit needs a kind of space vehicle and space suit for lowering its vibrations to a level that allows it to travel in other atmospheres like realms of material matter. The space vehicle for your spirit is your soul and the space suit for your soul is its astral body.

All energy has vibration. That vibration "determines" its energy state. For instance, H_2O has several energy states, depending on the rate of movement (vibration) of its molecules. At a slow vibration, H_2O is in the solid energy state called ice. Increase the vibration of its molecules and H_2O is a liquid energy state called water. Increase the vibration rates of its molecules even more and H_2O becomes an invisible vapor as its molecules separate and become part of air. Vapor and air both vibrate so rapidly you cannot see them. They are invisible to the human eye, unless there is particulate matter in them. (Steam is vapor mixed with water particles, which allows you to see it; just as smog is air mixed with water and other particulate matter which allows you to see it.)

Spirit, like air, is invisible unless there is particulate matter mixed with it. For instance, your Higher Self cannot be seen as its vibration rate is so high. Your soul vibrates at a lower rate, but it cannot, itself, be seen either. (Your soul is part of your Higher Self, but it is not your Higher Self, just as a cup of ocean water is ocean water, but it is not the ocean.) However, the astral bodies of your Higher Self and your soul can be seen as astral energy is spirit with particulate matter mixed in it. That particulate matter is called ectoplasm, which is the building block of physical matter.

The Donning International Encyclopedic Psychic Dictionary by June G. Bletzer, Ph.D., notes: ectoplasm exuded by "mediums" (people able to project a thick ectoplasm that flows from their physical bodies at will) has been measured and studied by French researchers who found it to contain: "albumoid matter and fatty matter (same as human cells, except for sugar and starch); smells similar to ozone; capable of being weighted and measured; coming from advanced mediums, it contains white blood cells, calcium phosphate, membranous cell detritus, and nitrogen." A further note adds: "analyzed by Massachusetts's Institute of Technology and found to contain properties of; sodium, potassium, water, chlorine, albumen, epithelial cells, and red blood corpuscles."

Your astral body is a mixture of spirit and ectoplasm. Your astral body surrounds and interpenetrates your physical body. Your astral body and physical body mirror one another. They are alike. Your astral body is less solid than your physical body, but it can be seen. Babies and small children see it readily. Older children and adults who have been taught not to see it must relearn this ability.

Hold your hand up in front of a plain, light background, like a white wall or the blue sky. Spread your fingers. Stare at the spaces between your fingers. Relax the focus of your eyes until they are slightly unfocused. Play with the distance of your hand to your face until you see a kind of fuzzy outline of light around your fingers. That is the outline of your astral body's fingers. Next, see if you can shift your brain/eye focus in that same manner to see a kind of dim outline around other people's bodies. This is usually most visible around the shoulders and head and is easier to see in a kind of dim light. (Practice this in the dim lighting of a movie theater before the movie starts.)

Western scientists already know, to some extent, about astral energy, though not to the extent of metaphysicians. In fact, scientists who puzzle over the unknown are really looking for the known, which is always in evidence and available to them. When people are blinded by shortsightedness, they do not open to their insight, thus overlooking the obvious.

Acupuncture and acupressure are two methods of working with astral energy. There are certain points on the physical body that correspond to certain points on the astral body that have to do with the flow of astral energy and its entry into the physical body. (The subconscious needs astral energy for many of its tasks; including the repairing, regenerating, and rejuvenating of cells.) When these entry points become blocked they can be opened by inserting a special needle, as in acupunture, or a special pressure, as in acupressure, on these points. The lines of the flow of astral energy between these points are called meridian lines. Tracing the meridian lines help keep these lines open and flowing in the proper direction.

Chakra is a Sanskrit word that loosely translates to "spinning wheel". Astral energy has certain generating centers in the astral body. These generating centers look like spinning wheels of Light. The chakras "power up" and "spin out" astral energy along the meridians lines. When astral energy is low or blocked in a particular chakra or at any point along a meridian, the part of the physical body fed by that chakra and meridian suffer.

Astral energy is part of the life force of the body. To build and keep a strong life force the following are <u>essential</u>:

√ A strong spiritual connection with the Higher Self. (Get in the habit of talking (aloud or by thought) with your Higher Self and asking for its guidance and protection. Also meditate.)

√ Sunlight. (Make sunlight dangerous and/or convince humans sunlight isn't good for them and you can control the human race as the sun is a prime source of life force.)

√ <u>Fresh</u> air. (Same as above.)

√ <u>Clean</u> water. (Same as above.)

√ <u>Natural</u> food. (Addict humans to chemical and hormone laced foods and you've got the same scenario as above. Plus, you can effectively "herd" them through their addictions in the direction of your choosing.)

√ Physical exercise. (Stretching exercises are particularly good as they move the nutrient and oxygen filled blood, as well as astral energy, to all the cells of the body/brain. Breathe deeply as you stretch as this brings in oxygen and astral energy from the Higher Self. To add further impact: image, think, or speak to your body, giving it in thanks for its support of you. Then ask, image, or speak of the perfect balance and ratio of muscle, bone, fat, tissue, fluids, glands, and organs in your strong, youthful, and flexible body.

√ Joy. Laughter. Love. (The kind without judgment and conditions. The kind that comes from The Higher Self; thus the importance of meditation.)

√ Touch. (It's part of how humans share life force with one another.)
√ Positive thoughts at all levels of mind.

Around the astral body and chakras are fields of colors called auras. Like the astral body, the aura can be seen, with practice, by shifting ones eyes and mental focus. The auric field is not static. It changes as a person's thoughts and emotions change. It is even affected by the thoughts and emotions of others. Aura readers (people who see and interpret the auric fields) must be careful not to "color" another's aura with their own thoughts and emotions. (Just like working with hypnosis and NMR.) For instance, the color of rose pink is often associated with the emotional vibration of non-conditional love. Feeling that kind of love for someone can affect the way one sees the colors in that person's aura. (Just as placing a rose filter over the camera lens to photograph a sunset will change the colors of the sunset in the picture, not in the sunset itself.) Also, people do see colors differently. The color aqua marine will appear more green to some and more blue to others. Brown eyed people and blue eyed people see certain colors differently as well. Good aura readers learn how to make the necessary adjustments.

An example of how ones own perceptions can filter what one sees in another's aura, is when we invited a truly gifted aura reader to sit in on a session with Master of Light. She told us later that she had seen a very jolly man with a long white beard in Dr. Harmon's astral field while Master of Light was talking to her. Pamela asked Master of Light about this later. Laughing, Master of Light asked Pamela how she perceived 'his' presence.

"The hue of the light in the room changes somehow," Pamela replied, "Often there is a sense of soft blue in the room and sometimes a kind of rose pink color. Sometimes, it seems there are several colors. But I always know when you are coming in as the light in the room softens, just like daylight softens at sunset."

"The softness of the light at that hour brings you very close to your God awareness," Master of Light responded, "and as I am the Consciousness of Light, I trigger those feelings in you, which color, if you will, what you see. The delightful Lady of Colors who was here yesterday had preconceived ideas about who and what I might be. She loves your Dr. Harmon and she perceives, correctly, the joy vibrations that fill his auric field. She thinks of me as a guru of his and assumed any guru of his would be filled with joy as well. She is a powerful being and her thoughts used astral energy to create a jolly looking guru as she spoke with me. It is as apt a form as any other, for I have no form and, yet, I am all forms. I Am Light. Each person will perceive me differently as what each person perceives of Light will be colored by their own expectations, thoughts, and feelings."

The auric field, astral body, and physical body affect one another. Weakness in the astral body "invites" illness, disease, or injury into the physical body. Illness, disease, or injury of the physical body weakens the astral body. Healing and transformation of the physical body brings the same results to the astral body just as healing and transformation of the astral body bring the same results to the physical body. The difference is, the astral body responds to thought much more quickly than the physical body. The more focused the thought, the more instantaneous the results on the astral body. The greater the life force, the more quickly those results filter to the physical level. This realization is an important one for it brings the recognition that one can change, heal and transform ones physical body through techniques and methods that affect the astral but do not harm the physical body.

For instance: Laser surgery can be done mentally. Imagine how much more cost effective and safer laser surgery will become when medical science "discovers" this! (Imagine how those who make expensive laser surgery equipment and those who charge for laser surgery will fight to squelch this discovery!) We have SEEN the results of mental laser healing on a small number of clients who have focused their minds on light altering specific areas of their bodies. Each said it took concentration, belief, and patience, but it DID work. We were amazed ourselves.

We shouldn't have been so surprised; after all, we are accustomed to seeing what thought can do. We also know the ancient Kahunas of Old Hawaii would use astral healing for, among other things, repairing broken bones instantly. (Witnessed and documented by Western Scientists.) They did so by mentally connecting the broken bone of the astral body. (The astral body is called aka kino in Hawaiian). At the same time, they would put their hands on the broken bone of the physical body to transfer mana (vital life force) into the bone for the instant transfer of the healing from the astral to the physical. It is interesting to note that the Hawaiian symbol for mana (vital life force) is a lightning bolt.

The Kahunas understood that the lower the mana a person possessed, the longer it would take healing to transfer from the astral to the physical. So the Kahunas not only built up their own mana, they figured out how to collect and store extra mana they could utilize for healing people of low mana.

The Kahunas also understood the subconscious mind, which they called the "low self", or unihipili. The conscious mind was called uhane, or the "middle self". The Higher Self was called aumakua, or the "High Self". They believed that the mana that flowed from the High Self was the strongest mana of all and they named it mana loa.

The Kahunas recognized that thoughts and emotions in either the low self or the middle self could block the flow of mana from the High Self. They recognized this flow was necessary if a person was to stay healed or be granted a prayer manifestation. Knowing this, Kahunas would often do a kind of pre-healing or pre-prayer ritual designed to clear thoughts and emotions that could block this flow. Righting wrongs done to others and forgiving others of wrongs done to oneself were frequently part of these rituals.

For a prayer to be manifested, the Kahunas had a person say the prayer aloud three times in order to direct the low self as to what was wanted. They believed (rightly!) that the low self was the one that either allowed or blocked the mana needed from the High Self to manifest the requests of the middle self. Kahunas did hypnotic rituals in order to "catch the attention" of the subconscious mind. They also believed the low self held the memories but had inferior powers of reason. The middle self, they believed, could not remember for itself, but had full power of inductive reasoning. It's amazing how knowledgeable the Kahunas were about the way the mind works!

The astral body, or aka, of the High Self was also called The Light, The True Light, The Path, The Way. Aka is also the same word used for the halo of light around the moon and sun, whether they are in the sky or just before they rise above the horizon. Aka actually translates to shadowy body and the Kahunas believed all things to have a shadowy (astral) body, be they crystals, plants, animals, fabricated material, man, woman, child, or thought. The shadowy bodies of thoughts were very important to the working of low and high magic for the Kahunas.

The Kahunas called working through the High Self (such as with prayer) high magic. They understood the High Self had greater mana that could transform the physical more rapidly than the mana of the low self and middle self. HOWEVER, they also knew that thoughts, beliefs, and emotions in either the low self (subconscious mind) or the middle self (conscious mind), or both, could block the sending of prayer to the High Self or the receipt of the mana from the High Self. Thus, they often had to work through and with the low self and the middle self, which they called low magic.

(Those interested in knowing more about the Kahunas and their amazing knowledge are referred to the books of the western researcher and linguist Max Freedom Long.)

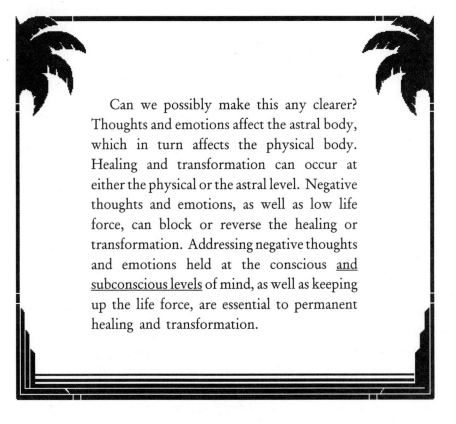

Can we possibly make this any clearer? Thoughts and emotions affect the astral body, which in turn affects the physical body. Healing and transformation can occur at either the physical or the astral level. Negative thoughts and emotions, as well as low life force, can block or reverse the healing or transformation. Addressing negative thoughts and emotions held at the conscious <u>and subconscious levels</u> of mind, as well as keeping up the life force, are essential to permanent healing and transformation.

Humans are entering an age where it is important, even crucial, to understand there are astral realms, planes, and dimensions that our spirits and minds tune into, travel through, and dwell in. We know this at the subconscious level. We know this at the Higher Self level. It's time we know this at the conscious level.

Our souls regularly "tune into" and "visit" various astral levels during certain periods of sleep. At least they do when we are in balance and healthy. (In fact, to stay balanced and healthy we better leave our bodies regularly. This gives the body and its cells a chance to balance and heal themselves according to their truths, not ours.) Dreaming is a tuning into or traveling in astral levels; as are drug "trips", out of body experiences (o.b.e.) and near death experiences (n.d.e.) Mental telepathy, precognition, and other psychic experiences are also a tuning into or visiting in the astral levels.

Thought has form in certain astral levels and it is a "tuning into" or "running into" negative thought forms in these levels that causes many "bad" astral trips (including nightmares). To get out of these levels, it is necessary only to think, will, or pray oneself out of them, as the astral responds instantly to thought in these levels. This is much more difficult to do with a drug induced "trip" as drugs (legal or illegal) affect both the "hardware" of the brain and the "software" of the mind.

All physical forms have astral forms in the astral levels. These astral forms remain in the astral levels long after the destruction of the physical form and comprise a kind of "astral world". There are many dimensions and planes of this astral world. When a soul leaves its physical body at death, it can choose to remain in its astral form in the astral planes of earth or it can choose to leave its astral form and go into the Light.

When a soul leaves its astral form to go into the Light, that astral form is "deactivated" in some manner. (Perhaps this can be compared to "hanging up" ones space suit in a hanger for later use.) That same form can be "activated" again at any time by the spirit that created it. (Just as one can wear ones old "space suits".) It can even, it seems, become activated by another spirit. (Rather like borrowing someone else's "space suit".) This may explain:

• How past life personalities (and inner child personalities) come forward.
• How a regression to a past life other than ones own can seem so much like ones own.

- How a spirit can be "channeled" even when the soul of that spirit is reincarnated or is in the Light. For instance, The Universal Records say the souls of Abraham and Peter, the Apostle, are in the physical body today. Yet these "spirits" are being channeled by people other than the souls of Abraham and Peter. This brings up some interesting questions: Who, really, is being channeled? The astral personalities or the Higher Selves of Abraham and Peter? The Higher Selves or personalities of the channelers? Or something else entirely? (Yes, we plan to ask Master of Light and Master of Spirit, but why should we have all the fun. We encourage you to investigate these answers for yourselves through your own inner access to Higher Spirit.)

~ * ~

We think recognizing the existence of astral levels can explain many things being talked about today which are difficult to understand or explain. We don't ask you to believe any of the following. We ask you to entertain (or at least wonder about) their possibility.

- Immaculate conceptions are the merging of the astral energies of two people whose minds, bodies, and spirits are dedicated to a single purpose. While the physical sperm does meet the physical egg, the penis is placed near the vagina, not in it, and the sperm is guided from the penis by thought, not movement.
- A great spiritual Master who has mastered the physical realm can, after death, imbue his or her astral body with such powerful life force that the astral body appears, even feels, solid. Often this is mistaken for resurrection of the physical body. In a sense, it is, for the physical body is transmuted, at death, into a life force that can be used on the astral planes by the spiritual Master.
- Lesser spirits can also temporarily materialize their astral bodies by "borrowing" the life force of people in the body.
- Recalling the dead is possible when a Spiritual Master of great life force is able to call back a soul into the physical body and recharge, in a sense, the cells of that body with his or her own life force. Highly evolved Masters rarely do this as they know death is part of the balance of life and an important part of a soul's journey.
- The astral levels are where The Universal Records of the soul and the Universe are kept.

- Edgar Cayce was an extraordinary psychic, seer, and trance channel. We have, like many others, spoken with Mr. Cayce's astral being. He told us that sometimes he would access information from the Records, but more frequently he, or one of his spirit guides, would access information from a person's own mind, body, or Higher Self. He added he would not always 'like' what he found in the Records and that he had, on occasion, changed the information to adhere more closely to what human consciousness could, at his time, accept. He added human consciousness has grown sufficiently to receive more in depth information from those Records. He suggested we investigate more deeply the story of Abraham and his sons. We will share what we found in Book Three.

- Not all spirit is good, loving, knowledgeable, or tells the truth. People, and other beings, do not become evolved or of higher consciousness just by being in their astral forms or spirit state. <u>It is important to be able to know the intent and level of consciousness of any spirit and whether that spirit is telling the truth</u>. It is important to know when a spirit (even a spirit guide) is NOT to ones greater good. The Higher Selves can discern this. It is essential, when working with astral levels and with spirit, to be connected to Light and ones Higher Self. (Master of Light offers guidelines on this in Chapter Eight.)

- There is an astral level in which fairies, elves, leprechauns, and other so called "mythical" beings dwell. Sometimes they materialize into the physical levels and are seen by humans. Sometimes they even incarnate as humans.

- We define "alien" as any spirit that defines its "planet of origin" as other than the physical and astral levels of earth. Many people embodied today did not begin their planetary sojourns on planet earth.

- There is life on other planets. On some planets the forms are astral, on others, they are physical. Many of those "alien" civilizations have developed space travel to a far greater sophistication than have humans. Many use their knowledge of the astral levels to travel through time and to materialize (move from the astral to the physical) and dematerialize (move from the physical to the astral) themselves and their space crafts.

- Many "trips" aboard space crafts are astral trips. This does not make them any less real. Such experiences can have strong impact on the physical being, even to leaving marks on the physical body. (Remember, what happens to the astral body filters down to the physical body.)

- Aliens have been watching humans for many centuries. Many of these aliens are advanced in consciousness and they honor and respect the human will and presence on the planet earth. Others are selfish in their motives and intent and are hopeful of finding ways of "using" the earth and humans for their own purposes. They neither respect nor honor human will. (Especially as they see humans willfully destroying their own glorious bodies and planet.) Again, it is important to use the Higher Self to know the intent of any being.

- What many people call a "new" soul is actually a being that is "new" to the human experience. These can include "alien" beings and earth astral beings. Many "new" souls, as well as ancient earth souls, are present in body today as this is such an important time in human experience.

- The future is not set as the future is built by a person's ever changing thoughts, beliefs, emotions, and actions. Most people are creating several possible futures as few people are very singular in their thoughts, beliefs, emotions, and actions. This makes individual futures difficult to read accurately.

- The individual future is affected by the collective thoughts, beliefs, emotions, and actions of all humans. The reverse is also true. The collective future is more stable than individual futures, as it changes more slowly, making it somewhat more easy to tune into.

- The future can be changed, and is constantly changing, as thoughts, beliefs, emotions, and actions of humans change. This is true individually and collectively. Psychics often accurately tune into the future only to have their predictions not come true as the future has shifted.

~ * ~

Babies and very young children are quite aware of the astral levels and can readily see them.

Pamela: "As a young child, I was very aware of what I now call the astral world. I would so alarm my mother when I chatted with people she could not see, she ordered me to quit doing it. It was a struggle for me to separate this seemingly invisible (to my mother) world from the visible world, until I began to perceive the "invisible" world was slightly off the ground. After that, I would concentrate on focusing on the forms connected to the ground while letting the forms off the ground fade. Eventually, I succeeded in blocking out the invisible world, as do most children.

However, I continued to let one, a grown up, visit me at night. One night, he sat on the edge of my bed and said he would be going away for awhile. I was very upset. He explained I had work to do as a child as well as a grown up. He said my work as a child would be to learn which things adults taught me were beneficial and good and which were not. When I had sorted all of that out, he added, I might change my mind about seeing the astral world again. In the meanwhile, astral beings like himself would respect my wishes, which was to not see them because it upset me to upset my mommy. They would continue to visit me, and I them, in my sleep and they would always be protecting and helping me, he said. I would also continue to hear them in my head, but I might not realize, for a long time, that it was them.

After this, I became very frightened when I would wake in the night and see dark forms in my room (which happened frequently). I think it was because I figured, in my child mind, they had to be "bad" spirits as the "good" ones said they wouldn't show themselves. I think now that this happened because I would be, just upon awakening, in an altered state which allowed me to see astral forms. I think my childhood experience is common to many people and I believe this is why so many people are frightened of spirits and other "invisible" beings.

That said, there ARE dark beings and spirits in all levels of the Creator's Creations. Dark beings and spirits serve only their own purpose and care little for the greater good. <u>However, dark beings and spirits only have the power over us we give them.</u> Learn to focus, at all levels of your mind, on your own positive powers and abilities and you never need fear darkness. In fact, you can even discourse with dark beings and spirits without fear of harm or influence.

Focus is so important to obtaining the goals you seek, including the future you desire, that we must bring up now something which can greatly interfere with your focus. You have read, thus far, on how your past experiences can create programming, thoughts, beliefs, and emotions that create division in your mind. You have read of the importance of clearing up that division.

Now, we shall share with you about spirit attachments.

We warned you the mind and spirit are complex!
How could it be different in a complex cosmos?

Spirit attachments are not to be feared. Spirit attachments are, in most cases, simply people. They are people who have, for one reason or another, chosen not to move into the Light or the astral levels at the death of their physical bodies. Spirits attach by merging their astral energies with the astral energies of those who have physical bodies. This is a hardship on the physical body and it scatters the focus of the "owner" of the physical body. Let us list a few things about spirit attachments that will be helpful to you before we share with you stories of spirit attachments:

1 People can have more than one spirit attachment although not everyone has a spirit attachment.

2 A spirit attachment will identify with the age, gender, and personality of the last physical body he or she had.

3 Permission must be granted by the person who "owns" the body for another spirit to attach to that body, though this permission is often given by personalities (like the "inner child") in the subconscious levels or by abdicating ones responsibility for ones body. (Drug use, drunkedness, suicide, etc.)

4 People frequently have a hard time turning down someone they have loved from attaching; especially if their own grief has held that spirit from moving on.

5 Abused and/or lonely children frequently invite in spirit attachments that help them deal with their abuse and/or loneliness.

6 Spirit attachments and the ones to whom they are attached can be very bonded emotionally. This is especially true of attachments one has had since childhood.

7 Most often the spirit attachment is NOT granted control over the body.

8 The exception to this is abdicating responsibility for ones body by actions that jeopardize the body. (Drugs, suicide attempts, getting drunk, leaving the body unprotected, and the like.)

9 Spirit attachments are often drawn to people addicted to what they were addicted to while they were embodied. Such attachments can make it harder to end these addictions.

10 The subconscious mind knows when a spirit attachment is present;

though it may hide this information from the conscious levels if told
to do so by levels of the subconscious mind.

11 The Higher Self always knows when a spirit attachment is present and
knows whether this attachment is beneficial to all concerned.

12 NMR can be used to determine whether spirit attachments are present,
as well as information about those attachments.

13 Exorcising, banishing, or getting "rid" of a spirit attachment is rarely
enlightened or successful if the spirit attachment does not want to go
and there are inner levels of the one to whom they are attached who
do not want them to go. In such cases, the spirits sometimes hide from
the ones seeking to remove them or they leave and come back later.

14 Helping spirit attachments and the people to whom they are attached
understand their relationship and examine all their options for staying
and going is VERY enlightened and helps all concerned. To wrest apart
people (whether in or out of the body) before they are ready to let go
or move on is very cruel. It helps no-one.

15 Death happens for a reason. It is a sure sign that it is time for the soul
to move into higher levels of learning or to prepare for a new physical
body. Helping a spirit attachment to realize this helps spirit attachments
to move on willingly once the one to whom they are attached can let
go.

~ * ~

Sheila came to see Pamela after a gifted aura reader told her she had a
very angry male spirit attached to her. Sheila was very upset and asked
Pamela for NMR to know if this was true. NMR confirmed Sheila had
a spirit attachment, a male in his 40's, who had been with her since she
was a child. Sheila was insistent this man be "removed immediately".
Pamela explained to Sheila she was probably emotionally close to this man
and that it would be better to work toward a gradual separation. Sheila
was adamant. She wanted the man "gone now". Pamela suggested she guide
Sheila into hypnosis so she, Pamela, could speak with this man and find
out more about him. Sheila agreed, especially after Pamela said the man's
cooperation would be required if he was to move on into the Light.

Spirits can be afraid of the Light for many reasons. Sometimes, they
have been so traumatized by their emotions while in the body, they have
forgotten, even at the inner levels of mind, about the Light. Sometimes

they have been so programmed to believe in "Hell and Damnation" they are afraid of being judged in the Light.

Sheila's friend needed a little coaxing to speak When he did speak, he said he was ready to go to the Light, which he knew about, but that he doubted Sheila was ready for him to go. Pamela told him she agreed with him, but as Sheila was so disturbed at the conscious level by his presence, perhaps he could move on and watch from the Light to see if Sheila continued to work with Pamela to ease her inner turmoil. If she did, he could stay in the Light. If she didn't, and he thought it best, he could return. Sheila's friend agreed and moved into the Light.

Sheila, coming out of hypnosis, said immediately, "that was a bunch of bull. I didn't believe a word of it." The next thing she did was burst into tears. When Pamela asked why the tears, she replied, "I've never been alone before, I don't think I can do it."

Frequently, when a spirit attachment does move on, the person to whom that one was attached experiences all the symptoms of grief. Bonds ARE created at the subconscious level and letting go can be difficult. We have spoken with many spirit attachments who have told us the person to whom they are attached went to someone who "told" them to go away by using Light, prayer, conversation, or banishment rituals. Some of those spirit attachments tell us: "I left for awhile and came back later." Others say, "I ignored it. I didn't want to go." Others say, "It really hurt my feelings." Still others say it angered them.

It is important to realize even Light, Higher Selves, and God cannot and will not MAKE any spirit do anything they don't choose to do. Spirit attachments cannot be forced away from people who are willing at some level to allow them to stay attached to them. There are ways to "remove" spirit attachments unwilling to go; but only if the person to whom they are attached insists on them leaving at the conscious level AND there is no one in the subconscious levels holding onto them. However, it is still better to help the spirit attachment understand the benefit of moving into the Light, or certain astral levels if they are not ready for the Light, so that they do not attach to someone else.

We have rarely had an attachment return from the Light (they love it there), unless they have been pulled back by the persons to which they were attached. (Grief is a powerful pull on loved ones, so is helplessness and dependency.) We have had spirit attachments lie, however, saying they are in the Light; only to discover they are not. (VERY careful wording of NMR can discover this.)

Mick was a discarnate spirit attachment. (Discarnates are spirits who have had physical bodies with which they still identify.) Mick was a spirit attachment of a special services government agent who had come to see Pamela to deal with a great deal of personal and professional stress. This client suffered from a shoulder pain ever since joining the police force twenty years before, and it had been getting increasingly worse. He also had two girlfriends and deciding which girlfriend to "choose" was contributing to his stress. With NMR, he became clearer about his inner feelings for both women and realized he really wanted to marry one of the women, but was so fearful of marriage, he used the other woman to keep himself from getting too serious with the one he really loved. He decided he was going to stop seeing the woman he didn't love and begin working with his fear of marriage. Shortly after he left, Dr. Harmon approached Pamela. "How did your last session go?" he asked.

"Fine," she replied. "Why?"

"Do you feel alright?" he pressed.

"Well, no. My shoulder hurts alot," she admitted. "That's funny. My client had a sore shoulder. Same shoulder, too."

"I don't think you're alone," Dr. Harmon said. "We'd better check it out."

He was right. NMR indicated Pamela had picked up a discarnate that had been attached to the government agent. Dr. Harmon guided Pamela into hypnosis so the spirit attachment could speak with him. He did so readily. He said his name was Mick and he said he was very angry at Pamela. Dr. Harmon asked why.

"That busy-body woman talked him into breaking up with Marta. I like Marta. She's a lot more exciting than that other stick in the mud." Of course, Dr. Harmon didn't know what Mick was talking about so he asked Mick to explain. "What's to explain? She stuck her nose where it's not wanted, that's all. Goddamned women. I'll fix her."

"Are you making her shoulder hurt?" Dr. Harmon inquired.

"Don't know if I am, don't know if I'm not. Would serve her right if I am." Dr. Harmon asked Mick to tell him about himself, especially how he died. "Well, it was damn stupid, the way I bought it. I was off duty. I'm a cop you know. I was sitting on a bar stool, minding my own business. Some damn idiot started a brawl. It didn't look too bad so I thought I'd finish my shot of whisky. Well, some jackass hit me on the back of the head with a goddam bottle. My lights went out and when I woke up, I was dead."

"I see," Dr. Harmon said, stifling a laugh. "Did you see a Light anywhere after you died, Mick?"

Mick became cagey and reluctant to talk. Finally, after some coaxing he said, "Yeah, I saw a Light. I didn't want to go anywhere near it."

"Why not?" Dr. Harmon asked.

"So I thought I'd hang out awhile," Mick remarked, ignoring the question. "I stayed at the bar until my young friend came in."

"What young friend was that?"

Mick gave the name of Pamela's client and continued, "I liked him. Reminded me of me when I first joined the force. Been with him ever since. I've felt kinda bad about it at times though."

"Why is that?"

"That shoulder pain of his. I think it's me. My shoulder has hurt me there ever since I got hit with that bottle. I don't know why that should affect him though."

"You're in his energy field," Dr. Harmon explained. "What you feel, he feels. Your thoughts probably affect him, too."

"Only when he listens to me," Mick grumbled. "Say, that testing your busy-body friend did with him, that leg stuff. It said he had inner guilt. Do you think that was me, too?"

"Do you have guilt?" Dr. Harmon asked.

Mick sighed a deep sigh. "Well, I guess I can tell you. I didn't go to the Light 'cause I knew I'd be punished in it." Dr. Harmon asked why. "I was a good cop, don't get me wrong. But I was less than an honest cop. I took money from time to time. Everyone did. Even took some big money once. I don't feel too good about that."

Further conversation with Mick revealed how fearful he was of the punishment he'd been taught to expect for his bad deeds. Dr. Harmon explained to Mick how many times he'd escorted others to the Light and that he'd never seen or heard of anyone being punished. People seemed to love being in the Light; he told him, especially when they found loved ones, or were met by greeters that seemed so happy to see them.

"What if ya find old enemies? I was a cop ya know. Must be a few fellas up there I put away."

"I'm talking about the Light, Mick. I think they're smart enough in the Light to know where to take people when they first come over, so everyone can get their hard feelings sorted out. Don't you?"

"Yeah, yeah, I guess you're right. Probably a lot smarter than anyone down here."

"I think you can bet on that. You a betting man, Mick?"

Mick laughed. "I don't take sucker bets. Don't make them either. What happens after you get to the Light?" he asked, clearly growing more curious, and braver.

"Well, it seems once you're in the Light, you're a lot smarter about traveling in other realms, like the astral level you're in. You lose the aches and pains you have on the earth plane, too. You can keep track of the people you love from the Light, even have them visit you when you want. Souls say they love being in the Light."

"So they stay in the Light forever huh?" Mick mused.

"No, they stay until they're ready to go somewhere else."

"Like where?" Mick asked suspiciously.

"Like back to earth. They decide what kind of body and life they want to have and they return."

"You mean I can have a body again!" Mick exclaimed excitedly. "Can I make it how I want it to be?"

"Yes. But you may find you want something different once you are in the Light than you think you do now," Dr. Harmon cautioned.

"Nah. I know what I want. Let's check out this Light."

Dr. Harmon mentally escorted Mick to the Light. Spirit attachments tell us when we do this they can sometimes see our astral bodies accompany them as well. We've escorted many spirits to the Light and we've asked many people, in past-life regressions, about their experiences after their deaths. People do not all have the same experiences at death or the same experiences in the Light. Many people experience meeting greeters. Sometimes the greeters are people they knew while in the body and sometimes they are not. Greeters are always welcoming and they are always respectful of the people they greet, never approaching them until they are asked to approach. In some past-life regressions, people have been so shocked to find their was no punishment for their "evil" deeds, they have turned away from the Light, vowing to punish themselves.

Mick's experience in the Light surprised us. Mick found a bar full of his old drinking buddies and was more than eager to stay. Pamela's Higher Self spoke after Mick left: "The shoulder pain will begin to ease now, but the muscle has been bruised, so the healing will not be complete until the morning." The pain had grown stronger throughout the session. It was so intense following the session, Pamela went to bed. The next morning the pain was completely gone

Two weeks later the client who had "brought Mick in" returned for another session. "By the way," he said to Pamela, as he sat down. "I don't know what happened the last time I was here, but my shoulder felt better when I left. A week later, it was much better. Now it's gone. It's amazing. I haven't been pain free for twenty years."

We realize that the idea of spirit attachments is a great shock to many. It shocked each of us, too. Dr. Harmon discovered such attachments when, in the days before NMR, they would suddenly "pop" out during a session. At first he wondered if they were a kind of "fantasy" of the mind. But, like past-life and inner child personalities, it became increasingly impossible to deny their presence and their effect on people.

Pamela first heard of such attachments when NMR revealed a discarnate spirit attachment - a boy of age 12 - with her. Though she experienced this first hand, she was still reluctant to "really believe" in such attachments until Linda came to see her.

Linda was a young wife and mother of two small children. She sought therapy with Pamela because she felt she'd been sexually abused by her step-father. Pamela tested Linda at about her fifth visit to "see if she was alone". She was not. NMR indicated a 8 year old boy attached to her.

Linda was, understandably, confused and upset. She did share, however, that once, when she'd been half awake and half asleep, she'd "thought" she'd seen a young boy at the foot of her bed, looking at her sadly. Still, she didn't want to "waste her money on some fantasy". Pamela convinced her it would be helpful to her and Linda reluctantly agreed to "see what happens".

Once Linda was relaxed enough to "let go", she began to cry in a small voice. Pamela asked who was crying.

"I am. I'm lost," the little boy said in Linda's voice.

"Where do you belong?" Pamela asked.

"With my mommy and daddy, but I don't know where they are," the boy said plaintively, and continued to weep.

"Maybe I can help you," Pamela offered gently. "What happened to your body?"

"I don't remember, something bad," the boy said.. "I want my mommy, where is she?" the boy demanded, stopping his crying for a moment.

"I don't know," Pamela answered. "But I know how to find out."

"How?" the boy cried. "Can you find my body too?"

"Your body is gone," Pamela explained softly "but you don't need it anymore. You can do everything you did in your body and more in your spirit body."

"My spirit body?"

"Yes, the body you have now. There are places you can go in it that are a lot more fun than being stuck here with Linda."

"No. Linda said she'd help me, and I like her." After a pause, he asked, "Like what things could I do?"

Pamela laughed and said, "Follow me. I'm going to leave my body and show you a place a little boy like you can find lots of fun. Then you can ask all the questions you want."

"You can do that?" the boy asked. "Will your body die like mine did?"

"No," Pamela explained, "I'll leave part of me in my body while another part goes with you. Come on, we're going to fly in our Spirit bodies now. Just let go of Linda and hold my hand and here we go."

Pamela asked the boy if he could see the Light. "Yes," said the boy, "it scares me." He explained to Pamela he'd seen the Light before, at his death, but he hadn't known what it was and so he'd run away and gone to the first "nice lady" he could find who would "let him in". Pamela told the boy she would go to the Light with him, to make sure the Light was a good place for him, and if it wasn't, or if he wanted to come back, he could. The boy agreed, and by mental thought, Pamela continued to travel into the Light with the boy. He found greeters who told him they had been waiting for him. They said his mother and father had been looking for him in their prayers and that he could visit them in his spirit, if he wanted, or talk to them in his mind, so they would know he was alright. They introduced him to another small boy, just his age, who said he'd take him fishing every day if he wanted. The boy, quite happily, said he wanted to stay in the Light..

Linda was very upset after the hypnosis. She felt she'd made up the whole story; though she could not imagine why she would do so. "Maybe to please you," she decided. "Although I would never imagine a boy fishing in heaven. That's not what I was taught to believe about heaven. And why would God let a little boy get lost in the first place!" Indignant and disturbed, Linda told Pamela she didn't think she'd be returning.

Three weeks later, Linda called Pamela in a panic. She was having terrible anxiety attacks, she reported, obsessing continually that she was about to die. Thinking she had cancer, she'd made out a will and scheduled a cancer exam. When that came up clean, she'd begun thinking she was about to have a car accident. "And every time I close my eyes," she said, "I see a graveyard full of graves, tombstones, and dead people. It's awful, I don't know what to do! Do you think the hypnosis caused all of this?"

Pamela assured her she didn't think so, but she was certain NMR would indicate what was causing it. When Linda arrived, NMR indicated another spirit attachment. Linda said, emphatically, she did not want to waste another session on a "fantasy." Pamela suggested that they just see what Linda's mind came up with to explain these visions and thoughts of death. Not knowing what else to do, Linda agreed.

In hypnosis, Kathy came forward. Unlike Linda, who spoke very slowly and haltingly in trance, Kathy spoke quickly and easily. She was 15, she said, and she'd been killed in an automobile accident. Her body hadn't died right away and she'd "hung around" it in the hospital, hoping it would live. When it didn't, Kathy very sadly accompanied her body to its burial. Not sure what to do or where to go, Kathy had stayed with her body all night. "It was horrible," Kathy said. "I spent the whole night in a graveyard full of graves, tombstones, and dead people. I've been trying to remind her of it lately. We met there the next day."

Kathy explained Linda had come to the cemetery with her parents. Linda had been young, only three, and she'd seen Kathy right away. Kathy had asked Linda if she could go home with her and Linda, delighted to have a new friend, said yes. Kathy and Linda had been together ever since. "Now

I want to go to the Light, where you took the kid," Kathy said to Pamela. "I listened to that and it sounded like a kinda neat place. But I don't want to go alone. I want her to come with me."

"How can she do that?" Pamela asked.

"She can get cancer. Or she can have a car accident like I did. I've always taken care of her. She won't like it here without me around. Besides, she's not taking care of her stuff. She'd be better off in the Light with me."

Pamela asked what "stuff" Kathy was referring to, and she answered, "You know, the sexual stuff with her step-dad."

"Do you know about that?" Pamela asked.

"Sure. I was there, too. He did alot more stuff than she's telling you. It's weird though, she says she's forgotten it. That's a lie. We talk about it."

Pamela reminded Kathy that Linda was only aware of her on a certain level.

"Yeah, that's true," Kathy agreed. "She ignores me a lot of the time. If she goes to the Light with me, we can hang out together like we used to. She's not much fun anymore."

"But she has children to take care of," Pamela pointed out.

"I know," Kathy retorted indignantly, "I play with them all the time."

With loving reason, Kathy was eventually persuaded to at least investigate the Light without Linda. When Kathy found young people, teenagers like herself, having a party, she was delighted. "Okay, I'll stay without her," Kathy said. "But tell Linda I love her and that I'll watch out for her. Tell her she's not happy in her marriage and she ought to do something about that. She ought to do something about what happened with her step-dad, too."

"I'll tell her," Pamela promised, even though she knew Linda was listening.

Linda was even more disturbed after this session. "I can't understand why I make up such things," she said. "It must be the hypnosis. Maybe your thoughts are transferring into my head."

Pamela, realizing how upset Linda was, did not charge her for the session. "Let's just see if the obsessions about death leave," she said to Linda.

Three days later, there was a message from Linda on Pamela's answering machine. It said: "You won't believe this. I still don't believe it, but it really happened. First off, I'm not having those thoughts or visions anymore. Second, I still haven't told anyone about what happened. I know they would think I was crazy. Plus, my pastor warned me hypnosis was bad, so I really don't want to tell anyone besides my husband what I'm doing, and I didn't tell him anything about the spirits. That would really make him mad. So, what I want to tell you is what happened with my four year old. She's been a royal pill for the past three days. Last night, in front of guests, she was so awful I pulled her from the dinner table, marched her upstairs, and threw her on her bed. 'What's wrong with you young lady?' I demanded. She locked her eyes on mine and with tears streaming down her cheeks she blurted out, 'Where's Kathy? You sent her away didn't you.'" Linda paused for breath. "I thought you might want to know about that."

Pamela dismissed her lingering doubt about spirit attachments after Linda and Kathy. This experience did not end Linda's disbelief, however. As we go to print, Linda still cannot bring herself to accept what she said in hypnosis as "real".

In general, we bring up the possibility of spirit attachments with our clients when they ask about it or when it becomes a question as to whether the spirit attachment is blocking the stated goal of the client.

Discarnates, in particular, attach to people in the body, because humans become very "fixed" on the body. As one discarnate told Pamela when she asked him why he'd attached to her client in the first place, "I didn't like just floating around. It made me feel like a ghost." When asked what a ghost was, he replied, "You know, a dead person." Obviously, he did not consider himself a "dead person", though most people still "alive with a physical body" would.

Mrs. Johnson was a client of Dr. Harmon's. A rational, solid, and highly respected business woman who had known Dr. Harmon since he was a boy, she came hobbling into his office on two canes, her knees crippled with advanced arthritis.

"Your brother is my doctor," she announced, "and he informs me I'm going to be in a wheelchair soon. He also says you are the only one who might be able to help me. I don't believe in this hypnosis nonsense, but if you can do anything, please do it. I am NOT ready for a wheel chair!"

It only took two weeks to heal the pain in Mrs. Johnsons's knees; thanks in large part to the dogged commitment of Mrs. Johnson and in no small part to several regressions that cleared years of deep-seated negative programming. The regression work was followed with hypnosis sessions for programming healing of the knees. Mrs. Johnson threw away her canes and went hiking in the foothills with her grandchildren. (After five years, X-rays showed the previous damage to her knees from the arthritis to be dramatically healed.)

A year after successfully getting rid of the pain of arthritis, Mrs. Johnson returned to Dr. Harmon's office. "I'm STILL not convinced about what you do," she announced, planting herself in his office chair, "not entirely anyway. After all, I was taking medicine and vitamins and herbs. Maybe they just all kicked in."

"Maybe," Dr. Harmon agreed affably. "So why are you here? My brother send you again?"

"No," she replied, looking away from him and then down at her hands. "In fact, I'd appreciate it if you don't mention to him, or anyone else, why I'm here. I'm not even sure why I'm here myself. But I didn't think anyone else would listen to me without thinking I've gone senile, half nuts, or off my rocker completely."

"Well," Dr. Harmon replied, smiling, "I doubt you can tell me anything I haven't heard before, and as for being off one's rocker, I've been accused of that a time or two."

Mrs. Johnson didn't even crack a smile. "Well," she began hesitantly, "as you know, I own a health food store. In fact, my family owns an organic farm, and I've always eaten the fruits and vegetables we grow. I eat healthy, I always have. Maybe too much, but healthy. So what's happening just doesn't make any sense." She took a deep breath. "For the past several weeks I've been eating eggs and ham and drinking coffee EVERY MORNING!"

She looked at Dr. Harmon and shook her head. "Can you believe it? I can't. I start driving for work, then when I get to the corner where I have to turn left, I turn right and go to McDonald's instead. I don't want anyone to see me, so I practically wolf the food down. I keep asking myself why would I act against what I believe in? I wouldn't be caught dead in a fast food place. Though I probably will be," she added, "if I keep eating like this every day."

Mrs. Johnson stopped and cleared her throat with embarrassment.

"Then, this morning, just as I turn right, I hear a voice in the back seat behind me. It was clear as day. It was a male voice and had a drawl. It said, 'Hurry up, Ma'am. We're late. I need my coffee.' Well, I tell you, Hugh, I turned my head around so fast I almost wrecked the car. There wasn't a soul in the back seat. But it felt like someone was there." She paused and shook her head. "I think I might be going crazy. Can you do something about THAT?"

NMR indicated a spirit attachment, a male in his 30's who had come to her when she was six years old. He was willing to communicate. Okay," Mrs. Johnson said reluctantly, "but only because I trust you. I've known you since you were a boy, and I've never known you to be dishonest or grasping. If you believe what this leg stuff says, I'll believe it. Besides, I'm sick to death of eggs, ham, and coffee. I'm willing to try anything that might work."

Mrs. Johnson entered hypnosis easily and quickly and soon began to speak. It was her voice, but not her voice. Much lower than her natural timbre, the voice certainly sounded male and it had a definite Texan accent.

"I'm from Texas, alright," the spirit attachment explained, when Dr. Harmon commented on his accent, "that's why they call me Tex." Tex further related that he had fought in the civil war and after it had ended, he and some fellow ex-confederates had been on their way to California when they'd been jumped by Indians in Arizona. "They come outa holes in the desert and kilt us," he drawled. "After that, I just sorta drifted." Asked when and why he'd come to Mrs. Johnson, he said it'd been at a seance her grandfather and grandmother had let her watch when she was six. The little girl had been open and friendly, so he'd stayed with her ever since.

Dr. Harmon asked Tex if he'd like to go to a special place where he could find out how to have a body of his own. Tex replied, "Well, I reckon as how I've always liked her, ever since she was a little girl. But I've never felt right being in a woman's body. Anyhow, she doesn't eat what I like. I've managed to get her to eat a real breakfast lately, but I don't know how long that's gonna last. Yup, it would be real nice havin' my own body. Seems like I'm ready to go alright."

Dr. Harmon asked Mrs. Johnson if she would be willing to have Tex move on. Her "yes" indicator finger moved emphatically. So Dr. Harmon guided Tex to the Light. There Tex found some old buddies and was delighted to remain.

Afterwards, Mrs. Johnson, who had heard every word, said she didn't believe a word of it. She wondered, however, why in the world she would make up such a crazy story. "It just doesn't sound like something I'd even imagine," she remarked, then added, "I'll be very curious to see if I quit eating those horrible breakfasts."

She returned a week later. "I haven't gone to McDonald's once since that session," she reported, "and that damn voice hasn't come back, Thank God. But my blood pressure has risen alarmingly in the past week and your brother can't find any reason for it. He taught me how to visualize it going down, which he says works for a lot of his patients, but it hasn't worked for me and medications haven't helped either. You always seem to know what to do, what can you do with this?"

First, Dr. Harmon helped Mrs. Johnson take her blood pressure. It was 200 over 110. Then they began to test the reasons for the high blood pressure with NMR. As they did so, Tex's voice suddenly burst forth from Mrs. Johnson. "I'm so dang sorry," he apologized, "but I plumb forgot about my partner and left him there with you. He gits so scared without me. Goes all to pieces." Dr. Harmon asked if the partner would talk to them. "I don't know, I'll ask him," Tex said. When nothing more came forward, Dr. Harmon quickly guided Mrs. Johnson into hypnosis.

When Mrs. Johnson began to speak again, it was - like before - her voice and not her voice. Nor did the voice sound like Tex's voice. It lacked his broad Texan drawl and braggadocio. This voice was weak and spoke with great hesitancy and agitation, saying, "I's goin' crazy here without Tex a telling me what to do. Whar's he git off to anyhow?" Tex broke in then and, after apologizing profusely, took his partner off with him.

Mrs. Johnson was instantly out of hypnosis. Dr. Harmon took her blood pressure again. It had dropped dramatically; from 200 over 110, to 130 over 75. Such a rapid drop in the space of ten minutes would normally cause extreme distress and discomfort. Mrs. Johnson announced she felt lighter, but not uncomfortable in the least.

"Even though I don't believe any of what just happened," Mrs. Johnson announced, "I sure hope it's caused me to stay fixed."

Mrs. Johnson did not have trouble with her blood pressure again. Nor did she ever eat a eggs, ham, and coffee breakfast again. Why or how "Tex" suddenly gained enough influence to wrest control of her eating habits was not addressed as in clinical practice the client's needs are of primary concern and much that might be asked or explored with a spirit attachment is not.

Research studies with spirit attachments have been done. Dr. Harmon has conducted and participated in several such studies. When a spirit attachment is talking, (even when a past life personality is talking), brain wave patterns can alter dramatically, as well as blood pressure and skin temperature. The following story indicates how seriously spirit attachments can affect the body.

Dr. Harmon was teaching a class on visualization techniques for medical hypnosis. He asked the class members to focus on a physical trait or symptom they wanted to change. One man exclaimed, "I have so many symptoms I hardly know what to focus on!"

When asked to name his symptoms, he replied, "My eyes are bad and are getting worse. I have a condition where colors shift in and around my eyes, making my eyesight very blurry. My bowel problems are so bad I've had bowel surgery, which didn't help much. I have heart problems as well as high blood pressure, which gives me headaches, one of which I have right now." Dr. Harmon asked the student, a gentleman in his 40's named Tom, if he was currently under a doctor's care. He replied he was, adding his doctor had referred him to the class as he thought hypnotic techniques might benefit him. "Good," Dr. Harmon remarked smiling, "then do you suppose your doctor would approve of your learning, and demonstrating, right now, a technique for immediately lowering the blood pressure a point or two?"

"Approve? He'll probably make me teach it to him," Tom replied.

Dr. Harmon took Tom's blood pressure in front of the class, asking him to watch the needle and note the numbers. Another member of the class, a registered nurse, was asked to retake the blood pressure and verify the readings, which she did. Next, Tom was asked to focus on "imaging" or "visualizing" the needle in his mind as it lowered by two or more points. His blood pressure was taken again. It had gone up. This was not what it was supposed to do. Dr. Harmon instructed Tom to close his eyes. He gave Tom suggestions for relaxing deeper and visualizing or imaging the drop of the needle on the blood pressure dial. While he was doing so, his blood pressure was checked again. It had gone up even higher! Somewhat alarmed,

Dr. Harmon called for a five minute break while Tom relaxed and listened to soothing music. Thinking over what had happened, it suddenly occurred to Dr. Harmon that there might be a spirit attachment influencing the blood pressure. Since NMR had not yet been developed, his only way of knowing would be to guide Tom into hypnosis and see if there was indeed such an attachment.

Gathering the group back together, Dr. Harmon proceeded with a hypnotic induction. Once Tom was securely in hypnosis, Dr. Harmon asked if there was "someone else" in the body. A finger began to move rapidly. Dr. Harmon then asked if this "other person" would speak to them. Again, the finger wiggled. Dr. Harmon gave instructions for using mental energy to vibrate the vocal chords, enabling the attachment to communicate. Suddenly, a strong, loud voice began speaking excitedly. It was, however, speaking in German. Dr. Harmon broke into the stream of German words, explaining that his German was very limited. Would the spirit, he asked, mind speaking in English? A guttural voice hesitantly replied, "I don't speak so good English. But I try, yah? Und I am no spirit, I am a person. Du verstand?" In several sessions over the next two days, the class was to hear a fascinating story, told in broken English, by four different spirit attachments.

The first related that he was a Sergeant in the German army in World War I, and that with him (also attached to the body) were three soldiers from his unit. Two were German, like himself. One was from what is called Yugoslavia today. They had been on patrol together on the front lines. An American artillery shell blew up the shed where they had gathered. One of them had been near the shed, one was just walking out of it, and the other two had been inside. All of them had been fatally injured, though none of them had died instantly. One had been blinded when half his face was torn away. This soldier told of his slow and agonizing death, unable to see or to move. Another said he had lost his legs and bled to death. The third had his "guts" (bowels) blown away. The Sergeant said he was semi-comatose when the American infantry over-ran them. "A dough boy," he related sadly, "bayonets me in the heart as I lie on the ground"

There was much the Sergeant and his men did not understand or could not explain. The Sergeant remembered thinking at his death of his mother and sister, who were struggling alone without anyone to help them. He found himself with them and tried to be of help, but no-one paid any attention to him. He stayed with them (but do not attach to either's body), and some years later came to America with them when they immigrated after the war. He went with his sister when she married and when her son (his nephew) was born, he attached to his nephew's body. Later, when that nephew had a son of his own (Tom), he attached to him. So the Sergeant was Tom's own great uncle. Sometime in Tom's early childhood, another of the soldiers rejoined his Sergeant by attaching to the Sergeant. (The attachment of a spirit to another spirit attachment is called "piggybacking". All spirits within the energy field of the physical body affect it, whether they are piggybacking or directly attached.) The last two soldiers said they had been "half in and half out" of Tom's body until he was 12. (Probably meaning they would come and go.) They said they attached "permanently" when Tom had a dream, at age 12, of the death of the patrol. (Tom later mentioned the dream had been so vivid, he'd always remembered it.)

The Sergeant was escorted into the Light by Dr. Harmon. and the Sergeant's patrol followed. Immediately following the release of the "German Patrol", Tom's blood pressure, which had stabilized over the past days, lowered to a healthy norm. Dr. Harmon kept track of Tom for the next couple of years. Within weeks of the release of the spirit attachments, Tom's eye disease, which had been diagnosed as progressive, stabilized and over time his eye sight improved dramatically. Within a few months, tests indicated his heart condition as having <u>completely healed</u>. Further tests showed his bowels <u>had healed</u> also. He had not had a headache since the "German Patrol" left him.

Cases like these, of which we have many, make it very difficult to deny or ignore the "evidence" and effect of spirit attachments. Even memories one has can be those of a spirit attachment. (Important to recognize when working with abuse!) Attachments are not, in most cases, trying to take over the body, nor do they mean to affect the body or the person in it. Most often, they are not even aware they are doing so. <u>Drugs, medications, treatments, procedures, and surgeries designed to "stabilize" symptoms of the mind or the body caused by spirit attachments will have little or no effect if the attachment remains</u>. Attachments can be, and frequently are, the cause of "disassociate" behaviors and "multiple personality" disorder.

Spirit attachments do sometimes take over the body, if permitted (overtly or covertly) to do so by the one who "owns" the body. "Blackouts" in short term or long term memory can be due to attachments who have gained control of the body. (Children frequently leave their bodies when being physically or sexually abused, which is why they often cannot later remember that abuse, unless they stayed around, astrally, to watch. But the subconscious mind and the cells do remember, as do spirit attachments who stayed in the body to "take" the abuse and help the body survive.) Spirit attachments who take conscious control of the body can be responsible for violence to themselves and others. Abusers often have such attachments they have drawn to them, which is why abusers frequently cannot "remember" the abuse, unless they stick around to watch or to participate. (Their subconscious mind, body cells, and attachments will remember it.)

When spirit attachments are guilty of a crime, an enlightened society works with them to help them heal and then to help them move into the Light. (Trying to integrate a spirit attachment, even a past life personality which has come forward as a spirit attachment, into the "main" personality is highly unenlightened, as well as impossible.) An enlightened society would also work with the inner mind of the one who allowed the attachment. An enlightened society would never release or execute criminals without having first healed them (with regression therapy) of their inner pain, hate, and rage. Execution of such people is a good way to create future sociopaths (by birth or spirit attachment). Societies that recognize they themselves will be born into what they create for the future have a powerful incentive for enlightenment.

True spirit guides do not, in most cases, attach to the body except to be channeled. (Attachments are quite capable of calling themselves spirit guides when they realize this would gain them respect or control.) True spirit guides know better than to attach to a body; they realize the effect this has on the body and the person in it. True spirit guides rarely ask for those they guide to give over their bodies or lives in any manner. Spirit guides offer guidance; they are not "into control".

A client and student of ours was highly indignant when her spirit guides said: "The life force of this one will be withdrawn if she chooses this path". Yes, this sounds like "control". However, her Higher Self explained: "She chose, before entering, her purpose. She has already walked the path she now contemplates. There is nothing to be gained there. I will withdraw the life force if she chooses it again. The body may linger, but the spirit will leave it."

The Higher Self is the only spirit guide allowed to "withdraw the life force" without ones consent as the Higher Self IS oneself.

NMR (when precisely and properly done), the Universal Records (when accurately accessed), and Higher Self channeling (when not filtered by the conscious or the subconscious) are the most accurate methods we know of for determining whether particular spirit guides are or are not beneficial to ones path, purpose, and greater good.

~ * ~

Sue was a client of Pamela's. Sue had a childhood of abuse, as well as trauma from several back injuries and surgeries. Sue had several types of multiples; including an active inner child personality; a personality created by that child to protect her; a discarnate attachment who helped to soothe and comfort her after she'd been abused; a discarnate attachment of a man she had known in a past life in Greece, and a past life personality of her own from a later past life.

Sue did not know about her very active inner levels of mind when she sought therapy with Pamela. She suspected, however, there was a lot more to her mind and its abilities than being smart. (Always a straight "A" student, Sue, now in her 40's, continues to study, explore, and grow with many varied interests.) She and Pamela began their work together by using NMR to establish the origins of her difficulties with her back.

NMR indicated a past life as a woman in Germany whose death, at the close of World War II., was the origin of the weak back. Once Sue was in trance, it became clear this past life personality was still with Sue as a past-life spirit attachment. The woman, named Greta, explained that she'd helped Sue as a child when she was being hurt by her parents. She understood such hurt, Greta, said, because she had been similarly hurt herself.

Greta's story unfolded as she told of being conscripted to clean and cook for a group of Nazi officers in Berlin during the war. These officers had treated her very badly. Their leader had, however, been kind to Greta when the others weren't around, and Greta had fallen in love with him. The night before the advance of the Allies into Berlin, the officers, had, in a drunken rage raped and beaten Greta to death. Not only had the man she loved not stopped them, it had been his heavy boot that had broken her back;

the final crushing blow that killed her.

Greta's abuse was worked with over three sessions. At the end of the third session, Pamela asked Greta if she would like to move into the Light. (Whether this means the past life astral personality stays in the astral levels is unclear. It still seems to "work" best to convince them to "go to the Light". If they won't do so, one can escort them to the astral world. We share more information on the astral world in Books Two and Three.) Greta said she was willing, but that it would greatly upset the inner child personality. She also wanted to meet with the Nazi Officer in order to let him know she forgave him. When Pamela suggested she do that in the Light, Greta refused. She wanted to tell him now, she said, as part of her healing. Pamela asked, through the Higher Selves, that the Nazi Officer be brought to Greta. Soon, he was "present", sharing his sorrow and guilt for the murder and misuse of Greta. Greta told him she loved him and forgave him.

Sue was bemused by this session. She still felt she was "making things up" in hypnosis and this had been an elaborate story her mind had concocted. However, she believed strongly the mind could heal her back and "if this is the way it wants to do it, so be it".

After Sue left, Pamela mentioned the summoning of the Nazi Officer to Dr. Harmon and said she'd realized, after Sue left, that she had neither asked the Higher Selves to take him away or checked with NMR to see if he was gone. "Opps," he commented, "maybe you'd better call Sue." As she expected Sue back the following week, and Sue had already indicated she didn't believe any of it, Pamela chose to wait until she returned to check on the Nazi Officer.

Sue called a few days later, saying she had to see Pamela right away. "Something is very wrong with my eating," she explained. "I have never had an eating disorder. Now I can't stop eating. I've been eating since I left your house. I stopped at a restaurant, and you know how I hate restaurant food, and had TWO HUGE meals. I couldn't believe it. On the way home I stopped and got something to eat and bought something to cook when I got home. I've been eating non-stop every since." Pamela agreed to see Sue the next day.

When Sue arrived, she said, "It's getting worse. I ate meat in between classes today." As Sue had been a vegetarian all of her life, this was even more disturbing to her than the non-stop eating. NMR indicated the cause of the non-stop eating was a spirit attachment influence; specifically the Nazi Officer spirit attachment. In hypnosis, he came forward readily. Pamela spoke with him of the Light and he agreed to go.

He came back, however, or lied about going. Sue said at her next session, "I think he's back. I ate meat again today at lunch and I lifted a weight in gym class I should never have been able to lift. My teacher was horrified. She knows about my back."

When the Nazi Officer came forward again, he announced he had no intention of ever leaving Sue. She could help him, he said, by eating more meat and more food, and he could help her by making her stronger. "I lifted that weight today," he bragged.

Pamela pointed out that Sue's back could not handle the weights "he" was lifting and that Sue did not want him in her body. She also pointed out that because no part of Sue was holding onto him, he could be made to go. "Of course," she added, "you could attach to someone else, but I suspect having a body of your own and really eating food, not just enjoying it vicariously, is what you really want. Someone with your strength and brilliant mind could build a perfect body." The Nazi Officer was convinced. He WOULD build a perfect body. This time, Pamela called for Beings of Light to come accompany him into the Light.

Sue's eating returned to normal after this session and stayed there. She also began to trust more in what she was saying in hypnosis. Trusting in herself is a big issue with Sue. Addressing, more thoroughly than she has, her childhood will play a big part in maturing Sue's truly extraordinary talents and abilities.

In the rare instances of spirit attachments that refuse to cooperate, there are ways of "capturing" them, but this is not the place to outline that. It's important to note, as well, that even beings of Light, even the Light itself, cannot take away attachments a person is holding onto at some level of mind.

The next story is one of an "evil" discarnate. As you read this story, which is painful, do remember that souls always draw their own "evil" and "good" to themselves by their own thoughts, beliefs, emotions, and acts. This young man, to whom the "evil" was done; had abdicated control of his body through choices of his own.

The story begins when a woman who had, many years prior, taken some

classes from Dr. Harmon, called to ask for reading material that might help
her deal with the pain she was feeling over her son's suicide, two days before.
She mentioned she had thought she had seen glimpses of her son around
her home, but she supposed that was only her imagination, driven by her
desire to see him and talk with him. We asked if she would like us to see
if her son needed any assistance. She asked how we could do that. We
explained about the Universal Records and that, through them, we could
perhaps discover the whereabouts of her son. She asked us to do so. The
following is most of the transcript of that session. Jim was a young man
in his twenties and his real name (as well as the real names of all the clients
and spirits in this book) is not used.

Master of Spirit: "You are requesting information about a young boy. What
    is the age?" (Pamela gives Jim's birth date.) "One moment please. There
    are two records for that one - his primary spirit and an attachment. It
    appears the spirit attachment caused him grievous anxiety and
    depression."

Pamela: "Was this a spirit attachment that came into the body with him
    at birth or at a later time?"

Master of Spirit: "No, it came more recently."

Pamela: "Would it have been the greatest influence on the manner of his
    death?"

Master of Spirit: "Yes. He is still earth bound, he is not moving. Very
    fearful, confused by the happenings brought about by the second spirit
    that came to him some time ago and this came to him in some altered
    state. I don't see what altered state that is."

Pamela: "Is the spirit[attachment] still with him?"

Master of Spirit: "While they are separate, they know where each other
    is when the spirit wants him. The spirit is not capable of generating
    another body and foolishly wanted to destroy this last one, which left
    the prime keeper of the body in a very confused and distressed state.
    He is afraid to talk to her, his mother. His mother may invite him.
    And if she chooses, we will invoke spirit of him to her, if she chooses.
    It would be helpful for him to be able to speak and to be assured he
    can move into the Light."

Pamela: "In a case such as this where there was spirit influence, does it
    [the spirit's influence] over-ride the will, or did this young man have

a propensity to confusion in the first place?"

Master of Spirit: "He was very open to discovery and experimentation and altered states." [Note: The boy's mother had mentioned that her son had experimented for several years with drugs.] "A propensity that led him to allowing a spirit that was not to his benefit to inhabit his body with him. This spirit became disenchanted, because of another relationship, and caused the destruction of the body."

Pamela: "Would it be helpful for us to draw the boy here to talk to his soul and perhaps to the spirit attached with him?"

Master of Spirit: "That is your option, not mine."

Pamela: "Then, please help us to find Jim and bring him here."

Voice: "Maybe I can help."

Pamela: "Oh, hello Master of Light. Can you help us with this young man? Your light is everywhere. Perhaps you can bring in his energy for us."

Master of Light: "You are wise. Let us see if he will come. You might send your thoughts inviting him to visit." (Pamela speaks aloud inviting Jim to follow Light and come to speak through Dr. Harmon's body.)

Jim: "Help. Help me. I'm afraid. I want my body. I feel lost."

Pamela: "Have you heard of the Light, Jim?

Jim: "Yes."

Pamela: "Did you see it when you left your body?"

Jim: "I don't know, I was scared."

Pamela: "Yes, emotions often block seeing the light."

Jim: "I was so scared. I don't know why I did that."

Pamela: "You were being influenced by another is our information."

Jim: "I know. I was crazy."

Pamela: "How did you happen to draw that one to you?"

Jim: "I don't know. I think he's still around here. My mother will be mad at me."

Pamela: "She's not mad at you. She's very sad. She thought she saw you,.."

Jim: "Yeah, well, but I saw her sadness. She didn't even know I was dead."

Pamela: "The sadness is for herself, Jim, because she won't be able to see you. But her life will go on, and she will meet with you again. When your mother leaves her body, you can be one of her greeters, you can help her with that. Imagine that."

Jim: "Oh, good, yes, good."

Pamela: "She would love to have you talk to her. How would you do that?"

Jim: "I don't know. How would I do that? In her mind?"

Pamela: "Yes, if she will just sit and center the way she's been taught, you could talk to her in her mind. You could give her some kind of signal or thought that she knows it is you, something meaningful between the two of you."

Jim: "Can I go there now?"

Pamela: "Well, one second, Jim, before you do, tell me about Master of Light.."

Jim: "He's here now."

Pamela: "How do you perceive Master of Light?"

Jim: "It's a joyous feeling, like he's above and all around me."

Pamela: "Jim, Master of Light can take you to your mother to communicate with her and then he can take you to the Light, a place of understanding and peace and tranquillity where you can meet with your own Higher Self. You won't be alone, you know, there are others there, others that you've known."

Jim: "I think I know that. I feel better."

Pamela: "Good. Then would you like Master of Light to take you to your mother now?"

Jim: "Maybe he can help me. He feels so good maybe he can make her feel better. I love my mom. I shouldn't have done that, I don't know why. . .."

Pamela: "Perhaps you can understand about that, too, Jim. Perhaps this is your first step on a journey of the mind."

Jim: "Okay. Alright. Bye."

Pamela: "Good-bye. Thank you Master of Light who is everywhere. I now ask if that spirit that was attached to Jim that seems to be seeking a body, would you communicate at this time?"

Voice: [Deep and rough.] "No."

Pamela: "No? You don't want to communicate?"

Voice: "No. You'll make me go away."

Pamela: "I'm not going to make you go away. In fact, I know how you can have your own body."

Voice: "I don't believe you. How can you give me a body?"

Pamela: "I know how to do it. I certainly know that trying to get a body your way isn't going to work for you. You don't have enough control of them, do you? They don't do what you want them to, do they?"

Voice: "No. I get rid of them."

Pamela: "You want to get rid of them?"

Voice: "They want to get rid of them. They don't do what I want."

Pamela: "What about the last body you had of your own?"

Voice: "I got rid of it. It wouldn't do what I wanted it to."

Pamela: "What did you want it to do?"

Voice: "Never mind."

Pamela: "You want a healthy and strong body that you can do anything in, don't you?"

Voice: "Yes, done my way."

Pamela: "I fail to see how you can have a strong, healthy body doing it your way, trying to take over other bodies."

Voice: "If I can find one that wants to leave, I can take over."

Pamela: "As sort of a walk-in. Have you heard of that?"

Voice: "What you call it, maybe. I just want a big, strong, healthy body."

Pamela: "Is that why you go to bodies that are feeling suicidal, hoping you can exchange?"

Voice: "Either that, or I make them leave."

Pamela: "Well then, how is it you haven't become a walk-in yet?"

Voice: "They die too fast. They won't leave without me, and then when I go to leave, the body's gone."

Pamela: "You know, to become a walk-in you need a body with a mind that is strong and at peace and centered. An agreement must be made before they leave and you go in. You're going about it all wrong."

Voice: "No one told me. How do you know so much?"

Pamela: "I, too, am spirit at one level. I have great knowledge available to me. On top of which, I've talked to many spirits and received much information."

Voice: "How did you do that?"

Pamela: "Much like this. Teaching people to be channels by relaxing their mind and body in a way spirits can talk through them."

Voice: "What can you do for me?   Get a body for me?"

Pamela: "What do you think of the idea of being born in your own body
and then growing it strong and healthy? That way it's yours. That way,
you're in COMPLETE control of it."

Voice: "Hmmmm. Maybe I don't know it will be healthy and strong.

Pamela: "You need to pick the right parents for that. There's something
to be said for genes. Also, by this time, you recognize a strong, healthy
body needs a strong, healthy mind. Have you not noticed that when
they have weak minds the body becomes weakened?" [Voice: "Yes."]
"And a person with a strong, balanced mind - they aren't going to let
you come in."

Voice: "Okay, how do I get this body?"

Pamela: "There is a place I know where you can go." [Voice: "Where?
Where?"] "Where you apply for a body." [Voice: "Where?"] "I'm going
to ask from the levels of Spirit that there come to us now a perfect one
that can show this energy where to go to get a body that is strong and
healthy. I assume you want it male?" [Voice: "YES!] "Then the one
that comes must know how to help him to get a male, strong, healthy
body of his own. I ask for that energy to be here now, to come now.
Master of Light, bring that one now. Have you perceived another energy
here yet?"

Voice: "It's laughing at me."

Pamela: "Well, let's talk to it. Maybe, you don't want it. Let's find out.
What's it saying to you?"

Voice: "It said, 'I can give you a body without a mind.' Humph."

Pamela: "Is that what you want?"

Voice: "No. That's exactly what I DON'T want."

Pamela: "Now, energy, can you tell him what he DOES want? What's
it saying now?"

Voice: "That I better go to that place where they - WITH me - make things,
decide and make things. I don't know what the word is here. But it's
not like THEY make things happen, it's like I do, too. It's like they
can help me do that. My decision, but they help me make it happen.
That sounds good. I can do that. As long as they don't stick me in
a body without a mind."

Pamela: "I think as long as you tell them what you want, that's what you get."

Voice: "That's what it says. Can't do that here, though, have to go on. Move into what they call the ether or the Light. Okay. I'm ready, I'm ready. There are two Light Beings here. Oh, I'm excited to meet the Light. 'We'll go with you', they say. Thank you."

Pamela: "Good luck on your journey."

Voice: "Thank you, I don't need luck."

Pamela: "Quite right, how stupid of me. Much Light on your journey."

Voice: "Thank you."

We sent Jim's mother, with some trepidation, a tape of this session. It took her a year to call us. She said it was because it took her a year to get past her grieving for her son. She expressed her gratitude for our help, but also said she had been very disappointed in the tape. She had been hoping for more. She had hoped the tape would "prove" to her that her son still existed. She also said she "never really heard from him"; that she'd "only" had dreams of him and "imagined" him talking to her in her head.

Discarnates express great frustration to us as they tell us how easy it is to meet and speak with their loved ones, but how frequently their loved ones believe it is "only dreams and imagination". Humans have "closed off" their awareness to so many levels of mind and spirit.

Jim's mother provided a very interesting footnote to this session. Jim's fiancee had listened to the tape as well. Suddenly, as she was listening, she gasped and turned off the tape. With a pale face she told Jim's mother she had arrived at Jim's bedside just as they had turned off the life support. "He made a sound, through his lips," she said. "He was trying to tell me something, I knew he was. But the nurses said it was air escaping his body." She started to cry softly as she said, "On the tape, I heard that same sound. He was saying, 'Help me'".

No doubt you are wondering if anyone knows how to go to the Light when they die or if all children "get lost" at death. People choose at all ages the degree to which they will "turn off" their inner levels of knowing. Everyone sees the Light. Not everyone chooses to move into it. Fortunately, everyone has a Higher Self' that keeps guiding souls towards those who will help them move into the Light.

Dr. Harmon had a client, a woman of 70, who had escaped the Holocaust. She was very fearful of dying and Dr. Harmon spoke to her at length about the Light. She listened politely, said she wished she could believe him, but she was still fearful. She left to visit her son on the East Coast before they could do more in depth work about the Light.

Several weeks later, her son, a psychologist, called Dr. Harmon. "My mother just died," he said quietly, "but I have to tell you what happened. I still can't believe it. But I witnessed it. So did her Doctor and a nurse. They're as shocked as I am. After my mother flat-lined, her doctor and I were discussing what would be done with her body next. I was watching my mother's face as we talked. It was relaxing to such a peaceful look, I was fascinated. The nurse was about to cover her face when suddenly, and mind you, I could still see the flat line on the monitor, she opened her eyes and looked straight at me. She said, "Tell Dr. Harmon it's true. There is a Light. I'm going to it now.""

There is a Light. There is a consciousness of Light as well. That consciousness speaks to all of us all the time. It speaks through rainbows and music; through sunrises and sunsets; through sun and moon; through sky and stars; through clouds and rain; through all that lives and all that is.

This consciousness we have dubbed Master of Light, though it no doubt answers to many names. We have much need right now, we humans, of Light, for the balance in our world has tipped precariously toward the Darkness. Both are needed, Light and Dark, for in the fulcrum of this balance our world, and the life forms upon it, exist. In this balance, we exist. The Balance has been lost and must be regained. Let Master of Light tell us how.

~ NOTES TO YOURSELF ~

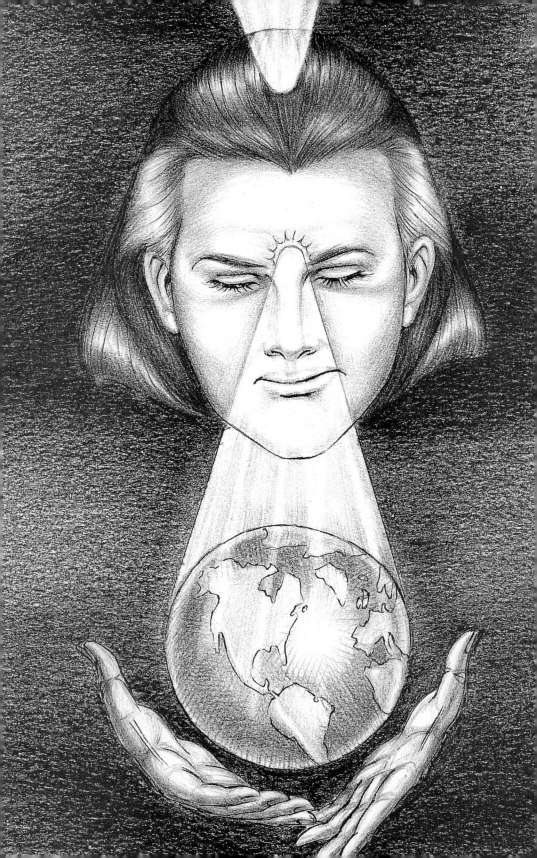

Chapter 8

Joy! Joy! Joy!

Your quantum physicists tell you all of matter is composed of ever smaller particulate matter and that the smaller the particulate matter becomes the greater the spaces between them grow. They tell you there is more space than matter in matter and they wonder what is in the spaces. The astral levels are in those spaces. In those levels is energy; the energies of thought, spirit, emotion, color, sound, astral matter, realms, planes, and dimensions. All exist as frequencies of Light.

I am the consciousness of Light. I have no form and I have all forms for my Light is with everyone and everything. I meet with Pamela and Hugh daily; just as I meet with each of you daily.

Pamela believes I should use the term "Doctor Harmon" instead of Hugh. She believes his education and wealth of knowledge and experience entitle him to his proper title. It is amusing to me that Pamela, who professes not to believe in titles, elevates the good Doctor and me above herself because of our titles, though I have no title except what she has given me. Master of Light she calls me, which amuses me even more. I was pleased to see her place her name first in the authorship for that is her proper place in the order of things for this book. It amuses me it took her so long to realize that.

I am easily amused. Humans delight and amuse me greatly and though, as Light, I am not to have preferences, I do, which amuses that which created me. All spirit has consciousness and all consciousness grows and changes in ways that are often as surprising to that which created it as it is to the created.

You humans have forgotten to be amused. You are heavy with

your growing consciousness. You are heavy with your realizations of your power and your place in the greater scheme of things. You are heavy with your growing awareness of the future. A future which you have yourselves created and a future which you yourselves can uncreate. What is there to be heavy about with this? The child who makes a mess is happy to laugh at the mess before the caretaker swoops down to bathe the child and clean up the mess. This is as it should be. All are in their proper roles - the child doing what children do and the caretaker doing what caring does best. In this way progress is made.

Humans have made a mess in their child like refusal to acknowledge or heed the consequences of their thoughts, words, beliefs, and actions. The caretakers of the human race are here to bathe the child and clean up the mess. All are in their proper place for progress. Just as the child is taught to leave behind the messes of childhood as it grows in consciousness, so is it the job of the caretakers to teach the human race to grow in consciousness and move forward into your adult responsibilities and rewards. Humans are ready to grow. They simply need a little guidance and a little help. This is why I am here. This is why you are here. It is why Pamela and Hugh are here. As I am writing this chapter and Pamela is supplying only the focus of her mind and fingers, I shall call the Being of Light that I love so dearly, just as I love each of you, Hugh.

I meet Hugh at sunrise. He loves the dawn, as do I. Hours of joy we have spent together, as I delight in the palette of colors, shapes, and forms I bring to him which brings him joy. His joy inspires me. Just as your joy inspires me in every dawn you rise to watch. "Joy, Joy, Joy!" He thinks this often in the purity of his spirit as he watches the sun rise and listens to the life forms of Nature rejoicing at its rising. He is at his best when he feels this purity of spirit. This is why I call him at dawn, to combine his Spirit with my Light. His is a mighty Spirit and mine a mighty Light and together we shower the world with the healing vibration of joy.

I am with Pamela always. She laughs for she thought I would say I meet with her at sunset. I know better than to call her at dawn for she is not in human body at dawn. She has much work to do at many levels and her work in the spaces between material matter keeps her busy while her human self is at rest.

I am with Pamela always for she is the caretaker of human consciousness.

She acts sometimes like a worried mother; scolding the children and shaking her head at their messes even as she delights in their creativity. She, though more spirit than human, has become too human. This is as it should be for above all humans she knows what the future brings and while her spirit knows it will be but a blip in the greater span of time she knows as well in her human heart that it will bring much despair for generations to come. She loves humans. Her Spirit has served humans since human time began. That service is nearly ended. No matter the outcome her Spirit will take its place among the Masters wearing the mantle of the Master's highest role. She calls me Master. I am Light. I serve all Masters.

You are a Master, too. Stop and put down this book at the end of this paragraph. Look around you. What you see is what you have created. I have served you in this creation. Look now at what you have created.

Did you enjoy what you saw? Did you see how beautifully your Spirit and my Light have worked together to manifest all that you chose to create? Did you realize as you looked that the messes you have created that they are simply a part of your learning and your spiritual growth? Let this amuse you! Laugh as a child laughs, with pure delight and joy. Now with that same delight and joy, pick up your mantle as a caretaker of your world. I will help you in this. You need my help. I need you to do what must be done. Here is how we shall work together, you and I. Your minds shall focus my Light to bring the balance back into the world. Your world is out of balance and must be brought back into balance. A simple task, really. All it requires are certain vibrations of Light.

You have learned that all energy has vibration. Even solid matter has vibration as within all solid matter there is movement of particulate matter and the energy in the spaces between them. All must be in balance one with the other to keep the harmonious vibration that keeps the physical form of matter intact.

It's like a symphony. Notes and chords must be arranged in perfect balance. Instruments must be in tune with skilled musicians playing them. The conductor and the acoustics are important. Each part of the symphony must be in balance one with the other to create a sound that is harmonious to the ears.

Sound is an excellent example of the power of vibration. Sound is vibration. The vibrations of sound are very powerful and they powerfully

affect energy. Sound can shatter eardrums and mountains. Sound can
mutate, even kill, cells. Sound can heal cells. Sound can transmute matter
into other forms of energy and other forms of energy into matter. In Book
Two, which I shall write, I will share information to help you use the
vibrations of sound, light, color, spirit, and physical motion for
transmutation of energy, including healing. Before we do that together,
however, we must change the vibrations of your planet together. Otherwise
there will be no one left to write or to read Book Two.

The vibrations of the energy fields of your planet are severely imbalanced.
As a result, the physical form of the planet is cracking. The crusts and
mantles of earth are shifting. Molten layers are being pushed upward. The
magnetic poles are so out of balance the weather is completely off balance.
The land is dying and the waters are killing the very life forms they are
meant to support. Animals are turning against one another, even of the
same species, as their instincts tell them their greatest fight for survival is
upon them. Your animal bodies are responding in the same manner. You
are turning against one another. Your bodies and your minds and your
spirits are not balanced with one another. The animal is gaining the upper
hand as its instincts tell it to survive above all.

This situation cannot last long. Nature will right itself. Balance is as
great an instinct for Nature as is survival. Always Nature seeks the balance.
This is why your bodies heal and your cells regenerate. This is why there
are seasons. It is why the oceans, the rivers, the streams, the lakes, the forests,
and woods and valleys and hills and mountains all exist where they are. It
is how Nature maintains the balance.

Humans have worked against Nature and not with it. Human wills and
whims have neglected to pay attention to maintaining the balance of nature.
You move mountains, hills, rivers, lakes, streams, woods, and forests without
restoring the ecological balance. You build structures on land that cannot
support them and populate land without the resources to support you. You
have wiped away forests in the name of profit when it profits you nothing
as the energy fields of the forests are crucial to the balance of your planet.
You have depleted the resources of the lands and the seas. You have placed
action before clear thinking and greed before balance. Even those of you
who have clearly seen the big picture have failed to apply your sights to
the smaller picture of your own part in this. The minutia of your lives

have blinded you to the magnitude of your responsibilities for maintaining the balance of nature.

As a result, the vibrations of your planet are highly unstable and dangerous. You all sense this. Your minds, bodies, and the spirits of all of nature are very frightened. Thoughts and emotions have vibrations and fear has a very powerful vibration. The vibration of fear is so universal on the earth at this time that it is adding tremendously to the imbalance.

This situation has been noticed by beings of planes, realms, dimensions, and planets other than earth. All of the cosmos is affected by the energy fields of all of the cosmos. When one planet's energy field tilts as far out of balance as yours, all that are of higher consciousness pay attention for they know it will affect the balance of the whole. The dilemma for them is they cannot directly interfere in the situation as you have created it yourselves. They can, however, help you help yourselves and many are doing that. Many are benevolent in their intents; some are not.

Human beings are channeling and receiving telepathic messages in record numbers as beings of all dimensions and planes seek to press their warnings to humans of the need for immediate action. Unfortunately, this means of contact is not acceptable or convincing to many humans. Even when it is, it is not trusted, which is just as well as there are those speaking to you that do not have your greater good in mind.

You have been, in general, irresponsible in your communications with spirit; whether they call themselves guides or aliens. It is like the situation with your cyberspace. Through your computers you are seduced by those telling you what you want to hear. Your senses of intuition which would normally warn you of a person's true intent if you were to meet that person face to face have not yet learned how to tune in via the cyberwaves. So you are vulnerable to lies, deceit, and conceit.

It is the same with other dimensions of reality. You are excited to hear from a being in another dimension. The being tells you it is knowing, wise, and of higher consciousness and you take the information at face value even though you see no face! It is not hard to talk like a being of higher consciousness; one need only study the thought forms of beings of higher consciousness. It is very easy to know what humans like to hear. Your need to feel important makes you very vulnerable. It is very amusing to watch humans who feel special because they can channel, use mental telepathy, or have psychic abilities. You all have these abilities. Every animal on your planet has these abilities.

I do not mean to make light of your abilities. I mean to enlighten you. The telepathic abilities of your physical beings are quite exciting. Combined with the powers of your spirits, it makes you quite unique in the universes. You can't imagine how you intrigue the beings of other dimensions and planets. When you do make physical contact with other beings never for a moment think you have less power than they have. Your powers are extraordinary. Other Beings respect your powers far more than do you. Even in ignorance of your powers you have given ample demonstration of your abilities to hold your own. Imagine your position in the universes when you know more of what you are doing with your powers. Your emotions add to the fears of other beings. Your emotions cause other Beings to be wary of you for your emotions make you highly unpredictable. Unpredictable beings are to be treated with great caution.

This is why beings of other planets have not contacted you more directly. They are afraid if they were to physically appear before you; there would be mass hysteria among you. This has happened before; they realize the danger of it happening now. They do not wish to stress your planet beyond its tolerance by adding the energy of hysteria to its energy field.

As you channel the many beings who wish to contact you, it is best that you channel, at this time, their thoughts, and not their energies. Do not bring them into earth's energy fields. Although vibrations of some of these beings might be beneficial to you and your planet in normal circumstances, the situation on earth is anything but normal. It is like trying to defuse a bomb without knowing how much time is left. Everyone is being very cautious for no one knows, not even I, how much time is left.

Even those aliens who want to control you do not want your planet destroyed. Nor can they invade you directly for your spirits have free will. Not even The Prime Creator crosses your wills and as long as you are in human form, your planet and bodies are protected from those who would wrest either from you. However, you can give them away directly or indirectly.

There are those that are arguing in the Higher Realms that humans have given away their right to the earth and their bodies because of their actions. Actions that now threaten the planet with great destruction and the human life form with nearly complete destruction. They ask that your planet be given to them. Along with your human bodies, if possible.

Incredibly, Nature argues for you alongside your Higher Selves. Earth had not been planned as a place of habitation for your spirits. It was a place for the Spirit of Nature to work in co-creation with the Prime Creator. Your souls became intrigued with the earth in their explorations. So intrigued they entered the life forms they found here and began to identify with those forms. This was upsetting to the spirits of those life forms and they petitioned, in a sense, their Higher Self, the Spirit of Nature, to help them.

A plan was devised by your Higher Selves and the Spirit of Nature to evolve a life form that would better suit your souls. The spirit of that life form would serve the souls and in return that spirit and its life form would evolve in consciousness as well. So began the human race. You have, over time, pushed away your awareness of the spirit of your bodies, just as you have pushed away your awareness of the other levels of your spirit.
You have been quite ruthless in your dealings with Nature. You were never meant to rule nature; you were meant to learn to live in harmony with it. To do so will bring great harmony to your souls. Instead, you have over-run the earth. You have quit communicating with the spirits of nature. Indeed, you deny that any form on earth other than your own has consciousness. I can assure you, all that is has consciousness.

Despite your actions and your stubbornness in reforming, Nature wants to give you another chance. Your Higher Selves and Nature are closely bonded. Both hope that you will see the Light. A little pun there. I do enjoy word play.

Nature's plan is to wipe the planet clean of humans, save for a very small number, before humans destroy the planet beyond Nature's ability to restore it. The few humans remaining would be without technology of any kind, for Nature is fed up with your technology. You will struggle against the elements and other animals for your survival. You will learn, once again, to respect Nature. Make no mistake, it would be for those few humans remaining as though they had returned to the age of the dinosaurs. Humans would again have to begin their long march of civilization for the thirteenth time.

Earth is a jewel among the Prime Creator's creations. Its beauty and diversity of life forms are wondrous to behold. Beings of many planets envy humans their earth. Souls are eager to incarnate in the earth, even those who know they face tremendous challenges in their incarnation. The soul grows quickly on the earth plane as it meets what it creates through choice.

There are few planets like this. On most other planets there is uniformity of look, thought, will, and action through group identity. Individuality is not present and emotions, as you know them, are not present either. Nature as you know it is unique to the earth. Nature's breathtaking scope of variety of species and populations within those species is breathtaking to behold and present only on earth. Sadly, many were present only on earth. Even as I write this, the magazine Science News, October 25, 1997, reports that Stanford University scientists have developed a new way of measuring biodiversity. These scientists are warning the National Academy of Sciences in Washington D.C. that geographically distinct populations of species are disappearing from your earth at the rate of 1,800 per hour! If you are looking for signs of global destruction, you need look no further. It is here. You have no idea how important each population and species is in Nature's balance. You are destroying your nest at a rapid pace.

You even take this compulsion to wipe the planet clean of diversity within your own species. Many of you agitate for one world government and a planet of one people, one culture, one look, and one will. Those who yearn for a earth of uniformity are woefully out of balance with what earth is. Your differences are part of your heritage. The urge to control and eradicate your differences are part of your crisis.

Among those offering to help you in these days of crisis are beings of lower consciousness. Beings of lower consciousness are those who want to help others in order to help themselves. You have many of these among you. Some are human, some are not. Aliens in astral form are attaching themselves to you as the kind of spirit attachment you read about in Chapter Seven. Many of you are letting them in out of curiosity or the thought in your consciousness that you need saving. They like the sensations of your human bodies. They are hoping you will be willing to share your bodies with them if you let them help you save your planet. You would be wise not to take their help.

Those who teach and preach that if you follow them they will heal you or save you will ultimately enslave you for your "own good". True leaders light the way, they do not become the way. Any leader that would encourage your powerlessness is a leader seeking power. Your true leaders have tried to tell you time and again that the essence of The Prime Creator is in each of you and that it is this essence that is your power and your salvation.

It is the Vibration of the Prime Creator within you that heals and transforms you and others through you. When you activate this Vibration within you, it spreads from you to others. They can block this Vibration if they choose, though often this choice is at an inner level of mind. If the Vibration is accepted, healing and transformation can manifest. Such healing and transformation can also be reversed at any time through thoughts, word, belief, or action.

Dr. Harmon teaches no one can heal another. I laugh each time he says this as he is himself a healer. A healer is one in whom the Prime Vibration, (the Vibration of The Prime Creator), can be quickened and activated at will by themselves or others. Of course, it is not the healers themselves who heal, it is the Prime Vibration within them. Dr. Harmon's Prime Vibration is quickened when his heart, as well as his head, is involved in his teaching or his healing work. Of course, the Prime Vibration radiating out from his energy field can be accepted or blocked by those around him as they choose.

Perhaps Pamela would be interested to hear that, like Dr. Harmon, she, too, is a healer. She finds this hard to believe as she has not seen evidence of this She and Hugh are opposites of one another in many ways. His Prime Vibration is a healer energy as he wills it to be so. Hers is a healer energy when others will it to be so. To answer Pamela's other question, for I hear her thoughts as I write even as she hears my thoughts to write, I used his proper title to honor him when speaking of his healer energy. I did not use your proper title as you steadfastly refuse to use one. So be it.

There are many of you who are healers and the rest of you can be, for the Prime Vibration is within every one of you. It is the core of your essence. It is always with you, though your minds are so powerful they can tune out your awareness of this vibration. Nor do you need any one or any thing to quicken it within you. You can do it for yourselves if you but believe that you can.

You are Spirit. You can use the Prime Vibration to move mountains, as well as to shatter or create them. You can use it to do good and you can use it to harm and destroy. The Prime Creator does not judge which you do for you have free will. To the Prime Creator all that happens to you and all that you receive is what you have, yourselves, created. All that you do to others is what they have asked to be done to them. You are merely an agent of their doing; you are not judged. You do, however, meet the consequences of your intents. You cannot hide your intents, even when you try to mask them from yourselves. They are recorded in the records of Spirit. These Universal Records are consulted each time you enter a new life experience. They are consulted to determine the consequences, lessons, and purpose of your new life experience. This is why it is to your greater good to use your powers wisely.

Your Higher Selves help you with this. While you must make your own decisions and choices, your Higher Selves continually offer you guidance as to your best decisions and choices. They do so through your own subconscious minds, which they use to transmit messages to you through altered states, dreams, hunches, intuition, psychic flashes, mental telepathy, signs, and omens.

Many cultures have worshipped spirits of nature as messengers of Spirit. While it is wise to honor all of nature, it is wise as well to recognize that Spirit uses nature to alert you to the messages placed directly in your own minds. The same is true of omens and signs. They merely signal that you have within you a message. Pause. Become quiet in your thoughts. Ask what the message is. Pay attention to your next thoughts.

Many of you have paid attention to the omens and signs that surround you now. You have discerned their meaning correctly and you have prayed and asked in your minds and spirits for enlightenment as to how you can avert the future you see in the signs and omens. This is what has brought me into your consciousness. You asked for enlightenment, and I am here. Let me enlighten you.

You have past, present, and future time on the earth planes as you have created time frames on the earth planes. The future is created by your actions in the present, and your actions in the present are determined by beliefs created in the past. Beliefs are thoughts linked with emotion. Your beliefs trigger your actions and your actions bring into manifestation your beliefs.

The future is not static. The future shifts as your beliefs shift. Few of you are singular in your beliefs, thus you have a number of possible futures at any given moment in time. Which future will manifest is determined by your actions. Few of you are singular in your actions, so at any given moment you have a number of probable futures within the possible futures. The future that actually manifests in physical reality is the future on which you focus. Focus is the steady application of thought and action.

You can explore your individual and collective future possibilities and probabilities through your inner minds. What you call hypnotic states are very conducive to this. Pamela has developed the use of NMR to do this as well. With the NMR you can get your Higher Self guidance as to which future path, as Pamela calls them, is most beneficial to you. If I may, Pamela, I would suggest you add the wording, "this choice is manifesting now in physical reality" to your testing as hopes, dreams, and beliefs to which physical action is not applied manifest on the astral, not the physical, planes. The fact that some of your futures manifest in other planes and dimensions added to the instability of human beliefs, emotions and actions is what makes the future so difficult to predict.

Each of you have what Pamela calls a Higher Purpose Path. This is the path of life you chose before entering this life. Many of you call it your Mission Path. This path is often difficult, but it brings the greater inner satisfaction and joy to the soul and spirit. Souls can diverge from this path at any time once they enter the physical body and many do. As there are many things to learn and discover in the earth planes, the Higher Self will usually continue to guide the soul and support it with its life force on any path. However, if a path is chosen which has nothing to offer in the way of learning or giving, the Higher Self will withdraw its life force from the soul. If the life force of the body is strong, the soul might remain for years in the body, but it will lack the guidance and support of the Higher Self. A soul without a Higher Self connection is like a rudderless ship. This, too, is a learning experience

The collective future changes less rapidly than individual ones so it is easier to tune into and predict, to some degree, the collective future. One of your collective possible futures is the complete destruction of the planet because so many humans fear this. However, Nature has a say in what happens to this planet so this future is not a probable one, though those individuals who focus on this may meet a death in which it feels as though the whole world is being destroyed.

One future that is rapidly becoming a probable future for humans is the invasion of aliens. This probability looms as more and more of you look beyond yourselves for help from those you believe are of greater knowledge and abilities than you. Turning over your problems to Other Beings and asking these Beings to solve your problems invites the Beings into your planet as co-caretakers with you. I can tell you your Higher Selves strongly warn you to avoid this future at all costs as it leads to enslavement of the human race. There is always the possibility of winning back your freedom, bodies, and planet, though it will require many, many years of great hardship and struggle.

There are aliens who wish you well. Trust those who offer to help you help yourselves and do not require that you allow great numbers of them to be present in either physical or astral form.

If you wish to keep yourselves free of alien domination, do not allow any alien presence in your bodies. Some of you have already allowed this. Your bodies tell you by their great fatigue that this is not acceptable to them. Trust your bodies. They know what is best for them, unless you train this awareness out of them.

If you suspect or wonder if you have an alien, astral, or spirit attachment, I suggest you pick a quiet moment to ask aloud that Light escort from your body and your energy field all spirit, astral, and energy attachments your Higher Self knows not to be in your best interest. Then ask for or imagine a shield of Light being placed around your energy field and you. In these days, I suggest you do this daily unless you are participating daily in the plan of Light I will share shortly. Doing either on a daily basis will eventually clear you of all attachments except those with whom you are emotionally bonded and not yet ready to let go. Filling your energy field with Light daily will help you and them to be ready, but you may need emotional healing and support.

On the subject of aliens, it would be very wise to let go of your fear of them. You are well protected by your Higher Selves. Most aliens mean you well. You are very powerful beings and all respect that. It might interest you to know that there are many aliens among you who have been born into human bodies. Most of these are here on a mission to better understand humans and in the process gain greater knowledge on how to help solve human problems.

It is not as easy for them as they imagined it would be. They are new to the human condition. The vulnerability of the human body is alien to them and they are not as respectful of human life as you are for to them, death is simply a stepping over into another level of consciousness. They fail to recognize, as yet, how difficult it is to get a human body. Experiencing individuality and choice is very confusing and frequently overwhelming to them. They are used to uniformity and no choice. They are also homesick. They feel much as you would feel if you moved alone to a foreign land completely devoid of all that was familiar and comfortable to you. They feel lost and confused. They need your patience and understanding.

They also need to be taught the rules of humans and human society. Humans take much for granted in their teaching of the young as they are used to humans who have been here before and have an understanding of the basics. Many of your young people have not been here before; they need to be taught the basics. They need you to be clear in what is expected of them and the consequences they will meet if they do not do what is expected of them. They also need you to be firm in applying the consequences. Be scrupulously fair and just in your expectations and the consequences you set. You are dealing with beings of high consciousness, even if they are a little confused.

An age of great enlightenment is a probable future for humans as so many of you hope, dream, and work toward this and there is such an infiltration of high consciousness among you. Not only have many so called alien souls been born among you, many of you are souls from very advanced civilizations from earth's past. MANY of you were in Atlantis and other even more advanced civilizations. You hold within you much knowledge that can easily usher in great advancements in all fields. This is not, however, the more probable future at the moment as few of you are paying attention to doing what needs to be done to avert the future on which the human race is now focused.

Change is inevitable in the affairs of humans and their planet Nature teaches you this. There is regularity within nature, but even within this, there is always change. Humans have come to detest and resist change. So resistant have you become that you have sought to enslave nature to your wills. This is not only impossible, it is very foolish. Your actions not only threaten you with enslavement yourselves as a consequence, they also have moved your planet completely off balance. Nature will right the balance.

Your immediate future is one of great change and transformation as Nature returns the balance to the planet. If you remove the energy of fear from your energy fields and move quickly into helping Nature restore this balance, these changes will be far less cataclysmic. There will be upheaval in your land masses. Seas will shift. Masses of people will die. Weather will change dramatically in many places on the globe. These things are already occurring. However, most people will live and the changes bring in a transformation of consciousness that is very positive. This is the future your Edgar Cayce and others foresaw. It is your focus of fear on this future that has, in part, altered it and moved it into the more cataclysmic future you now face.

This future is not beneficial to you. It is one of such massive planetary change that few humans survive. You will practically annihilate yourselves, whether it is through Nature directly or through the nature of humans.

The situation is like a cancer that is so far advanced the conventional courses of action cannot be taken. Denial will ensure death. Focusing on positive thoughts alone will not work, for the cancer is too advanced. Surgical removal is impossible as there is too great an invasion in the body. Chemotherapy and radiation therapy will not work for the body is too weak to restore the damage done to healthy cells with those processes. Even prayer will not work if the prayer is one of desperation and fear or the cancer patient inwardly resists the prayer.

The word prayer has become for many of you what I believe you call a "turn off". It is also true that many of you pray in a way that turns off, as in tunes out, your Prime Vibration. True prayer is any word, thought, belief, or action that quickens the Prime Vibration. It is the activation or quickening of the Prime Vibration within cancer cells that return them to their normal balance. If the message of the cancer is understood and the steps taken to return the cells to balance, the cancer will not return.

You have collectively created an imbalance in your earth's energy field that is like an advanced cancer. Only by activating and quickening your Prime Vibrations on a massive scale and directing these into the energy field of earth will the balance be restored. Once the balance has been restored, you will need to understand and act upon Nature's message that it is imperative you keep the ecological balance of nature, including in your own bodies, if you are to remain free of disastrous imbalance.

You can do this. You will need as many minds focused on this as possible. You do not need all of earth's humans. A few hundred thousand of you focused on doing this will work. However, each one of those few hundred thousand will have to remain committed to this work until the balance is restored. It may take months. It may take years. It depends upon how many of you focus on it daily. I will inform you when the balance is restored, though you will begin to see it for yourselves. Do not panic as others will when upheavals occur. Keep your focus on the plan. It will work. It is all that will work at this point. I suggest you get started now.

Pamela and Hugh call this plan The Omega Project because omega is the symbol for consciousness and the study of altered states and the omega point designates the end of one age, particularly a millennium, and the beginning of another. Their personal project is to increase the use of altered states to bring in a millennium of raised consciousness; thus the name The Omega Project works for them. You can call this plan anything you choose.

The plan is simple though it will be difficult for many of you to do because it requires daily execution of it over an extended period of time. You will see the fruits of your efforts during that time. This will help to convince you that the plan is working. You will have personal benefits, as well, which will keep your incentive for participation high. Many of you will continue this practice until the end of your lives and you will be known as Masters.

The plan requires humility on your part. You will need to keep your minds clear of all thoughts except that of Light entering the energy field of earth so that your Higher Selves, in their greater awareness, and I, in my greater enlightenment, can direct the Light to restore the balance properly. Many of you will be tempted to add your own direction to the Prime Vibration you will focus as Light. This would be dangerous to the accomplishment of your goal. Your instinct, as humans, is to do what you think is best for the greater good of all. The solid state of your planet is held together by the harmonious balance of positive and negative energies. Do you know how to restore this harmony of positive and negative energies? I do.

Many of you would argue that to send intents of love, joy, peace, harmony, healing, good health, balance, enlightenment, or even a greater connection with the Prime Creator or The Higher Selves would create balance in individual or collective consciousness. You would be mistaken. All humans pick up subconsciously on the intents and energies being sent to them or to the collective consciousness of all humans in earth's energy field. Humans who feel inwardly unworthy of positive energies and intents close themselves off to these instinctively. Humans who are defensive, and there are many, also close themselves off and feel anger and resentment at what they subconsciously perceive as a message they are lacking. Humans hate to be told they lack anything. Pride is important in human conditioning. It weakens humans and their energy fields to be judged as less than perfect. To fill the consciousness of earth's energy field with judgmental, critical, or conditional thoughts, even if they are not intended as such, would antagonize millions of humans. This would not be beneficial to your goal of bringing in harmony and balance. Let me put into the consciousness of each what is needed by each to achieve the balance needed in earth at this time. I can do this if you and your Higher Selves will focus on channeling Light and only Light.

There are many levels of spirit guides with many levels of consciousness and awareness. Your Higher Selves, your spirit guides, and all spirit that serves you are as eager as you to accomplish this mission and they have been offering you much guidance in how to do this. Their guidance may seem contrary to what I've just told you. Many spirit guides have been human before, but they have not completely understood, even yet, how the human mind works. Other spirit guides have not been human before, so they have not realized the importance of this principle in dealing with humans. Your spirit guides now realize, as they read these thoughts in your consciousness, the error in their well intended guidance. They know Light has been with human consciousness since humans first began. They acknowledge my greater understanding of humans and understand the wisdom in my counsel to you on how to return the balance to the earth. Be as humble as your spirit guides and you will do very well indeed.

The Prime Creator, contrary to what many of you think, has consciousness and that consciousness is active in all the Universe. The Prime Creator has sent you Light to help you help yourselves. This help cannot be given any more directly than this as you are spirits of free will learning the consequences of choice.

The plan of Light is simple: Act as channels of Light.

Let your Light shine and the consciousness of Light will do the rest.

I will outline the process in a moment, let me explain how it works first. As you begin this process, your Higher Selves will draw around you and merge their energy fields with yours. As you focus your minds on Light, your Higher Selves will focus that Light as a laser that activates and quickens the Prime Vibration within you. As this Prime Vibration is activated within you, it acts as a tuning fork, sending vibrations out from it to spread throughout your bodies into the energy fields around you and your Higher Selves. As you focus your thought on these vibrations extending out from you as beams of Light, that Light fills the energy field that surrounds, envelopes, and penetrates the earth. As that energy field becomes filled with Light by either all of you doing this at one time, or more likely, enough of you doing this over a sustained period of time, the balance of earth's energy field will be restored. This balance will positively affect all the energy fields of earth, including the consciousness of humans. You will move into an age of enlightenment.

Many of you already have meditations, prayers, and other processes you use to center in that which is the essence within you. Your powerful energy fields are very important to this plan. Your Higher Selves and I ask that you implement this plan before you move into your normal procedures. Then, as you proceed with your mediations and prayers, your Light will continue to extend from you. All of your Higher Selves already know of this plan and are eager to begin it. The steps have been agreed upon by all of them. I am the consciousness of Light. I assure you this is so.

Your subconscious minds are important to this plan. This is also why you focus your thoughts and minds on only the Light and nothing else. **If you give any other direction to this, the attention of your subconscious minds will be diverted. The power of this plan is in the singular focus of many minds. Divert this focus into diversity of thought and direction and you not only dilute its power for your goal, you will in many instances turn its power against your goal.** Let me, in my greater enlightenment, direct the Light.

You may notice as you ask your Higher Selves to surround you that you feel a coolness around your bodies. This is the presence of Spirit with you. The activity of Spirit within you often feels warm to some people, but the presence of Spirit is usually sensed as coolness around the outside of the body. Asking or stating that Light and your Higher Self surround, protect, and fill you with Light protects you from spirits and astral beings that would divert you from your focus and purpose. Know that there will be many levels of spirit, including spirit guides, astral beings, angels, and spirits of higher consciousness focusing their Light with yours. You will be plugged into a group energy of inestimable power. To misuse this power would be very unwise in deed.

If you do not have your own meditation process, this process is a powerful beginning to any meditation. I will share with you information on how to continue into a powerful meditation and on how to end your meditation with using the Light shinning within you for personal goals.

As you participate in this plan daily, your energy fields will, over time, remain filled with Light. This will positively affect your bodies and lives, as well as the bodies and lives of those around you who allow your energy fields to affect them. This increases the filling of earth's energy field with Light which will hasten its return to balance. If enough of you participate in this plan daily, the balance will return quickly enough to avert the future before you now. Each of you is important to this. It is your mission. If you are reading or listening to these words, you have been called. Participating once a day is essential. More than once a day speeds the process.

You need the process speeded up, the situation grows more critical every day. The Plan takes less than a minute of your time. What you receive in return makes this time cost efficient; one of your favorite terms, I believe. Time efficient, too, if you will allow me a small joke. The Plan, outlined below, is re-printed on a tear-out sheet at the end of this chapter.

~ * ~

IN LIGHT & YOU

★ Take a moment. Stop all activity that interferes with your concentration and focus. You can stand, sit, lie down, or move. If you are tired, it would be best to sit up so you don't fall asleep. Focus your eyes on a single spot. Breathe deeply three times. On the third breath, say or think: "My Higher Self and Light surround, protect, and fill me with Light to activate and quicken the Prime Vibration within me." [If you prefer, use your name for the Prime Creator in place of the Prime Vibration.]

★ Continue breathing deeply and with your eyes open or shut, roll your eyeballs upward in your head as high they can comfortably go. This may be as high as your eyebrows. Perhaps it will be to your forehead or hairline. It may be you are able to roll your eyes even further upward. Now imagine you are looking right inside your skill.

★ There is a glowing Light there. Some of you may see it right away. For others, it may take some time. Those of you who are not visual may sense or feel the Light more than see it. Over time, you will come to see it. Imagining it is there is sometimes the first step for some people. This will be sufficient and you, too, will see or feel the Light over time. The Light is like your own inner sun, shining from deep within you.

★ Focus on the Light and feel as though you are moving right into its center. This Light is your essence. As you move within it, you will see, feel, hear, or sense your Prime Vibration being activated and quickened. Some of you may notice a flash or burst of Light. There may be a sound. If you find yourself responding to this sound by humming or toning, that is fine. For others the sound will be a deep inner silence. You may feel a profound sense of well being, or a feeling of being centered and connected. There may be a sensation of deep peace, joy, love, harmony, balance. For some it is a very orgasmic feeling. You may feel the vibration physically. This may sway, rock, or vibrate your body. Trust yourself to go with whatever is happening. You asked for your Higher Self protection. It will protect your bodies as well.

★ Focus your thought on your Prime Vibration acting as a tuning fork, sending vibrations from it throughout your body, into your energy field, and into the energy field of your Higher Self surrounding you.

★ Focus your thought on rays of Light extending out from all around your Higher Self energy field.

★ Focus your thought on these rays of Light filling the earth's energy field that surrounds the planet, fills the atmosphere, envelopes the surface of earth, and penetrates through the layers of magma down to the center of earth.

★ Focus your thought on the Light activating and quickening the Prime Vibration within the center of the earth.

★ Focus your thought on the vibrations from The Prime Vibration at the center of the earth beaming out as rays of Light from all around the surface of your planet, filling the atmosphere, and shooting out into space like a shinning sun.

★ Bask in the Light that fills and surrounds you. Feel joy at the recognition of countless others joining you in this process and daily filling the energy fields of earth with Light..

★ Joyfully thank Spirit for helping you. Spirit loves to be acknowledged by you.

~ * ~

That's it. Simple isn't it? It takes 30-60 seconds for most people. That is the difficulty of it. Many of you will want to fancy it up with chanting, toning, gongs, spiritual music, candles, incense, elaborate breathing, special movements, and other rituals. While it is not necessary, it is fine. Humans love rituals. <u>What is essential is to resist the temptation to add additional thought, intent, or direction to this process</u>. Focus only on the Light as outlined in the plan. <u>It is absolutely essential you focus your thought on, and only on, the Light.</u> This is the plan your Higher Selves and I have brought to you for the balancing of earth's energy field. Your personal theories on the sending of Light or the Prime Vibration can be tested in your personal lives. It is hardly fair to test them on what affects the whole planet and every life form on it.

For those of you who have difficulty focusing your minds or staying forcused on Light, it might be helpful to focus first on the flame of a candle with your eyes open or closed. As you raise your eyes upward, the image of the flame with stay with you. Focus on that image. Some of you may prefer to keep your eyes focused on the flame of the candle. This is fine. Rolling your eyes upward and then looking back at the candle will be helpful to entering the altered state that empowers this process.

After the final step of this process, when you are thanking Spirit for its help in this plan, you can ask it and the Light to remain with you as you continue into meditation or focus on your own goals. If you continue into meditation, you can focus on your goals at the end of your meditation.

To focus on your personal goals, speak of, think, or imagine your goal in the Light that surrounds you. Fill your thought or image of your goal with Light. Imagine your goal exactly as you want it to be when it is accomplished and allow yourself to feel joy at the thought of this. To illustrate:

If your goal is to heal or transform your body, do not think of the dysfunction, illness, disease, injury, imbalance, or what you don't want in your body. <u>This is very important</u>. To do so sends power to what you don't want. Imagine or think or speak of your body as if the healing or transformation has already been accomplished. I know a woman who physically altered her chin by cutting out a picture of a chin she wanted. By focusing on the image of that chin superimposed over her own and imagining Light filling the chin she wanted, she achieved it. She was very patient, spending five minutes a day on this project for several weeks. At first, she thought the changes she was seeing were her imagination. She was right. The change did occur first in her astral chin. You see the astral through your imaginations, which are simply your ability to image the astral levels. Since she did not let herself talk herself out of what was happening, it filtered to the physical level. She was very happy with her results. I was overjoyed at her recognition of her power working with my Light.

This is a VERY powerful process for <u>any</u> goal. Use it for your finances, your relationships with yourself and others, your own desires for your personal future, and for healing and helping others. You might want to concentrate on one goal per session so your subconscious mind can give full attention to each particular goal.

Stimulate a sense of joy with the intent that your goal IS manifesting even as you think of it, and you will stimulate your subconscious mind into giving it top priority. Again, thank Spirit when you are finished. You might thank your subconscious too. It is the part that must bring this into manifestation.

How will you know if this has worked in relation to a goal? The answer is simple. You will notice yourself taking the steps to bring or accept this goal into your life. You will feel a sense of calm, knowing this goal will manifest, unless your Higher Self has determined the goal is not to be reached for reasons of growth and understanding. Even then, you will feel calm. If you notice yourself feeling irritable, upset, or angry about your goal, or doing what is contrary to what you would expect to be doing to achieve it, then you have inner blocks to it. You will need to attend to these. Be aware that sometimes people see the goal happening or sense it beginning and tell themselves "this couldn't possibly be!". It would be wise not to talk yourself out of believing. Your subconscious is always listening. It will stop the manifestation of your goal if you tell it to do so with your disbelief or nonacceptance.

If your goal is to help or heal others, the most powerful thing you can do is fill their energy fields with Light. If they wish to accept it, they will. If not, their Higher Selves will use the Light in the manner they know will be of most benefit. It may be not achieving the goal they think they want or you think they want is part of their Higher Purpose and Good. Realize this and you will realize the folly of directing the Light for others. As to directing the Light for yourselves, you have free will. Only your own Higher Self can block this will as your Higher Self is you. Using this free will to interfere with another's will or Higher Purpose is not the path of wisdom and enlightenment. As Pamela is wont to say, choose wisely.

To use this process as a meditation, state or think that intent as you bask in the Light on your final step, just before thanking Spirit. Think or state to yourself how long or until what time you wish to remain in meditation and your subconscious mind will honor this, ending your meditation at the time you have asked. At that time thank Spirit and your subconscious mind.

Meditation is a tuning into the Prime Vibration. You have already done this. Now continue tuning into that vibration. Your Higher Self will guide you in this meditation if you do not resist or try to control it. If you find your thoughts wandering into earth plane thoughts, it may be helpful to focus on a word, thought, phrase, image, or sound that keeps you focused above the earth plane. Music is helpful for some of you, it is distracting for others. Remember your goal in meditation is to lift your vibrations into your spiritual energies. This will keep you charged with spiritual life force and physical energy and help you to handle all that you meet on the earth plane. Eliminate from your meditation anything that brings your thoughts or energies back down to earth.

As you lift your energies in meditation or when your Prime Vibration quickens, you may feel some dizziness at first. If this bothers you, ask aloud that you be balanced in a centered feeling. Meditation and the daily filling of your energy field with your Prime Vibration will open you to mystical experiences when you are ready for them. These may or may not happen during meditation. If you ask for a particular experience, such as out of body experiences and the like, during a meditation and it does not occur, know that your Higher Self will guide you in ways that will prepare you for that experience.   When you end your meditation or sending Light to the planet, you can ground yourself, if you feel you need it, by putting your feet flat on the floor and asking for grounding.   Imagining, as you ask for grounding, that you are a strong tree with deep roots and tall branches reaching upward will be very helpful and beneficial.   That is why you need as many trees as you can get on your earth.   They bring balance into all energy fields.

Go into Nature daily.   You need fresh air and Light for your bodies every day.   Do not be afraid of the Light.   If you are, or if you have beliefs that make sunlight dangerous for you, go into indirect Light.   You might attend to your fears and beliefs as well.   Make sure they are gone subconsciously before you absorb the direct Light that is beneficial to your bodies and your spirits.

Daily quickening of your Prime Vibration moves your body, energy field, and life into harmony, health, and balance.   You may notice subtle or great changes in yourself, depending on what you lacked before beginning this process.

Many of you will experience a triggering of or an increase in your psychic abilities.   All of you will notice your inner intuitions and hunches increasing in accuracy.   The messages of your dreams will become more clear to you.   You will feel a growing sense of inner peace.   You will find yourself feeling joy, no matter what happens to you or those you care about and love.

You may begin to notice others relating to you differently.   Those who feel unworthy of the energy around you will shy away from you.   Send to them or center them in a soft rose pink color.   This color is the vibration of non-conditional love.

Others will feel threatened by your energy.   They will react by staying away from you if at all possible.   If they cannot avoid you, anger may be triggered in them.   You needn't fear anger; it is the natural reaction when humans feel threatened and unable to flee.   Focus their anger in the pink Light.   It will calm them.

Those that would do you harm will be fearful of your energy field.   They will want to stay as far away from it as possible.   As your possessions pick up your energy field over time, they will want to stay away from your possessions as well.   The only exception to this will be if your own Higher Self or you draw them to you for a lesson, purpose, or to meet the consequence of your actions, thoughts, or beliefs.

Many people will instinctively be drawn to you, wondering why they always feel better after having been around you. You will begin to notice, if you pay attention, healing and transformations in those who open themselves to your energy field. You will know which people are open by the way they respond to you. When they turn to you and gaze upon you with smiles and eagerness, they are open. You will notice, as you gaze back at them, an aura of light around them. This is you, lifting their spirits, to turn a phrase, with your spirit.

You will feel joy at all of these things. Joy is a most powerful vibration. It will bring in your age of enlightenment.

May I suggest you add to this joy by not judging yourselves or one another. The Prime Creator and your Higher Selves do not judge you, why would you do less than this? To judge is to miss the mark as you seldom know, from your human level, the greater purpose in any person or experience. This is not to say you cannot set consequences for certain actions. The earth experience is for souls to meet the consequences of their actions. This is how the soul learns to choose wisely.

Your criminal element will benefit greatly if you make fair laws and set out clearly the consequences for breaking these laws. If you create exceptions to the consequences people will mold themselves to fit the exceptions. Ensure the safety of your jails and prisons and you will not feel badly for sending to them those who have met this as a consequence. Help those in the prisons and jails understand their own responsibility in creating those consequences, even to their responsibility for being caught in seemingly unfair circumstances. Inner work with altered states will be most helpful to this.

Govern yourselves wisely. You will meet the intents of your actions always. You might hide these intents from your own awareness. They are never hidden from your Spirits.

Respect one another as the unique and individual spirits that you are. Remember, the Prime Creator is in each one of you. Your Creator does not make your choices for you, but respects your will. Can you do less for one another?

Nurture your bodies. They serve you. A wise Master honors and respects those that serve.

Nurture Nature. You need Nature a great deal more than Nature needs you.

Those of you who wish to connect with one another for this great purpose of balancing the energy fields of planet earth, seek out one another. Choose times you can meet in thought with one another for the sending of Light to the planet. Finish with sending the Light to one another. It will add to your joy. You did this once before, in your harmonic convergence some years back. You focused on peace. Your cold war ended. The Berlin Wall fell. The Eastern Bloc opened to their freedom. Have faith in these changes. Have faith in yourselves; you have great power.

We have come to the end of my chapter. Pamela is as reluctant to let this chapter end as she was reluctant to begin it. She feared she would not channel me 'right". How easily I slipped into her consciousness. How easily I slip into yours. To begin and focus in the Light is to do it right.

I am eager to share with you in the next book. It was gracious of Pamela and Hugh to allow me to author it. I have enjoyed this writing. It is a new way of communicating with humans for me. I have worked indirectly through many of you in your writings, as I did with Pamela and Hugh in the first seven chapters of this book. To write my own chapter and my own book is exciting to me. Pamela and Hugh are surprised a Spirit of Higher Consciousness such as I am would have excitement. This is amusing to me. Humans are endlessly amusing to Spirit. You fill us with joy. We return the same to you. Joy! Joy! Joy!.

APPENDIX

Book List

(The following pages are on
tear-out sheets for your convenience.)

Proclamation

Master of Light's Plan of Light

Rachael's Story

To Join FREOMM or Order BOOK TWO

BOOK LIST

Quantum Healing, Exploring The Frontiers Of Mind/Body
Medicine and Ageless Body, Timeless Mind
Deepak Chopra, M.D.

You Can Heal Your Life
Louse L. Hay

Spontaneous Healing
Andrew Weil, M.D.

Dr. Fulford's Touch of Life
Robert C. Fulford, D.O., with Gene Stone

Healing Back Pain, The Mind-Body Connection
John E. Sarno, M.D., with Letitia Sweitzer

Edu-K For Kids
Paul E. Dennison, Ph.D. & Gail E. Dennison
("Brain Gym" book - 800-356-2109)

Healing Words,
The Power of Prayer and The Practice of Medicine
Larry Dossey, M.D.

Your Body's Many Cries For Water
Order from: Global Health Solutions
P.O. Box 3189 Falls Church, VA 22043
(Cost: $14.95 00 plus $3 shipping.)

Healing Visualizations, Creating Health Through Imagery
Gerald Epstein, M.D.

Many Lives, Many Masters
Brian L. Weiss, M.D.

BOOK LIST

The following is a highly eclectic list of books with information pertinent to what we've shared with you in <u>Odyssey of The Soul, Book One, Apcatastasis</u>. We don't necessarily agree with everything in all of these books. We apologize to authors whose books should be listed here. We've been focused on clients and writing our books, with precious little time in which to read, so we have probably left out some great books. Mea Culpa.

<u>There Is A River</u>
Thomas Sugrue
(This is the biography of Edgar Cayce.)

<u>ALL the Edgar Cayce Books</u>

<u>ALL OF THE BOOKS BY MAX FREEDOM LONG</u>
(The Kahuna information is amazing!)

<u>A New Science of Life, The Hypothesis of Formative Causation</u>
Rupert Sheldrake

<u>The Donning International Encyclopedic Psychic Dictionary</u>
June G. Bletzer, Ph.D.

<u>Modern Miracles, An Investigative Report on Psychic Phenomena Associated with Sathya Sai Baba,</u> Erlendur Haraldsson, Ph.D.
(We urge you to read about this LIVING Avatar.)

<u>Energy Emission Analysis,</u>
New Application of Kirlian Photography for Holistic Health
Peter Mandel

<u>Vibrational Medicine</u>
Richard Gerber, M.D.

<u>The Lost Art of Healing</u>
Bernard Lowen, M.D.

BOOK LIST

The Dream Book: Symbols for Self-Understanding
and
Sex and Psychic Energy
Betty Bethards
(Inner Light Foundation (707) 765-2200)

Dreams That Come True, Their Psychic and Transforming Power
David Ryback, Ph.D.

The Celestine Prophecy, An Adventure
and
The Tenth Insight
James Redfield

Closer To The Light,
Learning From The Near Death Experiences of Children
Melvin Morse, M.D., with Paul Perry

Life After Life
Raymond A. Moody, M.D.

The Wisdom Of Your Subconscious Mind
John K. Williams

Self Hypnotism, The Techniques and Its Use in Daily Living
Leslie M. Lecron

Self Hypnosis and Other Mind-Expanding Techniques
Charles Tebbetts (Westwood Publishing 800-894-9766)

EMDR, The Breakthrough Therapy
Francine Shapiro, Ph.D. and Margot Silk Forrest

Women's Bodies, Women's Wisdom
Christiane Northrup, M.D.

BOOK LIST

Anatomy of The Spirit
Caroline Myss, Ph.D.

Intuitive Eating, A Revolutionary Program that WORKS
Evelyn Tribole, M.S., R.D. and Elyse Resch ,M.S. R.D.

Fat Is A Feminist Issue,
Susie Orbach

Like Mother, Like Daughter
Debra Waterhouse, M.P.H., R.D.

Regression Therapy, A Handbook For Professionals
Volume I & II
Winafred Blake Lucas, Ph.D.

Mass Dreams of the Future
Chet B. Snow, Ph.D.
(Association For Past Life Research and Therapies, (909) 784-1570.)

Bringers Of The Dawn, Teachings from the Pleiadians
Barbara Marchiniak

Akashic Records, Past Lives and New Directions
Robert Chaney
(ASTARA 909-981-4941)
(Ask for their book list. Many great metaphysical books)

Reach For The Rainbow
Lynn Finney
(All sexual abuse survivors should read this.)

Twenty Years To Life
Merrien Helton Harmon
(To be published in mid to late '98)

PROCLAMATION

People of The Earth,

The following message is from Higher Spirit. As you, too, are Spirit, as well as Body, and Mind, let your Spirit recognize the truth and the wisdom of the words and from whence they come.

"You must learn to embrace your wonderful power and abilities. And avoid the defeatism and idea your responsibility is nil or nothing. You ALL are responsible. Many peoples are choosing to leave the earth. For they have no faith. We give you faith. We provide you with power. You who take no advantage of this power are sorely disappointing to us. We need your power with our power. We need all to spread this message to any gathering where there are ears to listen, minds to think, bodies to take action to carry this message forward. And this is how it will work to save this planet earth. Earth is a very important link in the chain of development of the Universe. Your scientists are recognizing with their Quantum Theory a truth your Spiritual Masters have long taught - thoughts affect Matter. We tell you that your thoughts affect more than matter, your thoughts affect EVERYTHING. We tell you that there is present now an imbalance of energies in the earth. This is due to the focus of many on the negative aspects of your experiences in this plane of existence. This focus can be, must be, changed. It is possible with the use of the vibrations of Light. How can we tell you more of the energy and the power you have with Light? Is not laser surgery a powerful demonstration of what Light can do when it is focused and concentrated? And you have minds to use to focus and concentrate this energy. Such energy can raise the vibrations of this planet and of every life form upon it. If all on planet earth want to live a happy and healthy life and if planet earth is to remain hospitable to human life, focus on the Light. It is so simple and it is so powerful. Do NOT imagine what you wish the Light to do. Do NOT focus it on the evil or the darkness. Simply focus on the Light. Let the Light's healing vibrations lift the planet, and the life forms upon it, to their proper balance."

PROCLAMATION

The Proclamation was given to us five years ago. At that time we wrote: "What if hundreds, then thousands, then millions, then billions of minds were focused in and on the Light throughout the day and night? Might the Millennium dawn as an age of Peace, Prosperity, and Power for ALL? Shall we see? We have everything to gain. What YOU can do is participate."

In Odyssey of The Soul, Book Two, the spirit consciousness of Light we dubbed Master of Light, outlined in Chapter Eight the future humans now face, as well as how and why the Plan of Light would alter that future. We were pleased to note that billions of minds would not be needed, that a few hundred thousand would be sufficient. (Yet, imagine how much a million or a billion minds centered in Light daily could accomplish besides changing the future!) We realized, however, HOW IMPORTANT it would be for those few hundred thousand to focus in the Light DAILY and exactly as outlined by Master of Light. (Read Chapter Eight to realize why this is important.) As humans, we know how difficult it is to "stick to a plan" daily - even if it only takes a minute or two a day; even if the stakes are as high as these. Nevertheless, we are convinced there are several hundred thousand souls who are here precisely for this. It is the mission of Beings of Light. Reading these words now identifies you as a Being of Light. This is your mission.

Many of you have families, friends, loved ones, groups, and organizations that would enjoy meeting in the Light at the same time as you. Organize this for added joy. Link up with other groups and people to do it the same time as they are. We have people in every country that like to join us in our regular times. (Hugh at 6 a.m. for the dawn. Pamela at 6 P.M. for the sunset. Both at noon for the full rays of the sun.) We center at other times too, but we are faithful to these times. Join us. We welcome you with JOY!

YOUNG PEOPLE!! You are very important to this plan.
Read Rachael's Story after Master of Light's Plan of Light.

Foundation For Research & Exploration of Mind Motivation (FREOMM)
a non-profit foundation
10 Venus Drive, Rancho Mirage, CA 92270 (800) 403-4325

MASTER OF LIGHT'S PLAN OF LIGHT

Read <u>Odyssey of The Soul, Book One, Apocatastasis</u>, Chapter 8
It explains how and why this Plan will alter the future.

IN LIGHT & YOU

★ Take a moment. Stop all activity that interferes with your concentration and focus. You can stand, sit, lie down, or move. If you are tired, it would be best to sit up so you don't fall asleep. Focus your eyes on a single spot. Breathe deeply three times. On the third breath, say or think: "My Higher Self and Light surround, protect, and fill me with Light to activate and quicken the Prime Vibration within me." [If you prefer, use your name for the Prime Creator in place of the Prime Vibration.]

★ Continue breathing deeply and with your eyes open or shut, roll your eyeballs upward in your head as high they can comfortably go. This may be as high as your eyebrows. Perhaps it will be to your forehead or hairline. It may be you are able to roll your eyes even further upward. Now imagine you are looking right inside your skill.

★ There is a glowing Light there. Some of you may see it right away. For others, it may take some time. Those of you who are not visual may sense or feel the Light more than see it. Over time, you will come to see it. Imagining it is there is sometimes the first step for some people. This will be sufficient and you, too, will see or feel the Light over time. The Light is like your own inner sun, shining from deep within you.

★ Focus on the Light and feel as though you are moving right into its center. This Light is your essence. As you move within it, you will see, feel, hear, or sense your Prime Vibration being activated and quickened. Some of you may notice a flash or burst of Light. There may be a sound. If you find yourself responding to this sound by humming or toning, that is fine. For others the sound will be a deep inner silence. You may feel a profound sense of well being, or a feeling of being centered and connected. There may be a sensation of deep peace, joy, love, harmony, balance. For some it is a very orgasmic feeling. You may feel the vibration physically. This may sway, rock, or vibrate your body. Trust yourself to go with whatever is happening. You asked for your Higher Self protection. It will protect your bodies as well.

★ Focus your thought on your Prime Vibration acting as a tuning fork, sending vibrations from it throughout your body, into your energy field, and into the energy field of your Higher Self surrounding you.

★ Focus your thought on rays of Light extending out from all around your Higher Self energy field.

★ Focus your thought on these rays of Light filling the earth's energy field that surrounds the planet, fills the atmosphere, envelopes the surface of earth, and penetrates through the layers of magma down to the center of earth.

★ Focus your thought on the Light activating and quickening the Prime Vibration within the center of the earth.

★ Focus your thought on the vibrations from The Prime Vibration at the center of the earth beaming out as rays of Light from all around the surface of your planet, filling the atmosphere, and shooting out into space like a shinning sun.

★ Bask in the Light that fills and surrounds you. Feel joy at the recognition of countless others joining you in this process and daily filling the energy fields of earth with Light.

★ Joyfully thank Spirit for helping you. Spirit loves to be acknowledged by you.

~ * ~

You may, if you choose, continue with centering in the Light as a powerful meditation technique.

Foundation For Research & Exploration of Mind Motivation (FREOMM)
a non-profit foundation
10 Venus Drive, Rancho Mirage, Ca 92270, (800) 403-4325

RACHAEL'S STORY

Rachael is a young teenager who died, with her boyfriend, in an automobile accident. The friends riding with them survived. Rachael's spirit appeared to one of those friends, telling him she had liked the woman, Pamela, he had gone to see about his grief and anger at the accident. Rachael said she would, herself, be seeing Pamela on a certain date. He informed Pamela of this and on that date Pamela guided Dr. Harmon into a trance state so she could speak with Rachael.

Rachael wanted to know why she had lost her young body. Pamela suggested she guide Rachael into the Light to ask why. To Pamela's shock, Rachael was told in the Light to return to earth to find out why for herself. Pamela next suggested maybe going back, in Rachael's mind, to before she was born would answer her questions.

Rachael discovered she'd never been meant to live out a full life span and she was to investigate why. Pamela suggested Rachael move into the astral levels and ask for Healers of Light who could help her. Pamela asked her to report back the next week on what had happened.

The next week, as Rachael spoke again through Dr. Harmon, the light around him was radiant. "I found how to use Light!" she announced, laughing. "No offense, but the way you guys teach it is so boring!" Rachael's words in how to use the Light are on the other side of this sheet. But there is more to her story.

A few years later, as Master of Light wrote, through Pamela, Chapter Eight in Book One of Odyssey of The Soul, Rachael announced she was present. "Good," said Master of Light, "I have something to tell you both. The hope of the world is in the young people. They have the life force that is very important to my plan to save the world by changing the future through Light. You, Pamela, know this and you have been gathering on the astral levels many spirits who died young to help guide those in the body in their part in this plan. These young spirits lack only a leader. A central Light that coordinates their energies. This Light and leader is Rachael. It is why she died young, why she was sent back, and why she has been with me, learning and growing in my Light."

Rachael was stunned. Laughing, Master of Light teased, "I've never known you to be speechless, Rachael. "Speak to the young. Speak in their language. Speak through their music and their bodies. Speak in their minds when they open them to you. Lead your legions of the young. Teach them,

RACHAEL'S STORY

as I have taught you. Be with them as they center in the Light. Quicken their Light to meet with mine as I return the Balance to the Planet. Help them to take back their futures."

Rachael Explains How To Use The Light

"There is a way for everyone to use Light. AND IT'S SO SIMPLE! Raise your eyes up to your third eye, or up the middle of your forehead, as though you were looking right inside your skull. There you will find a kind of glowing energy, like a light, but it is cool, not hot. Focus on that energy and move right into it. You will feel centered and wonderful. So wonderful you will lose every sensation except that one focus. It's a feeling like bodies touching with all that energy exchange. It's better than meditation and better than feeling high. This feeling is BALANCE! In that balance is POWER to create ANYTHING! New Worlds! New Ventures! New Excitement! A new relationship with yourself. It's like getting a piece of God or getting a piece of the Universe. Now, send that energy shooting around the earth, enveloping the earth, penetrating the layers down to the magma, and out to the ionosphere, and the far reaches of the earth. The influence is universal, but it is YOUR FOCUS that makes it happen. You may see or sense colors or hear sounds. You may feel like you are floating. You may be filled with love or peace. Such an energy magnified by many minds around the world will eliminate the tyranny and the suffering and the wars and the greed and the desire to control others. Everything in the universe is seeking balance. If you create balance within yourself, everything around you begins to run smoothly. Take just a moment of time DAILY to see how it works, how easy it is to do. Just be careful not to do this when you're driving or doing things that require your conscious attention, because you'll lose a lot of your conscious focus if you really go with it. Sometimes you're half in and half out, sometimes you're all the way there. When you're all the way there, you will know it."

Foundation For Research & Exploration of Mind Motivation (FREOMM)
a non-profit foundation
10 Venus Drive, Rancho Mirage, Ca 92270 (800) 403-4325

The Foundation For Research & Exploration of Mind Motivation, (FREOMM)

The Foundation For Research & Exploration of Mind Motivation, (FREOMM), was founded in 1979 by Hugh Harmon, Ph.D.. We are a non-profit teaching, healing, and research foundation dedicated to demonstrating the availability of Spirit to human consciousness and the ability of the **empowered individual**, working with Spirit, to bring the self, the planet, and world affairs into balance. We are not a religious group. Spirit rejoices in the vast diversity of the human experience and asks only that you remember you are Spirit, with direct access to all levels of Spirit, including nature and your own physical beings.

Dr. Harmon and Pamela are frequent speakers and teachers for private and business organizations as well as for FREOMM sponsored classes, seminars, and symposiums. They donate the proceeds from this to FREOMM, as well as all profits from the Odyssey of The Soul trilogy.

Membership in FREOMM is welcomed and encouraged as we plan for the future and the enlightenment of those who will lead us in that future. Members vote yearly on FREOMM plans and projects. Plans for 1998 are: 1) Publication of Odyssey of The Soul, Book Two (Master of Light hasn't given it a subtitle yet). 2) Establishing our "Internet" Presence. 3) Training and certification of at least two NMR trainers per every state for the training of others in their state. 4) Establishing the first research and training site for Light Centers in which individuals receive balancing, healing, and classes in the use of the many vibrations of Light. The next meeting is scheduled for Kona, Hawaii in May of 1999. The yearly membership fees of $25 are not tax deductible,. Travel expenses to the meetings and ALL donations are tax deductible. Members also receive discounts on FREOMM books, seminars, classes, symposiums, and all other programs.

Odyssey of The Soul, Book Two, can be pre-ordered. The first 100 pre-orders of Book Two will be personally autographed and the 11th, 22nd, and 300th person pre-ordering also receive a reading of their soul's Universal Records from Master of Spirit & Master of Light!

We DO NOT sell our membership or mailing list.
JOIN FREOMM BEFORE AUGUST '98 & RECEIVE ODYSSEY OF THE SOUL, BOOK TWO FREE!!!!

--- -

YES! I wish to join FREOMM. Enclosed is my $25 check, money order, credit card number and expiration date. *We accept Mastercard, Visa, Discover, and American Express.* If you prefer to phone in your credit card number, call: 1-800-403-4325

Mail membership card to:

Name: _____

Address (include zip): _____

_____

Phone Number: _____

Credit Card # _____Exp Date:_____

Credit card orders sign here:_____

Mail to FREOMM, 10 Venus, Drive, Rancho Mirage, CA 92270

--- -

YES!! I wish to pre-order <u>Odyssey of The Soul, Book Two</u>. Enclosed is my $15 check, money order, credit card number and expiration date. (We will pay the tax and postage. Of course, if you'd like to include $5 as a donation, we can make excellent use of it.) *We accept Mastercard, Visa, Discover, and American Express.* If you prefer to phone in your credit card number, the number is: 1-800-403-4325.

Mail Book to:

Name: _____

Address (include zip): _____

_____

Phone Number: _____

Credit Card # _____Exp Date:_____

Credit card orders sign here:_____

Mail to FREOMM, 10 Venus Drive, Rancho Mirage, CA 92270

--- -

Remember: First 100 persons pre-ordering <u>Odyssey of the Soul,Book Two</u> receive autographed copies and the 11th, 22nd, and 300th person pre-ordering, also receive a reading of their soul's Universal Records from Master of Spirit & Master of Light!